Organic Gardening

The Natural No-Dig Way

Charles Dowding

with drawings by Jane Hassall

Green Books

First published in 2007
by Green Books Ltd
Foxhole, Dartington,
Totnes, Devon TQ9 6EB

Reprinted 2008

Cover design by Rick Lawrence
samskara@onetel.com

Illustrations © Jane Hassall
Photographs © Charles Dowding, Lucy Pope and Tim Sandall

The photographs are by Charles Dowding, except the following:

Photo section 1, between pages 32 & 33:
Lucy Pope page 6 (bottom)
Tim Sandall pages 3 (bottom), 4,5, & 8

Photo section 2, between pages 64 & 65:
Lucy Pope pages 4 (top left and bottom), 5 & 8
Tim Sandall pages 6 & 7 (top right)

Photo section 3, between pages 96 & 97:
Lucy Pope pages 4 & 6 (bottom)

Photo section 4, between pages 128 & 129:
Lucy Pope pages 4, 6 & 8
Tim Sandall pages 2 & 3

Text printed on Corona Natural 100% recycled paper

Printed and bound by TJ International Ltd, Padstow, Cornwall

British Library Cataloguing in Publication Data
available on request

ISBN 978 1 903998 91 5

Contents

Acknowledgements

To my father who amazingly tolerated my untried skills in his old orchard

To my mother who was always there and cooked so many fine meals

To the Argyll Hotel Iona, in whose gardens I was introduced to organic vegetables

To Charlie Wacher who encouraged me to believe I could be an organic market gardener

To many friends in the organic movement for camaraderie and inspiration

To Mary Langman and Elisabeth Montgomery for help and wisdom

To Fanny Charles for being such a champion of local, well-grown food

To Alex Baulkwill and Tim Sandall for their enthusiasm

To Lucy Pope for photographic help and inspiration

To Phil Butler, 'Bill the Butcher', for so much encouragement of my salad leaves

To Lawrence Woodward and Zizi Montgomery for setting me on the path towards this book

To Amanda Cuthbert for invaluable help and advice in constructing this book

To Susie for her deep reserves of love and support

To Rosalie, Jack and Edward for just being themselves.

Foreword

I am quite sure that this book will play an important role in reconnecting us with our food through instinctive contact with nature in the vegetable garden.

I first became aware of Charles Dowding's existence in the early 1980s through stories of his extraordinary vegetable garden in Somerset. Visitors spoke of his pioneering 'French intensive biodynamic method' raised vegetable beds and of how he expected his 'volunteer' workers to work extraordinary hours, only exceeded by his own total commitment to his garden. I was also told that his vegetables were large, beautiful, delicious, and much sought after!

When I subsequently met Charles, my image of this man of imposing strength was softened by the reality of his kind and benevolent presence. However, it became clear that I only needed to adjust my imaginary picture of the man, not his vegetables!

Charles is a brilliant gardener, a thoughtful and natural communicator, and he has emerged as one of the leading pioneer growers in the UK organic movement and a frequenter of the conferences, farm walks, seminars and other gatherings that came to dominate the lives of the hundred or so people whose work laid the foundations of the UK organic movement.

One of the fascinating aspects of organic growing is that it represents a bridge between farming and gardening. In an era where most citizens have become estranged from agriculture, I can think of no better person than Charles to forge new links through a better understanding of the vegetable kingdom. As he explains in this book, the secret is to be creative, and to garden by nature's rhythms as they work in your garden rather than by textbook rules. All one needs is a basic understanding of the seasons and relationships to make a success of your garden. Above all, the aim is to create a healthy environment.

Health is more than absence of disease. It is a positive, glowing state, and the best fruit and vegetables grow in healthy soil. Healthy soil is defined by soil life more than by chemical nutrients. A really fertile soil needs no digging or cultivation – in fact it does better without it! Compost is the magic potion to bring extra life and health to soil and crops – simply spread it on the surface.

I do hope that you derive inspiration from this book, whose author is a man who truly practises what he preaches!

Patrick Holden CBE
Director, The Soil Association

Organic is . . .
Simple, Natural Practices

What does it mean, 'To garden organically'?

It means understanding enough about your locality, your soil, your climate and your plants to work with them all in a way that ensures your garden, its produce and you yourself are bursting with health.

The actual methods you use can be chosen from thousands of possibilities, some of which are suggested in this book. When you get it right, which takes practice, your garden will bloom and yield and be a fun place to work in and enjoy. You will love being in it, and that will help the garden to be even more special, because you will be there enough to really understand what needs doing next.

One aim of this book is to suggest the general underlying principles, so that you can adapt them to your garden, allotment or patio, and make creative choices about what to do next.

Many gardening books give advice without justification: for example that compost and manure should be 'dug in'. I never do that, having found that it works brilliantly to spread it on top and let worms take it in, with many advantages accruing that will become apparent as you read this book.

I advise you to forget the 'rules'. Instead, understand better what is going on in the soil and with your plants, in your own garden, and work out your own methods instead. You may even invent some new ones or make an interesting discovery.

DIGGING

Most books suggest that a vegetable plot needs digging over every year. This is simply Not True. I have not dug, except to clear perennial weeds and turf, for twenty-five years, and my crops are better than ever. I use a system of permanent slightly raised beds and permanent paths of soil between them (see Chapter 2). Worms and other soil life do the 'digging' and keep the soil open. There are few weeds, because the soil is not panicked by being disturbed into 're-clothing' itself, which happens when the reservoir of weed seeds lying dormant in every soil are exposed to light, when soil is disturbed.

WEEDS

I do not enjoy weeding, so I manage my garden in a way that discourages weeds. I do not dig (see Chapter 1), avoid weedy compost, and do a little hoeing or hand weeding every ten days in the summer – and much less in the cold times – so that weeds are never allowed to scatter their seeds into the garden (see Chapter 2).

AN ART, NOT A SCIENCE

The world of gardening is full of chemical ideas. It is vital to ignore most of these and cultivate instead an approach that is based on Life, specifically the life in all soil, the essence of organic gardening. Respect and encourage Life as much as you can, chiefly by spreading good compost or manure. Up to 50mm of compost a year will make fantastic differences to plant health and size. Just spread it on top: within a few months it will mostly have disappeared, in the same way as leaves fall to the forest floor and are taken in by worms.

Organic gardeners used to worry that their composts contained too few nutrients as compared to chemical fertilisers, whose only ingredient is lots of nutrients. This concern is now being reversed, as appreciation grows that artificial fertilisers are lacking in the 'humus' of compost that brings vitality and health to the soil, as well as helping to hold moisture.

Which brings us to a most important issue – our very own:

HEALTH

Health is often implicitly assumed to be an absence of disease. My gardening experience suggests that in fact it is a state in itself. Plants can, as well as being free of pest and disease, have a lustre to their leaves and a pattern of growth that says 'I am growing very happily, just full of exuberance'. In the case of such fruit and vegetables, the flavour is also impressive, and I am convinced that the nutritional content must be as well. Analyses of home-grown produce are rare, but it is known, for example, that vitamin contents of leaves diminishes after picking, so growing your own fresh vegetables affords great opportunities to improve your own and your family's health. If you take mineral supplements, try remineralising your soil instead (see the box in Chapter 2, page 21).

NEIGHBOURS

You will learn more from the garden or allotment next door than from many books or articles. The soil and climate will be very similar, so if it works for him or her, it will work for you. You can learn even more from their mistakes, and your own! Don't worry about buying a soil testing kit or any fancy gadgetry. Talking to the neighbour or fellow allotment holder is often a great start for ideas. I never trained in a horticultural college, and am utterly grateful not to have done so, because it kept my mind clear of preconceptions and allowed me to base my gardening on simple, natural ideas that work, through decades of watching and learning.

That is organic gardening.

SUSIE'S RECIPES

Since marrying Susie my vegetables have come to know a powerful creative force! A first meal together at our small farm in Gascony was stuffed cabbage leaves with a memorably rich garlic flavour, as Susie took readily to the French way of creating a fine midday meal. She has an ability to fashion tasty meals from whatever is to hand, since we both dislike shopping and like to live off our own produce as much as possible. Her recipes are sound combinations of healthy ingredients, and I hope you enjoy them.

Chapter 1

The Art of Not Digging

The popularity of soil cultivation, and the common conviction that digging is absolutely necessary to grow vegetables and many other plants, shows how habits can become powerfully ingrained. Let us ask what digging and rotovating are supposed to do:

- loosen the soil so that roots can more easily travel through as plants grow
- incorporate manures and compost
- remove and / or bury weeds to clean the soil
- create a tilth for sowing

I now consider each point in turn from the perspective of a confirmed, long standing no-digger, who finds these arguments very puzzling and some-what contradictory, as well as causing some damage to the soil.

Soil loosening

If your soil really is so hard that plant roots cannot penetrate, then something has gone so badly wrong that mere digging will probably be a temporary solution. It would be more productive to ask: Why is my soil so hard?

A possible answer could be that you live in a new house and the garden was recently a building site, so that it is full of rubble underneath and has some dubious topsoil above. The clear solution in this case is to import a large quantity of compost (see below) which will serve to create a much softer, more fertile, lively and true topsoil above the existing topsoil, which should probably have been classed as subsoil anyway. The word 'topsoil' is often inaccurate and much of it is pretty dead, for instance if it has been kept for too long in a heap so that worms have disappeared. Soil is not a commodity that can be stacked, stored and shipped around. Soil can also suffer from being walked on in wet weather – a sound reason for having permanent beds and pathways.

It is worms and their lively allies in a living soil who are going to do your digging, on a permanent and ongoing basis, far more thoroughly and productively than any spading or forking can achieve. Worms need food: normally decaying organic matter which they turn into humus, another name for which is 'black gold' because it is the source of all that is best in plant growth. Even the worst soils have a few worms in there somewhere, so spreading up to 150mm of compost above them will provide the cool, dark, moist humus-potential that they thrive in and on. Quite soon your worm population will be increasing, and plants will start to grow – including weeds, but they should be easy to pull out of the crumbly compost.

Be aware that we are talking reasonably long-term here. Results in the first season of using compost on very poor subsoil may be only fair, yet all the time you are building for the future. Each year's crops are an increasingly interesting dividend while the real wealth is in your soil, a balance of health and fertility that increases all the time.

In terms of fertility, chemical farmers and gardeners tend to concentrate on the requirements of individual plants. One encounters phrases like 'potatoes are heavy feeders'. Sometimes this can become complicated, as conventional wisdom dictates a different 'feeding regime' for each kind of vegetable. Things are much simpler for a composting no-digger, who is simply looking all the time to improve the soil and holds an understanding that well-structured, undisturbed soil has a balance of possibilities that will serve any crop. 'Feed the soil, not the plant' is another way of looking at it.

Incorporating manure or compost

Do we need to 'incorporate' our compost or animal manure or whatever organic addition we are bringing to the garden? Twenty-five years of not doing so, on a range of soils and in different conditions, convinces me that there is absolutely no need to 'dig manures in' as so many gardeners do, and advise others to do, taking it for granted that it is automatically right and makes perfect sense.

In fact it makes little sense, and I find that results are better from surface application, since that is how nature works. Falling leaves are pulled in by worms, as are many other pieces of surface debris. Charles Darwin describes the worms' approach quite beautifully in his 1882 book *The Formation of Vegetable Mould Through the Action of Worms, with Observations of Their Habits*, where he comes to the conclusion that earthworms add between 25-50mm of topsoil a year in healthy pasture, as they secrete their fertile 'casts' at surface level. This is one reason why archaeologists have to dig so deep.

I find that quite soon after applying a 25-50mm dressing of well-rotted manure or compost on top of the soil, it starts, quite simply, to disappear.

Usually within a few months it is all gone and the soil is visible again, only a little darker, more friable and richer, with many crumbly and humus-rich worm casts. That is what we are aiming for, so compost can be applied two or three months before sowing or planting, and will be sufficiently broken up or dispersed or will have disappeared into the soil when our seeds or plants are ready. The soil will be thoroughly ready to receive them.

Occasionally, if time is short, plants can be set into recently composted soil, as long as the compost is not too rough; otherwise there is a risk of slug damage from the slimy beasts hiding under large lumps of half-decayed compost. Any lumpy compost tends to break down best on top of soil rather than being left in a heap, so it is best spread in late autumn or winter, well before planting time.

The other significant danger from digging manures or compost into the soil is 'nitrogen robbery'. Think of the woodier, tougher, fibrous bits of compost as rich in carbon and needing nitrogen to break down into humus. On top they do this quite slowly, helped by the weather, but inside the soil they are known to use the surrounding soil nutrients that would otherwise be available to plants, to finish their rotting down. Hence a golden piece of advice is to NEVER dig sawdust into the soil. Its large surface area of wood can absorb huge amounts of plant food. However on the surface it rots more slowly, mostly where it touches the soil surface, and the problem of nutrient robbery does not arise. Ultimately, after a year or two of weathering on the surface, it turns much darker in colour and becomes a valuable plant food. So in many ways it is safer to apply our goodies on top, just as happens in nature, when man is not digging or ploughing.

Burying weeds?

Farmers plough to bury surface weeds and residues, as much as to 'open' the soil, although some opening is certainly necessary after tonnes of tractor and machinery have passed over the soil. However, in our gardens there is no heavy machinery apart from a wheelbarrow! Keeping this and our own footfall to restricted pathways will solve any potential compaction problems. But what about weeds and grass?

The answer is to not let them grow in the first place. This requires an extra degree of commitment, especially in the winter half of the year, but has SO many benefits that it is at least worth careful consideration.

The main point is simple: no weeds growing means no weeds seeding. Yet how often does one see, in late autumn and winter, the gardener turn his or her back on their plot, while grasses, chickweed, groundsel and bitter cress are happily growing, then flowering and shedding seed, leading to many difficulties and discouragements in the spring.

One year's seeding is seven years' weeding. No maxim is truer or more forceful. One groundsel plant can yield hundreds of fluffy little seeds over a wide area, and a hundred groundsel weeds is not a pleasant problem to deal with. It can be quite difficult to catch all of them before they seed. Meanwhile there are other seeds lying dormant for up to seven years, waiting to spring up at unsuspected moments.

Weeding is mostly a great waste of time and stops us doing the fun bits, as well as causing disturbance to the soil as we dig them out or hoe them off.

So act preventively: a stitch in time saves about ninety-nine. Do occasional weeding through the darker months, removing that occasional small clump of grass, chickweed, bittercress or anything except the flowers and vegetables that you sowed or planted. Then nothing has time to seed, because you get to it before that could happen, and in springtime the soil is clean of weeds, which are not therefore offering shelter to slugs, and is ready for immediate sowing or planting, into the free tilth provided by Jack Frost.

Tilth

Here we confront the last fallacy of 'reasons for digging'. Tilth means a crumbly soil surface, suitable for 'drawing out a drill' to sow seeds into, with lots of fine particles that small seeds can nestle into as they moisturise and then send out those first fragile roots.

Diggers and rotovators sometimes spend a long time knocking the soil around to make their tilth, because they destroyed or buried it in the first place through digging or rotovating. Large lumps of less crumbly soil have been brought up to the surface and need time and weathering, or application of mechanical force, to be broken down. In a dry spring, the lumps can go hard before disintegrating; meanwhile a lot of moisture is lost, as well as precious time.

On the other hand, a no-digger can step out into the first mild weather after frost has lifted, to rejoice in a wonderful soft surface that is crying out for seeds or plants. This is particularly apparent if a bed system has been adopted, whereby all squashing of wet soil in the winter is confined to defined pathways, leaving the much larger growing area soft and friable (see next chapter). No moisture is lost to cultivation, and there is even another bonus: fewer weeds.

If we return to the logic of seven years weeds from one year's weed seeds, it can be surmised that digging (and rotovating) is incorporating quite a few more seeds each year, with the honourable exception of those diggers who do not let their weeds go to seed. At the same time, in moving soil up and down, a previously buried cache of weed seeds is brought to the surface and exposed to the daylight which is their trigger for germination – unless cultivation is done at night!

Weeds are healers after the digging

I have also come to conclude from watching what happens when I have been obliged to disturb soil, for example to remove tree roots or dig potatoes, that weed germination is almost a defensive reaction by the soil, to remedy the uncomfortable distortions caused by inversions of different layers of soil life and the breaking, even destruction, of some of its existing structure. Weeds are attempting to cover up the pain and heal the wounds. We really can treat the soil, our planet's skin and source of all our food, better than this.

So, apart from the processes of setting up your garden, please don't dig! This book is littered with advice to help adjust to a zero-cultivation approach, and once you get the hang of it you will find new alternatives to many 'traditional' gardening techniques.

Green manures

This is a good moment to mention an oft-quoted axiom of organic gardening, which is manuring the soil through digging in of a green crop grown to increase soil life and organic matter. The aim is good, but I rarely do it because of the digging.

One exception is a crop like mustard, which is killed by moderate frost. If sown late August or early September it will be just flowering as winter arrives, full of leaf and about 90cm (3') high. After being killed by frost, it will turn to inert organic matter and be taken in by worms so that, come spring, only some strawy stems will be apparent on the soil surface. It has enriched the soil without any digging, but that brings me to the other difficulty with green manures – I rarely have room for them! Any ground cleared over the summer is quickly re-planted with fast-growing vegetables such as beetroot, French beans and salads for autumn and winter.

Perhaps it depends how large your garden is, relative to what you want from it. Mine seems too small, and that is a good feeling to have, ensuring that beds are covered with crops through a long growing season. Other gardens have spare space that is growing weeds, and while weeds are a valuable green manure in themselves, we do not want their seeds as well – and it is extremely difficult to have one without the other.

So if you are likely to have an unused patch of vegetable or other garden for more than two months of the growing season, it is worth sowing a 'catch' crop like mustard, or a longer-term crop such as broad or field beans, both to prevent weed growth and to enrich the soil. Beans can be removed without digging, or left on the surface for their leaves to rot in, after which the stems can be composted.

Chapter 2

The Basics

Everybody gardens in a different and unique way. We all need to experiment a little to find which methods are most suitable for our temperament, site and preferences. Visiting somebody else's garden is always interesting, because it says a lot about the person's character.

Yet underlying this variety is a consistency of natural laws that apply to everybody. Appreciation of these allows us to garden more successfully, and also more expressively, because we can adapt nature's demands to our own needs and desires. The former are fixed, the latter change.

Enjoy the view – varied and beautiful

The vegetable plot offers more scope for inventiveness than almost any other part of the garden, not least in its location. Traditionally in large gardens it was put far away and out of view, because the labourers were then out of sight, and boring rows of predictable crops were considered unappealing to behold. Now, thank goodness, things are different. Few of us have servants so it is a positive advantage to have the food crops close at hand, where we can tend to them regularly and gather the harvest more easily.

Fruit and vegetables can also be beautiful and inspiring to behold. There are few finer sights than beds or rows of well looked after crops whose colours, size and form are varied and fluid. If your garden is small, consider a couple of raised beds wherever the light is best – and light is important. Many gardens are graced with tall trees and shrubs, but their shadows and also hungry roots can take away a lot of the best growing conditions from fruit and vegetables, which definitely thrive in full sun. Should your garden be overgrown, it may be worth considering an allotment – or a small intensive bed in the lightest part.

If you have plenty of space, take a look and imagine where food plants could make an aesthetic contribution. Herbs are normally grown close to the kitchen; salads can be as well. Fruit trees can be grown as hedges, borders, or against walls, using choice of rootstock to ensure the right-sized tree. Globe artichokes make a stunning hedge or specimen plant, and certain vegetables left to seed, such as leeks or ruby chard, add extra grace and beauty wherever they are.

The companion effect

Another benefit of mixing things up is plant friendships, whereby certain plants help others to grow well and keep healthy. I have often tried many of the better known combinations, such as French marigolds with tomatoes to deter aphids, or onions with carrots to deter carrot root flies, and find mostly that the effects are not as cut and dried as some people claim. However, if you feel good about, say, growing flowers among your vegetables, or vice versa, then it is most probably beneficial to the vegetables and it looks nice too. Insects above all are liable to live in better balance where many plants of different kinds and varieties are growing together. I find it works best to think in terms of many small ecosystems, than to be too exact about precise combinations of plants.

Seasonal changes

Flowers are always a happy and attractive addition to the vegetable plot, yet the edible crops are often really beautiful on their own, with so many shapes, colours and constantly changing characters, vividly illustrating each season. Spring can be lit up by the vibrant colours of a lettuce bed, and exciting meals are provided by asparagus spears poking through bare soil, although a transformation occurs in late June, when picking stops on the longest day, and within about two weeks the asparagus patch has become a jungle. At about the same time, the first courgette flowers, suddenly opening, dramatically large and bright yellow, are an inspiring pointer to summer. Moving into autumn, the different hues of ripening squashes, multicoloured chicories and apples light up the darker days, while winter is softened by leek leaves gracefully bearing frost and snow.

Bare necessities

So edible crops can be complementary to the general garden, but there is another side to the coin: it makes sense to keep vegetables grouped together. Constant sowing of tiny seeds and setting out of tender plants does not work well in congested borders where slugs and snails are lurking. One dedicated patch that is mostly bare in springtime will give more chance of success. The same applies to certain flowers. I like to plant annuals in the gaps of our herbaceous borders, but my choice is limited to ones that are less attractive to slugs – nasturtiums, for example.

It is a paradox that organic vegetables, grown the 'natural way', still require somewhat unnatural conditions. Nature does not do vegetable gardens, and permaculturists have made brave attempts to balance this by clearing small plots at different times, growing plants that can tolerate congested soil, and making full use of perennial vegetables. These are difficult skills to use exclusively, so we have to acknowledge that the bare soil we need is rarely found in nature and tends to re-cover itself with weeds. Regularly cropped soil that is having plants removed from it will deteriorate unless humus is regularly applied. Traditionally there was plenty of animal manure; now this only applies if you or a neighbour have horses.

A modern alternative is to source your compost from the increasing volumes produced at recycling centres from household wastes. It is less rich in nutrients than manure, so 50mm annually would not go amiss. The composting process is usually very thorough so there are almost no weed seeds, and a thick mulch on top will also help prevent the germination of dormant weed seeds in your topsoil. Usually this compost is offered in different grades according to how much of the wood has been sieved out. I would recommend 8mm grade, which is much finer than 15mm and contains less plastic – a certain number of pots, bags and toys always seem to pass through the municipal shredder.

Start clean

Before practising no-dig, the garden must be cleared of unwelcome perennials – principally docks, stinging nettles, dandelions, couch grass, ground elder and bindweed, in order of increasing difficulty. They must be diligently cleared out; remember that almost any remaining roots of the last three will grow again into new plants. Only bindweed and marestail / equisetum are intractable, because many of their roots are so deep and brittle that they cannot be extracted and require weakening by regular removal of new shoots.

Should your soil be infested with roots of perennial weeds, it is worth initially and temporarily digging out any bushes or plants you want to keep, so that cleaning can be effective. Thoroughness at the beginning will be amply rewarded later, with a much reduced workload. Any new shoots of couch grass or ground elder that were missed initially can be carefully removed, together with the scrap of root they have issued from.

Raised beds

Say you now have a nice patch of clean soil: what next? There are many choices here. I would make some raised beds, for ease of working in the long term, and because the soil responds better for not being trampled on.

The simplest and cheapest way to make a raised bed is to mark out the plot into 1.5m beds and 450mm paths with some string and bamboo, and then use a spade to lift the top 150mm of soil from the path area onto the bed next to it. Level off the bed, knocking out the largest lumps but not worrying about making a fine tilth, because adding a thick mulch of compost at this point (on the bed only) will help the soil to settle down again by nourishing its vital fungi, especially the mycorrhizae that are so vital to plants' well-being.

If the plot is initially all poor soil, instead of digging out a path you could create a bed by importing a serious amount of compost, up to 150mm depth, even spreading some on the pathways.

You will now have a nicely defined bed that looks dark and inviting, and a path that can remain as bare soil or can be mulched with, for example, wood chips or sawdust. Any woody material needs to take nutrients from the soil to help its cellulose and carbon to break down, so it is best applied to paths only. No more digging is now needed, ever. Use compost on top only, leading over the years to the creation of a fine, dark topsoil, even if there is clay or builders' rubble underneath.

According to the size of your plot, you can keep marking out new beds and paths until arriving at the outside edge, where it is best to finish with a path, so that the whole area is surrounded by lower pathways that are easier to keep clear of, for example, invading grasses. The resilience of grass never ceases to amaze me; it often feels as though I spend as much time keeping my grassy edges in order as I do weeding all of the vegetable beds. Some people like to bury 100-150mm planks of thin wood as edging strips to keep the grass at bay, making sure that the top of the plank is at soil level and almost invisible. My preferred method is to run a sharp scythe along the edge every two or three weeks. Also I pass occasionally with a trowel to dig out the shiny white roots of grasses such as couch, that are invading all the time in certain parts.

Less of this will be necessary if you have paved or gravel edges around the plot – although remember that even gravel needs some weeding, unless it has a synthetic porous 'membrane' underneath it. Another alternative, especially for small plots, is to make more elaborate beds with wooden or plastic edges, which can serve as the border of the plot with grass right up to them if you wish. For the long-term, I recommend 200x50mm planks, treated naturally with organic wood protector and kept in place with stout wooden pegs.

ORGANIC WOOD PROTECTOR

I brush on a product made by Osmo in Germany, called Wood Protector, which is composed of natural (not man-made) waxes and oils. One or two coats of Osmo paint, similarly of natural origin, will preserve wood extremely well. The Osmo products work more by soaking in than by attempting to cover wood with an impermeable layer. Hence they do not flake or peel: I used two coats of Osmo paint on my greenhouse six years ago, and it looks as good as when it was put on.

However there may be a snag to the visual appeal of wooden raised beds and their ease of maintenance. Soil next to wood tends to dry out and be unnaturally warm – just right for red ants, whose excretions are acidic and toxic to many plant roots. Ants' nests are becoming more common, and the most effective solution is to dig them out where feasible, but that rather spoils the idea of a no-dig bed! There are 'organic anticides' on the market, but I have found they are not always effective.

Improving fertility

Perhaps you will not even make beds, and run your vegetable plot as a level area. In this case, a 50mm mulch of compost over all the bare soil will help avoid any 'need' to dig by keeping the worms busy and giving sound structure. A well-structured soil has enormous resilience.

Most such soil, as well as offering a fine home to plant roots, will offer them sufficient nutrients as well. Correct treatment of the soil and using good compost is the basis of excellent growth, but occasionally you may be growing plants that demand a little more food, or help in some way – plants or trees in pots, for example, can benefit from organic liquid feeds.

THE VALUE OF GOOD SOIL STRUCTURE

J. Arthur Bower was a well-known flower and vegetable grower in Wisbech. He made superb compost, and spread it thickly every year. One morning in the 1950s he was horrified to see a fully loaded brick lorry in his wet field, after a wrong turning! The wheel ruts were deep, but visitors later in the day were amazed to hear the story because the ruts had disappeared, as his humus-rich soil recovered its structure in record time.

I have done liquid or supplementary feeding at different times, for example using comfrey and stinging nettles steeped in a barrel full of water for ten days, which creates a disgustingly stinky brew. The job of watering it onto plants is no less smelly, and altogether I feel that one's time is better spent in attending to the compost heap, meeting plants' demands through a soil-based approach.

An exception to this is occasional spraying of seaweed- or seawater-based sprays, say at the dawn of a calm summer's day, to ensure that all plants have full quota of minerals and trace elements, which is such an important part of their health and thus of our health. The sea is a fantastic resource that I became aware of when watching vegetables grow abundantly on the Isle of Iona, in the Inner Hebrides. The plants were growing in what looked like sand, to which the only addition was barrowloads of seaweed every winter.

SOURCES OF EXTRA MINERALS

British government figures, based on testing a wide range of foods every decade since the 1940s, suggest that mineral contents have fallen noticeably. Re-mineralising our own soil and crops is the least we can do to compensate, but exact measurements of what works best are hard to find. Work by SEER in Scotland has found benefit from spreading the volcanic rock dust waste of basalt quarries, and research by the Good Gardeners Association is assessing mineral contents of vegetables from no-dig, single-dig and double-dig plots to learn what effect cultivation has on the soil food-web and the potential loss of nutrients. As part of their 'Moving Beyond Organic' project, which aims to grow food for nutrition, the GGA are tracking the flow of nutrients, including vitality, from soil to crop and then relating this to human nutrition. Full results are due to be published in 2008; however, key findings suggest they are growing food with higher mineral content than the 1940s, and that a knowledge of soil biology is far more useful than a knowledge of soil chemistry if what we want to grow is nutritious food (see Resources).

Tools

You should require only a few tools, so it is worth buying good ones. The best I have found are made of copper in Austria, and last extremely well because copper does not rust (see www.implementations.co.uk). My copper trowel has kept sharp, has a useful pointed end, and has outlived two stainless steel trowels from a well-known store, which simply snapped at a poorly designed weak point below their handle. However, copper is softer than iron, so is not suitable for stony soil.

Here is a list of the tools I use to tend an acre and a half of vegetables, fruit and flowers:

- a long-pronged compost or manure fork
- a wooden dibber for making holes to set plants into, 65cm long
- a copper trowel
- a wheelbarrow
- a sharp copper spade for trimming grassy edges, chopping plant remains etc
- a copper ridging tool for drawing drills to sow into
- secateurs for pruning
- a short-pronged digging fork for lifting roots or stones
- a short-bladed scythe for grass and brambles
- a rotary lawnmower for grass, occasionally also for collecting leaves.

So, what next? Lots of healthy soil awaiting seeds and plants: which ones, and when?

Chapter 3

Deciding What to Grow

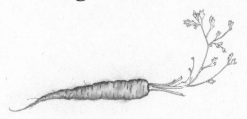

Gardening for food is brilliant because there are so many plants to grow, so many ways to improve the soil and make them grow better, and so much opportunity to enjoy the rewards. Every season I enjoy the challenge of new plants or varieties or ways of doing things. Success is sometimes elusive, although one is constantly learning, and it really is exciting when a new idea comes to fruition. But before that, some things need consideration before making your choice of what to grow.

How much experience do you have?
How big is your growing space?
How much time do you have?

Some examples to help you choose

For all of us, especially the beginner, nothing is more heartening than healthy growth and a worthwhile harvest. So I encourage you, initially, to grow what will grow most easily in outdoor Britain. For beginners there is huge scope for rapid and interesting harvests of salads, because from sowing to picking is often less than two months, and many different plants are suitable. Some salad plants will crop for two or three months, and many leaves can be gathered from relatively small areas, so I warmly recommend a close look at Chapter 9. Remember how much time is required for picking, making it worthwhile to have them as near to the kitchen as possible, possibly in a large pot outside the door.

If you have the space, a tasty and easy crop is new potatoes. They grow fast and reliably, and are out of the ground before their main disease, a fungus called blight that withers all the leaves, is even around. Potato plants are among the largest and quickest of all the root crops because they grow from old potatoes or tubers, which have enough food resources to propel young plants into rapid growth. Compare that to carrots – slowly growing from tiny seeds, which take an age to create enough root and leaf to make worthwhile growth – and parsnips, which take an age to even germinate.

Another space-hungry plant that is not too difficult is courgette, and it illustrates a highly important aspect of vegetable growing. How often can you be in the garden? Courgettes need picking every day, or two at the most, before they turn into small tender marrows and then, surprisingly rapidly, into large hard-skinned marrows. You may be caught out by the amount of time required for picking and dealing with your harvests, as one courgette plant can yield about sixty fruits between July and October. There is more work in picking and dealing with its output than in growing the plant.

Similarly, runner and French beans need frequent picking. The bean pods do not just develop and wait for us to gather them: they pass quickly through the tender pod stage on their way to becoming a tougher ripening pod that contains maturing seeds. It is such a pity that summer holidays occur when the garden is bursting with beans and other produce – another thing to bear in mind when you are planning.

The allium family are friendly in this respect: leeks, garlic and onions all grow slowly but steadily, and one harvest of garlic and onions, well stored, will afford many months of meals. And once they are picked, there is still time for another crop of late salad or French beans or oriental greens. Familiarise yourself a little with all the possibilities so as to make the choices best suited to your family's tastes.

Successional cropping

Keeping the ground full of something growing at all times is highly worthwhile.

- First, there is more to eat.
- Second, the soil is more often covered by leaves, helping to conserve moisture and to protect from heavy rain.
- Third, there is less room for weeds, which are shaded out by growing crops.
- Fourth, the plot or bed is more beautiful.

One way to achieve a succession is by ongoing propagation of sturdy plants, preferably in a greenhouse. Work out when crops will finish and have another plant ready to fill the space. Most salads, beetroot, French beans, spinach, kale, fennel, kohlrabi and other vegetables are around for only half a season, giving lots of interesting combinations to play with. Look at the table overleaf to pick out a few. Apart from corn salad (lambs lettuce), salads are not included in this table because there are simply too many possibilities, arising from their great number and rapid growth. So they can often be slotted in before or after other vegetables.

Combinations for succession

Match up any last 'H' with a first 'S' or 'P' to see what vegetables can succeed each other. Even more combinations are made possible by doing the 'S' part in a greenhouse and following 'H' with 'X'.

S = sow
P = plant modules, tubers or sets
X = growing vegetable
H = main harvest
OW = overwintered

VEGETABLES	Jan	Feb	Mar	Apr	May	Jun	Jul	Aug	Sep	Oct	Nov	Dec
Early Potato			P	P	H	H						
Second Early Potato				P	P	X	H	H	H			
Corn Salad	H	H	H	H				S	S	S/H	H	H
Broad Bean		S	S	S	X	H	H	H				
Broad Bean (OW)		X	X	X	X	H	H	H			S	X
Early French Bean					S	X	H	H			S	X
Late French Bean							S	X	H			
Summer Beetroot		S	S	X	H	H	H					
Winter Beetroot						S	S/X	X	H	H	H	
Summer Carrot			S	S	X	H	H	H				
Winter Carrot							S	X	X	H	H	H
Spring Cabbage	X	X	X	H	H			S	P	P/X	X	X
Winter Cabbage					S	X	P	X	X	H	H	H
Early Cabbage			S	S/P	X	H	H					
Late Cabbage					S	S	X	H	H	H		
Early Onions	X	X	X	X	X	H		S	X/P	X/P	X	X
Maincrop Onions		S	S/P	P	X	X	H	H				
Early Leeks			S	S	X	P	P/X	X	H	H	H	
Late Leeks	H	H	H	H/S	X	X	P	P/X	X	X	X	H
Garlic	X	X	X	X	X/H	X/H	H			P	P	X

Rotation

Rotation can be made into a frighteningly complex subject – indeed it often is. It simply means moving vegetables around the garden in succession, rather than growing the same ones in the same place every year, to avoid a build-up of pests and diseases.

A four-fold rotation of roots, brassicas, potatoes and miscellaneous vegetables used to be commonly recommended. The difficulty with this, and indeed any strict rules, is that it tends to divide the vegetable plot into rigidly defined areas, making it necessary to grow fixed amounts of certain crops every year.

I recommend instead that you keep an awareness or a plan of what has grown where, aiming to avoid repeat cropping for as long as possible. Listed below are the important categories of plants that are often closely related. For example leeks and onions are both alliums; therefore avoid following one with another, but intersperse them with successions of vegetables from other groups. More details are offered in the relevant chapters. Note that some plants cannot be rotated, such as perennial vegetables that grow in the same place for many years.

SOME VEGETABLES SHARING THE SAME CHARACTERISTICS

Brassicas: All cabbages, cauliflower, brussels sprouts, calabrese, broccoli, kale, rocket, most of the common oriental greens, swede, turnip, radish, kohlrabi

Alliums: Onion, spring onion, shallots, leek, garlic, chives

Umbellifers: Carrot, parsnip, celeriac, celery, parsley, fennel, dill

Solanaceae: Potato, tomato, sweet pepper, chilli, aubergine

Cucurbitae: Cucumber, melon, courgette, marrow, squash, pumpkin, gourd

Legumes: Peas, broad beans, runner beans, French beans

Beet: Beetroot, spinach, chard

Other: Lettuce, chicory, endive, basil

Perennials

Growing perennial vegetables will avoid any worries over sowing and planting, once they are established. Their roots survive the winter and send out new leaves in early spring. Rhubarb is ridiculously easy to keep going over several years, and choosing an early variety can give stems by the end of March. Asparagus, once established over two or three years, will crop from late April for two whole months, although quite a large area is needed to grow worthwhile amounts. Globe artichokes also need a fair amount of space but will spring up most years, and freshly picked chokes have a wonderful taste and tenderness.

Perennial possibilities abound in fruit – above all raspberries, which are so well suited to the damp British climate. Early varieties crop for a month from late June, and autumn varieties give a steady harvest throughout late summer and early autumn. Strawberries offer similar choices of different harvest times, but are a little harder to grow – you need to keep control of their runners and watch out for slugs and fungal damage in wet seasons. Consider carefully the pros and cons before planting, as outlined in Chapter 19, since you are committing to a few years' work and harvesting.

Chapter 4

What's in Season?

Growing your own food is a complete antidote to the seasonal uniformity of supermarket shelves. Out in the garden there are still four seasons, and it is vital to understand how they affect our sowing, planting and harvesting.

Sowing at the right time for healthy plants

Confusing signals abound, from nurseries offering plants out of season, to seed packets advising unnaturally long sowing seasons, presumably in the hope that we use up more seed. What we really need is information about when is the best time to sow for the plant to achieve its full potential and grow most healthily. I have in front of me a packet of rocket seed that says on the back "Sow April–September". Presumably they mean that their rocket seed will grow into nice rocket leaves at any time from late spring to early winter, but this is simply not true.

Like all plants, the growth of rocket is governed by changing day length. Days growing longer, from midwinter to midsummer, make it want to reproduce, so its energy goes into producing a stem with nice flowers that will turn into seeds as the plant dies off; whereas days growing shorter, after the 21 June solstice, but more especially after about early September, send it a signal to take it easy a bit! There is time to make plenty of leaves and roots in preparation for that great seeding season in the spring . . . and plenty of leaves for the gardener to pick in the meanwhile.

As an organic gardener, it is vital to appreciate this calendar of activity that affects the behaviour of everything we sow; also, sowing out of season often results in plants succumbing to more pest and disease. Consider rocket again: it is a member of the *Cruciferae*, also called brassicas or the cabbage family, all of which are affected by flea beetles making lots of little holes in their leaves, but chiefly from mid spring to late summer. So even if you do achieve some rocket leaves in May and June, they are likely to be peppered with these beetle holes that enlarge as the leaves grow bigger, whereas an August sowing will produce cleaner leaves in the autumn and winter, when flea beetles are much less active.

There is a major link between sowings made at the right time and healthier growth. Spring salad sowing should be lettuce above all, as it grows most healthily then and is not in a rush to make seed until later in the summer. Furthermore, frequent and careful picking of its leaves will delay the seeding attempt by at least a month (see Chapter 9). However all the oriental greens have an internal clock that is similar to rocket, so it really is not a good idea to sow mizuna or pak choi in the spring. Your leaf harvest will be quite small, and they will be of relatively poor quality. Sow them in July and August.

As a rule the most discouragement stems from sowing too early, before conditions are right or the soil is warm enough for plants to flourish. Until you have some experience, err on the side of caution. In my first year of learning to grow vegetables I sowed carrots in January, as recommended on the back of the seed packet. I never saw any seedlings although they probably came up briefly before slugs ate them off – a complete waste of time and seed. Now I make the earliest carrot sowing in late March and even then, if the weather turns wet, allowing slugs to prosper and eat the baby carrot's leaves, it can be necessary to re-sow.

Bringing the 'right time' forward

Carrots (except for round ones) are difficult to raise as greenhouse plants, but I sow almost all other seeds in my greenhouse, into modules or seed trays. They grow into vigorous plants that can resist slugs and give an earlier harvest. Spinach in April, beetroot in May and courgettes in June are most satisfying to harvest, at a time called the 'hungry gap', because few other crops are ready. Look at Chapter 6 (pages 34-44) to pick up some ideas on both how to grow your own plants and also how to extend the season a little with such simple materials as a roll of fleece.

Weather and climate

Plants grow and mature quite differently from one season to the next. One year my onions keep brilliantly, the next I lose half to a fungus that arrives in midsummer. Potatoes can be blight-free one autumn and full of it the next; leeks and celeriac may struggle through a dry summer or flourish in a wet one. I strongly encourage you to learn the basics of what conditions each plant likes, so that you can adapt your growing to their different requirements, but there will always be the unforeseeable consequences of extra rain or sun.

Over the last three decades I have experienced a range of vastly different years, and have also recorded an interesting rise in temperature that has extended the growing season by about a week at either end. For example, sweetcorn used to occupy ground for almost the whole growing season, whereas, for now at least, it matures early enough for significant crops of late salads to grow in the same bed through autumn.

But there is still no certainty as to whether next spring will be cool and damp or warm and dry. What works one year may fail the next; all we know for sure is the seasonal requirements of different plants, with experience giving a glimpse of the timings and methods that have most chance of success. I invite you to benefit from my years of trying different things to learn how sowing at the right time is an invaluable but often ignored part of successful growing, and even helps in dealing with slugs and snails.

Chapter 5

Living with Pests

A sound organic approach is to minimise opportunities for pests to prosper, rather than having to deal with unexpected damage. Put simply, gardeners have the ability to reduce pest problems through good gardening.

SLUGS AND SNAILS

Slugs are a fact of life, even for those who regularly use poisons to control their numbers. A better approach is to understand more about them, both to stop their numbers escalating and to adapt to their ways.

Correct timing of sowings is one strategy for co-existence, so that seedlings thrive in helpful conditions and are able to grow away from any nibbles. Look closely at the recommended dates for different vegetables in Part 2 (Chapters 9 to 19). Also, if possible:

Sow seeds in controlled environments such as a greenhouse, where they can grow unmolested into strong plants that are large and vigorous enough to resist the slimy marauders. This is a vital aspect of growing any early crop, whose health and vigour says to Mr. Slug, "Hold off here! I am growing well so leave me alone, or just nibble my fading outer leaves. Your job is to clear up the debris!" In other words, slugs have a place in the garden, but hopefully not too many places.

Reduce slug habitats as much as possible. Areas of unnecessary weeds, rubbish, long grass or overgrown plants can all be shelters to surprising numbers of the larger multi-coloured sorts which can destroy even large seedlings in a short spell of damp weather. For instance, once my rhubarb is growing I have an occasional look under the lowest leaves to find snails that are lurking in the dark coolness, waiting to come out for a nightly feed on anything nearby. Keeping the soil clear of weeds in springtime is vital; so is removing the leftover leaves and stem of any finished crops to the compost heap or bin, as soon as possible after harvest.

Greatest slug damage often occurs where ground has recently been cleared of grass or overgrowth that was home to large numbers who, suddenly, have nothing to eat. Least problems arise in a tidy garden where only the crops are growing, but nearby habitats can still make difficulties. Walls and stony borders are an invitation to snails to set up home, so it is best to grow resistant flowers together with fruiting trees and bushes near to walls, and site the vegetable patch a little way from them.

SLUG AND SNAIL RESISTANT FLOWERS

Slug and snail resistant flowers that I grow include penstemons, wallflowers, auriculas, campanulae, cornflowers, sweet william, foxgloves, verbena bonariensis and a wide range of other perennials. Note that certain plants whose leaves offer little culinary interest to our slimy friends can often serve as shelter to large numbers, so it is beneficial to conduct a clean-up in damp weather. A little foraging under leaves should soon reveal favourite hiding places. Slug-tender flowers such as French marigolds and dahlias need to be grown in more open ground and planted a little later than often recommended.

Night-time forays Another trick, for the brave gardener of nocturnal instinct, is to venture out with a torch and maybe gloves as well, and pick off everything that has appeared under cover of darkness – there can be a surprisingly large number of slugs. Putting them in a bucket of water will drown them.

Frequent harvests Even in bare soil there are always slugs – more commonly small grey ones who are notably conscientious in their tidying up role. When lettuce matures and develops a heart, I find that the decaying outer leaves become home to large numbers, whereas the heart which is still growing strongly and has the youngest, healthiest leaves is mostly free of damage. My sales of lettuce used to be always limited by the presence of at least one slug, even after trimming off the damaged outer leaves. People just do not like dealing with them, supermarket buyers above all! So it has been a great joy for me to discover how to grow frequently picked lettuce, whose small and less numerous leaves afford little shelter, as well as finding that it is feasible to mix leaves in water so that slugs are washed out. The Summer Salads chapter (pages 52-65) explains how you can achieve this and produce your own salad bag.

Predators You may be wondering if it is possible to encourage sufficient predators into a garden. Personally I feel that this helps, but not to the point that we can ever cease to be alert to the dangers, because slugs and snails are themselves simply part of the garden. Our role is to keep their numbers at a manageable level. Sometimes when picking spinach I disturb a toad sheltering under the leaves – they like the same conditions as the slugs they eat. But there are always slugs on the spinach as well, which makes sense because if the toad ate them all he or she would have to go elsewhere. Ducks or hens will clean up a garden, but I never let them into the vegetable patch because of the damage caused by hens digging and ducks nibbling. When we lived in rural France it was clear that poultry were encouraged to range all around our neighbours' farms and gardens, but never in the carefully fenced *potagers*.

INSECTS

The importance of sowing dates

After slugs, the most common difficulties are caused by cabbage-family caterpillars, to the point that I simply do not grow late-summer cabbages and calabrese. At that time of year, cabbage white butterflies are abundant and laying many eggs, especially in sheltered gardens. Measures can be taken to keep them out of crops or even to kill them, but I work instead to grow cabbages and other brassicas in the winter half of the year, when their predatory insects are much rarer. Suitable dates for all brassicas are covered in Chapter 14 (pages 133-148).

Put another way, for all the vegetables you grow, think which is the best time of year to sow and grow them for the least difficulty with insects. For example, peas sown in late winter have a fair chance of cropping before pea moths lay their eggs; cabbages for spring which are sown late August will mature when there are no caterpillars at all; and carrots sown in mid June avoid the spring flights of carrot root fly, and should be clean until October.

If, on the other hand, you sow seed on dates which do not respect the potential insect problems for any crop, you will need to spend time and money on remedies. Sometimes this can be justified, other times not, and in later chapters I suggest the sowing dates which offer most chance to each different vegetable of avoiding serious insect attack.

Attracting beneficial insects

There are many ways of maintaining a better balance of insects so that you have enough predators nearby to ensure a healthy balance. Pests are often there, but in small, scarcely noticeable numbers because other insects are eating them – aphids and hoverfly larvae for example. More predators can be encouraged by having the widest possible range of plants, including many flowers and a few stinging nettles.

DISEASES

I adopt a similar approach to disease, aiming to understand where problems are likely and then gardening to avoid them. For instance, potatoes are notorious for succumbing to blight, such that whole crops can be lost. This can be avoided by growing one of the new blight-resistant Sarpo varieties; or if you do not like their slightly floury texture, another solution is to grow a more waxy second early variety such as Wilja, which matures in August, often before the worst blight arrives, and its early harvest can be kept for use through the winter.

If you lose crops to pest or disease, you need neither despair nor reach for an expensive cure. Learn from what has happened and do it differently next time, to avoid the worst pitfalls. There may be slight damage, but we should be able to afford some losses if our soil is well composted and growing abundant, healthy crops.

OTHER ANIMALS

Badgers

In cold winters in Somerset, badgers often come into the garden searching for worms and slugs, perhaps because recently spread compost, on top of the soil, is an easier source of food – slugs and worms – in frosty conditions than their more regular haunts. Some of the first plantings are occasionally dug up as badgers look for little worms in the module's compost. Yet in spring they usually return to the fields, having in fact reduced the slug population at a wonderful time: just before the major plantings of early spring.

However, I am still nervous of badgers because they are powerful and can be extremely destructive when, for instance, they are foraging through a row of peas to satisfy their sweet tooth, or rapidly destroying rows of sweetcorn to devour its slightly immature cobs. As a protected species, they may not be hunted.

Rabbits

Rabbits are another concern. They can enter my garden because I hate putting up fencing, which would also need to be dug in so they cannot burrow underneath. A solution is provided by our two cats, who live outdoors and occasionally bring home young rabbits to eat. Numbers vary, and one spring I suffered some damage, initially watching onion, leek and garlic seedlings almost disappear; then parsley and lettuce. Then suddenly the damage ceased, only to reappear briefly in the autumn: rabbit numbers and eating grounds fluctuate all the time, but severe infestations may need fencing out to have any worthwhile crops.

Spring Cabbage, Onions, Mizuna in Modules.
Raised in greenhouse, planted late September

Scarole Endive Bubikopf in September

Lettuce Rouge Grenoble & Salad Rocket plants in different-sized modules for planting in tunnel, late October

Spring Cabbage netted against pigeons in October

Clearing grass by mulching with carpet & black plastic, then compost spread and ready to plant in June

Lettuce – Amorina

Lettuce – Rosemoor

Lettuce – Cos – Chartwell

Lettuce – Freckles

Lettuce – Bijou

Mizuna in September

Lettuce Bridgemere, 5 months old

Oriental Leaves before and after cutting

Lettuce – Frillice

Broad Beans in foreground, Potatoes under net, Redina Lettuce,
Onions, Parsnip, Lettuce and Kohlrabi under net

RABBIT FENCING

I admit to ambivalence over fencing rabbits out because it is such a major job: digging a narrow trench about a foot deep and lining it with mesh fencing, which should emerge above ground to about 80cm (2'6"). Or you can run two strands of permanently electrified wire around your plot, about 15cm and 30cm above ground level. However this is clearly bad for children, can be broken by badgers, and any grass below the fence needs regular cutting to prevent the electricity disappearing down blades of grass into the soil.

Birds

Pigeons above all, but also partridge and pheasant, can systematically strip leaves off peas, brassicas and salads, particularly in springtime. If this happens, you will need anti-bird netting. For example, drape a roll of four metre wide mesh over semi-circular wire hoops spanning the beds.

In springtime, fleece is effective against birds, as well as helping to protect plants from cold winds.

The essence of gardening is learning how everything fits together and how to respond as different situations arise. It is a continual learning process, never devoid of interest and always changing. Every season throws up new challenges and opportunities; the next chapter looks at ways of increasing the chances of success.

Chapter 6

Sowing Seeds, Raising Plants

The early summer can be a curious time. In those first long days of hot sunshine, just when one feels like some fresh, juicy vegetables, nothing is ready in the garden.

The days lengthen more rapidly than the soil warms up. And crucially, plant growth from seed is initially very slow. In the cool springtime, small seeds need many weeks to germinate, develop roots and attain any notable size. How can we speed up the early slow part of growth, to reach more rapidly the point where plants have enough roots and leaves for growth to take off?

Buying plants

The simplest way is to buy plants; however, there are three potential pitfalls:

- Firstly, they may have been raised in such ideal conditions for speedy but soft growth that finding themselves outside in cool, wet soil is terminally shocking. Keeping them outdoors in pots or trays for a few days before planting is always wise, so they can acclimatise at least, after which they may look less glossy but will be stronger.

- Secondly, there is the question of seasonality. The nursery's business is to sell plants, not to ensure the gardener has a fine crop. Every year I see plants for sale that are wrong for the season (such as pak choi in springtime) and hence doomed to relative failure, however well the gardener may look after them. So you will benefit from learning the right seasons for planting the right crops (a theme that runs throughout this book) and sowing your seeds at the right time, and ignoring some nice looking plants of dubious value.

- Thirdly, there is the question of vegetable variety or cultivar. Plants offered for sale need to look sturdy and appealing, but these characteristics do not always result in the best crop later on. Commercial seed catalogues describe certain varieties as "good for plant sales", which says to me 'avoid this variety, because they are listing no other benefits'.

The seed is usually cheap and I know from growing some of them that I prefer varieties with different characteristics. However, unless you have enough experience or knowledge of which varieties are the good ones, it can be tricky. Sometimes they turn out alright, but it is far more reliable to grow your own, space and materials permitting.

Buying seed

The principles of successful sowing and plant raising are the same for almost everything you will grow, so I will go into some detail. The first thing is to choose some good seeds, and this is not entirely straightforward. I sow a lot of seeds every year, often of the same vegetable but from different seed companies, and I have experienced a surprising number of irregularities.

For example, there are seeds which germinate poorly and unevenly, when sown at the same time as and next to other seeds of the same vegetable that are doing well. One year a large sowing of parsnips failed to germinate at all, while the neighbouring seed of a different cultivar grew strongly. A batch of lettuce seed came up as something completely different to what was on the packet. Two packets of Musselburgh leeks from different companies had completely different colour, stem length and frost resistance.

It is almost impossible to get any admission of such happenings out of a seed company. So buyer beware! If germination is poor or growth uneven, it may not be you who is at fault.

The other side of this story is that there are a lot of good seeds of a wonderful and growing range of vegetables and their many different cultivars. Seed catalogues offer a wider choice than most garden centres and it can be great fun to spend time in the winter picking out the seeds of an exciting summer. Hope springs eternal, and I love to try new and unusual offerings, at the same time as continuing with my tried and trusted regulars.

I recommend organic seeds because I feel that they have more vigour and integrity. No chemicals were used to protect their parents, who must therefore have prospered in reasonably natural conditions, and will have passed on some of this ability to thrive without artificial help to their progeny. Also, in buying organic seed, you are supporting a chemical-free farm somewhere in the world. The only difficulty is that many cultivars are not yet available as organically grown, although the choice is expanding.

When looking through seed catalogues, read the small print carefully – and read between it, the unwritten bits! For instance, "succulent and prolific" with no mention of taste suggests 'unremarkable flavour'. Any description involving the word popular makes me suspicious, look instead for terms such as "hardy strain", "productive" and "tasty".

Normally seeds come from 'open-pollination', meaning that insects have been allowed to move freely amongst them and move the pollen from plant to plant, resulting in a little uncertainty about the exact identity of male and female parents of any seed produced. F1 hybrid seed, by contrast, is bred in a controlled way to several specifically selected parents over many generations, a more expensive process.

Hybrids are not genetically modified!

F1 hybrids can achieve certain characteristics that make the extra cost worthwhile, such as the rich flavour of Sungold tomatoes, the sweetness of sugar-enhanced sweetcorn and the tightness of hybrid brussels sprout buttons. Note that seed saved from hybrids will not grow true to type; instead each plant will have different characteristics of the many parent varieties.

Hybridisation is an artificial method but is still working within natural laws, unlike the processes involved in genetic manipulation. It is exasperating to hear (so often!) the claim that plant breeding has been going on throughout history and that GM is just another refinement – suffice to say here that it is a dangerous attempt to manipulate plants outside the boundaries of the world as we know it.

How long will seed keep?

Many seed packets contain far more seeds than are needed for one year's harvest, and if kept reasonably cool and dry they can serve for another season. I find that lettuce and tomatoes will germinate reliably when up to five years old, but parsnip definitely works better with fresh seed – as long as it is fresh when you buy it! The best germination is usually from home-saved seed (see part 2, pages 114 and 125) such as peas and beans, whose vigour and reliability is often way ahead of most commercial offerings.

From looking at the list below, you can work out that it may be worthwhile to buy many lettuce and tomato seed packets to have a range of varieties over several years. Best storage conditions are cold and dry, but the figures below are based on ambient temperature and humidity, so they may not agree with other published sources!

LENGTH OF TIME SEED KEEPS
IN AVERAGE DOMESTIC CONDITIONS

Lettuce	5 years	Tomato	7	Leeks	2
Onions	2	Spinach	3	Brassicas	3
Parsley	2	Carrot	2	Parsnip	1
Beans	6	Peas	6	Sweetcorn	3

In ideal storage conditions of minimum humidity and around freezing point temperature, seed will keep for much longer. Yet five years is long enough to mean that packets of many different lettuces, for example, can be purchased and used over a number of seasons, sowing just a few seeds each time, so as not to be overwhelmed by lots of the same lettuce all at once. Or you can buy a packet of the seed company's own mix and see how it suits you, again sowing just a small number of seeds each time.

Sowing

Once you have your seeds, there is an important choice to be made between sowing them directly in the soil, or in compost in a greenhouse or on the windowsill.

As an example, the first outdoor sowings (not plantings) of lettuce in early spring will often be at risk to slugs if it is cold and wet, partly because it takes only one nibble for a tiny seedling to lose most of its two tiny leaves. In a cold spring, it is wise to wait for some warmer and reasonably dry weather.

While April can be warm and dry, it is usually a fickle month and it often pays to have raised seedlings 'indoors', in reliable conditions. A greenhouse offers the possibility of sowing some vegetables as early as late February, since seedlings of many vegetables can survive some frost, especially when they have the chance of growing strongly by day in warm, dry conditions. By April you can then have plants rather than seeds, and will be looking forward to some early harvests.

Using a windowsill for propagation is more difficult because a lack of light causes plants to become somewhat drawn up and spindly. Bearing this in mind, it is still a fair option if there are no other alternatives, and if you can 'harden off' the plants outside before planting. Hardening-off means accustoming plants to harsher conditions, such as the rain and cold winds that have not affected them inside. It ultimately makes them stronger and tougher and more able to resist the more bruising aspects of life outdoors.

Chief among these are undoubtedly slugs and snails, hereafter referred to as slugs for simplicity, since a snail is really a shell-covered slug. Their enduring presence must ALWAYS be borne in mind. At the same time, remember that their role is to 'tidy up the debris', so we want to ensure that our plants do not come into this category. Well-grown and hardened plants are definitely less appealing to slugs than spindly, weak ones. Remember also that plants growing in their right season are always more likely to succeed, when there is a much greater likelihood of the right level of warmth, moisture and of lower populations of harmful insects or diseases.

Using a greenhouse

To spread the load of growing your own plants it might be possible, on an allotment, to get together with the neighbours and share out some plant raising. Once everything is set up, it takes little more time to raise two hundred lettuces than forty. It would be marvellous if every allotment could have just one good greenhouse with automatic ventilation and a large water butt outside the door, or a tap nearby. The amounts of water needed are actually quite small, but watering needs to be regular, daily at least in fine weather, so water nearby is a great blessing.

Light from all sides makes growth in a greenhouse or polytunnel superior to the drawn-up leaves growing on light-depleted windowsills. Glass greenhouses hold more warmth than plastic structures, although bear in mind that even under glass, from November to February, sunshine is too weak and limited to build up significant heat, or to mitigate night frosts. Nonetheless, keeping cold rain and winds off plants and seedlings makes a huge difference, and once the days start to lengthen rapidly in March, the greenhouse can become an exciting port of call with visible spurts of growth and pleasant working conditions.

Late spring frosts, if hard enough (-3 or -4°C) can penetrate glass or plastic, so frost-sensitive plants such as tomatoes and courgettes may need a paraffin or electric heater set working at dusk, only when an air frost is forecast. The last 'normal' date for such an event is worth ascertaining from a local gardener, who will also be well aware of the later date of possible ground frost which would scorch or destroy the leaves of potatoes, tomatoes, runner beans and so on.

SURVIVING FROST

Vegetable seedlings which survive frost include most of the spring leaves like lettuce, spinach, cabbage, parsley, coriander, and also broad beans, peas and sweet peas. They will germinate and grow slowly in the greenhouse from a sowing in late winter.

For rapid germination and growth of seedlings, a bench of moist sand with electric soil-warming cables, controlled by a thermostat, will soon repay the investment if you are growing a larger number of plants.

Smaller versions of the same idea, such as electric propagators the size of a seed tray with a plastic hat on top and an electric heater underneath, need more careful use because water cannot drain out of the bottom. There is a risk of waterlogging, or at the other extreme of roots drying out from the powerful heat rising out of its base.

Failing a greenhouse, coldframes are a fair second option for successful plant raising. They are just not so good for the gardener on a cold, wet day! Also they risk harbouring more slugs than larger, warmer structures, so attention must be paid to damp corners and undersides of pots, planks or trays. Have a look regularly, even every couple of days, to remove slugs and snails, only one of which can eat lots of small seedlings quite quickly.

Composts for sowing

What to sow the seeds in? Do not use soil, because it will hold insufficient food and moisture to raise a reasonably large plant in a confined zone of root growth. Use a good commercial plant-raising compost – preferably organic – for slower, stronger growth. It will usually be called "multi-purpose", suitable for sowing and plant raising. Special sowing compost has less nutrients and superior drainage, but I have always managed with multi-purpose, and using one grade makes things simpler.

The nutrients in organic compost are similar to those in a non-organic compost, but their proportions should be more natural since they come from the field or farmyard rather than a factory. Some have added seaweed or rock dust to offer a range of trace elements, which are important for healthy growth.

Modules, seed trays and gutters

Regarding a container for the compost, the two main options are seed trays or modules. The main difference is that modules are divided into partitions of variable size, enabling each plant to develop its own roots and then to be planted without any root disturbance. Both seed and module trays come usually in A5 or A4 size, about 50mm deep and with drainage holes in the bottom.

Different vegetables need modules of different sizes. For lettuce, I recommend about forty 3cm modules per A4 size, to enable development of a fair-sized plant. Courgettes can start in modules of this size, but grow rapidly and will soon need transplanting to pots or larger 5cm modules, fifteen per A4 size. Fill trays or modules to at least 10mm above the top with compost and then press it down quite firmly, since roots thrive best in a medium that offers solid support, as long as there is no waterlogging.

INSTANT ROWS OF VEGETABLES

Plastic guttering of different lengths, filled with compost, is a useful way of raising short rows of peas, salad, spinach or any vegetable that grows at close spacing in a row. When plants are growing strongly, place the gutter outside for two or three days before drawing out a large drill in the soil and sliding it in whole.

Correct watering

Good watering is critical, and above all avoid over-watering. It is more likely to cause problems in seed trays, where water can lie near the bottom despite all the drainage holes. You can absorb most of the water that drains through the holes by putting newspaper underneath the seed tray. If the compost has been thoroughly wetted before sowing any seeds and then covered with glass, no watering will be necessary for quite a few days after sowing.

Thereafter it depends on the weather and temperature. If ever the compost's surface dries to a paler colour then water is certainly needed; avoid letting it dry out to the point where the compost has shrunk and become hard to make wet again. Peat-based composts can be difficult in this respect, and are best avoided for ecological reasons. Watering with a fine rose is kindest for seedlings and young plants. As plants develop more leaves they require noticeably more water and after a month or so they can be hardened off outside (longer for certain plants such as tomatoes, aubergines and peppers).

It takes some experience to learn how much water to give. Different plants need different amounts in different weather conditions. Getting it right takes practice and is worth mastering, as watering wisely makes a great difference to all plants. Seed trays and seedlings in general want a light touch from the watering can because germinating seeds are growing so slowly, and really require dampness more than wetness. Too much of the latter and they will 'damp off': their tiny roots suffocate in airless compost, where water is filling all the holes.

Modules are easier to water correctly because they drain more freely than seed trays, and usually contain slightly larger plants whose greater demands for water will suck up any temporary excess. Later, as they grow into small plants rather than large seedlings, it can become difficult to give sufficient water for even half of a sunny day, and this is one sure indication that a plant is ready to go out. Most plants will tolerate quite dry conditions and keep healthy but will not grow much, so on hot spring days a twice daily watering of modules will certainly help larger plants.

Otherwise a once daily routine is excellent, preferably in the morning so that cold water is not cooling the compost of an evening, and leaving damp conditions through the night, in which slugs and moulds may thrive. For this reason as well, be careful not to over-water on mornings of cool dark days as late as early May, when plants draw up little moisture: it is sometimes better to miss a day's watering. If you are not sure, lift up a pot or tray to see if it is heavy or light – you may be surprised either way.

Pests under cover

Slugs: if ever you see holes in the leaves, or plants eaten off, have an imme-diate and careful look for the slimy intruder (often only one) before it mows its way through several plants. It should be possible to maintain the small area of a greenhouse or coldframe slug-free, 99% of the time at least. A thorough spring-clean before first sowings affords great peace of mind.

Other pests can be trickier. Woodlice have multiplied recently in milder winters, to the extent that certain plants can have their stems terminally nibbled. I find most damage to tomato and spinach seedlings. Usually lift-ing the module tray will reveal clusters of woodlice that can be swept up and put on a compost heap. Doing this occasionally in late winter will help you keep on top of the problem for most of a season.

Ants are another beneficiary of rising temperatures, making their pres-ence known each springtime and then throughout the season. The sand of my propagating bench is home to a colony of flying ants that rise up into the compost of modules in contact with it. After midsummer they can make compost toxic with their secretions, and I place a pallet or open-meshed plastic trays on the sand, with plants sitting on that, to keep my plants out of contact with the sand and ants below.

Ventilation and shading

Many greenhouses now come with helpful automatic window-opening and -shutting devices that are sensitive to temperature. In their absence, open-ing and closing is vital in sunny weather, much less so in dull conditions. Each structure is different: my home-made greenhouse has ill-fitting win-dows that serve extremely well for natural ventilation. The small air vol-ume of coldframes makes opening every day more important. The homoge-nous plastic sheet of a polytunnel admits no air at all, so at least one door should be left open by day.

Some gardeners paint their greenhouse roofs with lime wash, or hang up shading to prevent overheating in summer. Personally I find this a job too far and have always managed fine without it, although it means I need to be vigilant about seedlings drying out rapidly in the hottest weather. Genuine lime wash is effective because it is most opaque on dry days and admits more light in damp weather.

Sowing indoors v. sowing outdoors

It may seem strange to spend so much time, effort and money on propa-gation when seeds can simply be sown outside in the soil. This is true to a point, but look at the advantages of good indoor propagation:

- *Earlier harvests* – first salad in April and May not June, courgettes in June not July, and so on.
- *Less slug damage*, because a larger well-grown plant can resist them in a way that tiny seedlings cannot. 'The seeds did not come up' is often, really, 'the seedlings were grazed off completely by slugs and snails'.
- *More crops over the season*, because as soon as one crop is finished, say carrots, another can be planted that is already a month underway indoors, such as plants of winter salad. There has been less of a pause while the new crop is germinating and establishing.
- *The possibility of growing exotic crops*, both because plants such as melons will have more time to fruit well in Britain from an indoor sowing, and because any spare greenhouse space in summertime, after the busy plant-raising of late spring, can be used for aubergines or chillies for example. This may be in pots, grow bags or in the soil.

Planting out

Some plants such as lettuce are tougher than they appear, and should survive any outdoor weather from about early April, except in parts of upland or northern Britain. A few days of acclimatisation to sun, wind, rain and frost will see them ready for growing in the soil.

Other plants such as courgettes and French or runner beans are much more temperature-sensitive. Firstly, they will be killed dead by any frost. Secondly, even without frost they will perish in the absence of sufficient warmth to enable their growth. They simply do not function when the soil temperature is too low; hence the advice to wait until late May or June before planting them out. This important detail is covered for each vegetable in their different sections.

Even when plants are set out at the right time, slugs will be interested because any plant that suddenly appears, as if from nowhere from a slug's point of view, needs time to settle in and start growing strongly. While in this phase of transition it has less spare energy than usual for resisting slimy attacks, so one or two leaves may be lost. The aim is to start with a reasonably large and healthy plant which has sufficient reserves to overcome the shock of transplanting, and at a time of year when the climate favours its steady growth.

The planting of modules and many other small plants is made easier with dibbers, which come in many sizes, to make small holes in the soil, each hole a little larger than the plant's rootball. I recommend a good dibber as one of your basic tools (see page 21).

A critical time: young plants settling in

For what seems like a long time just after planting (up to two weeks in the coolness of spring), your precious young plants will scarcely grow. Instead, they will be consolidating and adjusting to their new situation, organising their roots above all. This is an important principle that applies to everything newly placed in the soil: the settling-in period, when a plant's energy is used more for self-therapy than for growing. Through this critical period, plants have less ability to resist pest and disease – slugs above all – which is why they need to be reasonably large and strong in the first place.

It is also why your home-raised plants are almost certainly more likely to survive than many you may buy. Yours will have grown slowly in less than ideal conditions – some cold nights, dark days, the odd watering missed, in compost that may not be 100% perfect for the plant. All this helps to make them stronger. And this is why some of the beautiful-looking plants offered for sale by professionals may well struggle when confronted by the less than perfect conditions of a cold, wet spring, or a hot, dry one for that matter.

Fleece

Fleece is an invaluable and simple tool for helping young plants to grow in slightly adverse conditions. Most fleece is thin, porous and translucent woven plastic, which admits rain and air but not wind, and traps some warmth. What more could we ask for? It works best over young plants, whose leaves hold it slightly above ground level and allow the soil surface to dry out enough to discourage slugs, but the opposite can occur if it is laid over newly sown seedbeds in cold, damp weather.

Young plants seem happy to hold the slight weight of it by their leaves, and in growing they will push it up like a bubble. Keep a sheet of any length in place with, for example, a stone or brick every metre or metre and a half, and use these to pull the fleece fairly tightly over your seedlings. It works better to squash them a little, rather than allowing loose fleece to flap in the wind, hitting tender leaves. Simply roll the stones back on one side to pull the fleece to the other side and access beds for weeding, or even for picking. Usually it is best taken off after a month or so, by which time plants will be growing strongly and the weather will be warmer.

Fleece has less value in really wintry weather because there may be snow that will squash it onto plants below, and winter gales can cause holes and gashes. In high summer it can be useful for keeping insects off cabbages and oriental greens, but can also lead to overheating, and fine meshes are usually recommended for this purpose – although I find them disappointingly fragile. A drawback of both is perhaps an aesthetic one: that carrots or salad are not attractive when covered by what looks like white sheeting. Environmentally it is a reasonable choice; although made from oil, fleece and mesh are lightweight, containing little weight of raw material, and should last for several years. Many of my sheets have covered at least five crops already; the odd hole is not too critical, and some fleece has put up with trampling by badgers!

Fleece is suitable for covering all early salad plantings, spinach, cour-gettes, calabrese and sometimes French and broad beans, early potatoes and peas. Allied to good plants from the greenhouse, it helps the year to begin with a (nice) bang and to make the most of any half-helpful weather in springtime. It offers slight frost protection: leaves will be scorched where they are in contact with frozen fleece but reasonably protected otherwise. Fleece is also useful for keeping insects off brassica crops in summer – see Chapter 14.

One further use of fleece is in a greenhouse or polytunnel, as an extra layer of insulation in really cold weather. The 30% loss of light is more than offset by higher temperatures, helping plants through severe frost especially.

Other possibilities

An older version of fleece is the cloche, made of glass initially and then of polythene. The former are expensive to buy, of interest mainly to listed gardens. Plastic cloches are cheaper, but still a lot of work to erect and look after compared to fleece. The plants underneath them will require occasional watering and some ventilation as well, on hot days, since polythene is impervious to air and water. Many catalogues sell them, but I recommend sticking with fleece. Through March and April my garden can be at least a quarter fleeced, although by early June it will almost all have been removed, its job done.

Chapter 7

Making Compost

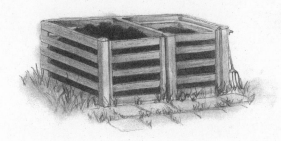

Whole books have been written on composting – this chapter is a brief outline to help you make the most of your possibilities.

Compost heaps and bins are magical means of turning garden waste into something of great value. Opening up a heap of successfully ripened compost is, for me, almost as satisfying as growing fine food.

How compost is created: balanced ingredients quickly assembled

The ideal heap has the right balance of green and fibrous material – about two or three parts green to one part drier, fibrous matter – and is built up within about a fortnight. It heats rapidly to 60-70⁰C, killing weed seeds and pathogens. When a month or so later it is just lukewarm, and turning it into an empty bin will introduce air and encourage a second, less hot fermentation.

From start to finish the process can take as little as two months, but in most gardens four to five months is more realistic. Various starters and accelerators, of varied composition, can be used to speed up and perfect the process. Best composting happens in summer, while in winter a lack of green matter and low temperatures make good fermentation unlikely.

Good compost is dark brown, almost black, crumbly and sweet-smelling, like a damp forest in autumn. If yours is not like this, keep trying – and remember that few gardens have an ideal mix of ingredients, all available at the same moment. Make the most of what you have.

Types of heap or bin

Larger gardens have space for and need two or more heaps, preferably side by side. Enclosures of slatted wood keep them tidy and conserve some heat. Solid sides are less good because air and moisture need to circulate. A roof to keep rain out would be fantastic – old carpet does well – or finished compost can be covered with polythene.

Bins are usually made of plastic, with lidded tops for putting green matter in and holes at the bottom for drawing compost out. One large bin may suffice for small gardens.

Rats

Heaps are vulnerable to rats, whereas in theory bins are rat-proof; but if rats do find a way in, they will certainly make themselves at home, especially over winter. They enjoy both the warmth and any edible additions, so you can make a difference. As a general rule avoid all food scraps (see kitchen wastes below), but if rats are already in a heap, avoid everything remotely edible such as peelings of potatoes, apple cores and avocado skins. Encourage cats or a terrier to patrol, particularly when you are turning or spreading compost in spring. (As late as May I once chanced upon a nest of ten baby hairless rats.)

Suitable ingredients

There are many recipes for making compost but, most importantly, the aim is to use up and rot down all of a garden's waste. Sometimes this means mostly grass mowings, sometimes mostly prunings, sometimes mostly kitchen waste. Aim for all ingredients to be moist and of small size.

- *Grass mowings* are valuable for heating rapidly, and combine well with crop residues, cardboard, paper, leaves and small twiggy wastes.
- *Prunings of trees and hedges* need chopping into 15cm lengths at most, otherwise they allow pockets of air in heaps that prevent the build-up of heat. Large quantities of woody material are best taken to a recycling centre.
- *Kitchen wastes* are excellent, such as fruit and vegetable peelings, coffee grounds, teabags and eggshells. Avoid food leftovers because they encourage rats and foxes – put them in a bin for your local council to compost.
- *Leaves* are fine in small quantities; too many will slow and cool the fermentation. Large amounts can be turned into leaf mould over one or two years, in sacks or bins.
- *Weeds* rot down well, even perennial roots such as dandelion, but there are exceptions. Bindweed roots are best burnt, and weeds with excessive amounts of seed may be better off taken to recycling in bags, because their seeds will survive unless heaps heat up thoroughly.
- *Crop residues* such as pea haulm and tomato stems are often on the woody side, and need both chopping up and mixing with sufficient green matter.
- *Newspaper and cardboard* need to be moist and scrumpled, and rot nicely in the presence of some green waste.

- *Air* is a vital ingredient, dispersed evenly through heaps. Intermix soggy and wet ingredients with fibrous ones. Turning heaps introduces valuable air.
- *Soil* is sometimes recommended as an ingredient for its bacteria, but usually there is enough on roots of weeds and crop remains.
- *Minor additions* of wood ash (not coal), yard sweepings, and vacuum cleaner bags are fine as long as they contain no metal or plastic.
- **Do not add plastic** because it does not rot down.

Heaps built in layers

Many texts recommend compiling regular layers of different ingredients. This can make the process sound more complicated than it is, and in practice the available ingredients are best mixed a little as heaps are assembled. In July, for example, you may have a large amount of grass mowings followed, two days later, by a lot of broad bean stems (chopped into 15cm lengths preferably, or smaller). These are ideal companions, and mixing them together with a manure fork would help the hot mowings to speed up the decomposition of the woodier bean stalks.

The aim is to have a variety of ingredients all the time, rather than a large amount of one followed by a large amount of another.

Last additions

The eventual height of any heap depends on how long it has taken to assemble, because some rotting down occurs long before arrival of the last ingredients. Any height between 1.2 and 2.5 metres is feasible, and the heap will soon decline to half that or less.

A waterproof cover will prevent cold rain from removing heat and air. The heap should stay warm or hot, up to about 60°C, for at least a fortnight. Once cool it can be turned, or spread on the garden if sufficiently decomposed.

This does not apply to bins where compost is regularly removed from the bottom, because in theory their contents should keep recycling forever. Should they stay full and decline to compost, they may be too dry, or with

---

TURNING COMPOST

Heaps can be turned as soon as they cool to lukewarm. Although most gardeners do not find time for this, it is well worth the effort. Air that is introduced will help further decomposition, as will further mixing of any uneven parts of the heap. Turned heaps are ready after another month or so, and are less work to spread since their contents are more even.

too many large stems making pockets of air, or containing a wrong balance of ingredients, such as too much wood (see Problems below).

Problems

I find that the compost of every heap has different qualities and defects, always reflecting its ingredients, the kind of protection, rainfall and the time of year. Here are remedies for some common problems.

Soggy compost, often bad-smelling, results from:

- too much fine green matter with too little fibre. Remedy: add more crumpled paper, cardboard or other high carbon ingredients.
- too much rain percolating through the heap. Remedy: cover and leave less long before spreading.
- a poor site with bad drainage. Remedy: make heaps in a drier area.

Uneven compost, large lumps unrotted is a result usually of insufficient chopping, shredding or mixing, meaning too little air and poor combinations for successful decomposition. Remedy: mix and chop more thoroughly.

Pockets of undecomposed dry ingredients. Remedy: Make sure when adding large quantities of dry waste such as pea haulm that it is sufficiently chopped to pack down and absorb any moisture added. Some stemmy wastes make a fibrous ball which water simply percolates through.

Generally poor decomposition may have several causes, ranging from insufficient moisture and / or green matter, to waste added in too large pieces. It should be possible to deduce which of these is to blame from the exact condition of un-rotted compost. Every heap is an interesting reminder of earlier seasons, and a wonderful way of processing waste.

Chapter 8

The Moon

When people ask whether I take the moon into account in my gardening, I am mostly surprised that the question even arises. Consider how the moon pulls great masses of water in the oceans. Plants are mostly water, so how could they not be responding in some way to the moon's force?

But what effect exactly is the moon exerting on plants? I think that nobody knows for sure, although I have observed that it certainly does. I love to cut open roots of beetroot Barbietola di Chioggia, whose sweet white flesh is ringed with pink circles that correspond to each moon of the plant's life. Leeks seem to create one leaf for each half moon, but some vegetables reveal no obvious pattern – carrots, for instance, show fantastic explosions of lines from their centre, but no series of rings.

How as gardeners can we best work with moon forces, to help them work in our favour? There are two different schools of thought, which I explain below. You will have to decide which makes more sense for your own gardening.

The traditional approach

The traditional approach, in Britain at least, mostly relies on whether the moon is waxing or waning. Waxing happens over fourteen or fifteen days between the new moon, when no moon is visible, and the full moon when it is 100% visible as a round white sphere. So a waxing moon is growing brighter and larger every night, and is considered to have an uplifting or drawing-up effect on plants. Its signature effects are strong leaf growth and general vigour above ground.

A waning moon occurs between full and new moon, so the moon that we see is becoming thinner every night, until it disappears again on the next new moon. This fortnightly period is one of 'contracting forces' which favour consolidation below ground. Growth of roots is enhanced, so for example carrots and onions sown during a waning moon will tend, over the course of their life, to emphasise root development a little more than leaf growth.

One moon above all is traditionally of great importance for plant growth: the first full moon after the spring equinox, seen as harbinger of spring and new life. The Christian festival of Easter still follows it, on the first Sunday after that full moon.

If you want to take the moon into account, the simple framework described above, and in the hundred-year-old poem below, is an excellent place to start. It was much used by farmers and gardeners before we all became more scientific:

If ye plant yer corn on the growin' moon,
And put up the lines for crows,
You'll find it will bear, and yer wheat will too,
If its decent land wher't grows.
But potatoes now are a different thing,
They want to grow down, that is plain;
And don't you see you must plant for that,
When the moon is on the wane!

Paying attention to waxing and waning may also alert you to other changes in your mind and body, and in the weather as well. I have often remarked shifts in weather patterns that correlate with new or full moons, and when this occurs the pattern often persists for most of the next fortnight. The new moon seems to have a greater effect than full moon, while both cause a noticeable difference to rainfall, usually increasing it.

One drawback to working exclusively with a waxing and waning moon framework is the long period of each. If you miss sowing carrots before the new moon, a whole fortnight must elapse before another opportunity comes around. Another snag is that most gardening work is governed by the waxing moon, which is benefiting leaves, flowers and fruits, indeed everything except plants whose growth below ground interests us.

The astrological approach

Another school of thought about moon forces looks at how the moon translates the energy of the constellation in which it resides at any one time. Much of the work on this has come from biodynamic farmers and gardeners, who follow the teaching of Austrian mystic Rudolf Steiner. He developed a whole system of farming in tune with cosmic forces that is extremely successful and used worldwide, although somewhat less in

Britain*. Biodynamic gardeners watch the moon very closely, how it looks and where it is in the sky, as well as how it relates to other planets and the universe as a whole.

Just as the sun passes through twelve constellations each year, so the moon passes through all of the same constellations each lunar month, spending about two and a half days in each. From each one it picks up one of the four dominant characteristics, or elements: Earth, Air, Water or Fire. So the moon in Taurus has an earthbound, rooty influence; in Gemini an airy, flowering one; in Cancer a watery, leaf-promoting effect and in Leo a warm and fruity aspect. After nine or ten days the 'earth, air, water, fire cycle' is finished and repeats itself, so that if you miss an opportunity to plant, another comes along quickly.

For moon enthusiasts there is plenty of evidence to suggest that this four-rhythm cycle has a strong effect on plant growth, but you need a current year's guide book (see Resources, pages 217-219) to know which constellation the moon is in, on any given day. There is also the peculiar fact that it can contradict the waxing/waning approach, because it is possible to have 'root' days during a waxing moon and 'leaf' days during a waning moon.

If working with the moon appeals to you, I recommend starting with the waxing/waning approach. Many ordinary calendars show the dates of full and new moons, giving you an immediate sowing guide for the year ahead. Or look out of the window on a clear night!

Green fingers

Just as important as the moon – perhaps more so – is the gardener. You and I carry thoughts and feelings everywhere and not least to the garden, where sensitive plants respond to them. If we are depressed or upset, our plants may succumb to some of the same malaise. When our mood is warm and sunny, growth is enhanced. True concern for plants and a desire for their health and wellbeing is felt by them as a positive help, which is probably what it means to have green fingers.

Feedback happens in both directions, because plants can also help us. Many people experience a calming and beneficial effect when surrounded by plants in a well tended garden, so we have the chance, through cultivating better thoughts and feeling ourselves, to set up a virtuous circle of mutual help.

---

* Rudolf Steiner became prominent in the early twentieth century. He divined his understandings intuitively, and specifically related many of them to the land, because of the importance he attached to eating good food, in order for people to realise their full potential, both earthly and spiritual. Biodynamic scientists have a way of measuring life forces in plants, using silver chloride on filter paper, that reveals striking differences between, for example, carrots that are biodynamically, organically or chemically grown. See BDAA in Resources.

Chapter 9

Summer Salads

Top quality leaves every day

Growing salad leaves in the summer half of the year is perhaps the most rewarding part of vegetable gardening. They grow quickly, they are beautiful to behold, and when picked fresh from the garden they have a quality that is rarely found in bought salad. The more healthy your soil, the better they become. After many years of adding compost to the soil, the leaves develop even more exciting flavours, and each one boasts a crispness, a colour and an allure that will make you simply want to eat more of them.

Furthermore, seed catalogues are now bursting with a huge and growing variety of flavours, colours and textures to try out. In the world of lettuce alone, I have grown and enjoyed over fifty different varieties, and love to experiment with planting varied combinations to serve as ingredients for different salad mixes. Or, more simply, you can buy mixes of different seeds in a packet, which vary according to which seed company selected it. I recommend, for any sowing before July, that you choose a lettuce-only mix, without rocket or oriental greens, because they have different requirements and will not thrive from being sown before the longest day.

LETTUCE

Lettuce is ideally suited to the British climate and conditions, growing quickly and healthily from about April to October. It thrives in both moist and sunny weather, has only one notable pest, the redoubtable slug, and only one significant disease, mildew of the leaves which can be avoided in most conditions (see pages 55-58).

Pests

Special advice on dealing with pests, and slugs in particular, is given throughout this book and at the end of this chapter. Such vital information is often too important to be put separately under *problems* because it affects everything else from sowing to growing and the varieties used. Pest issues are also integral to how soil is cultivated or not and to how and how much compost is used.

Categories of lettuce

Most seed catalogues list lettuce in five main groups:

Butterheads are the classic soft, round-leaved ones with floppy and slightly waxy, or buttery leaves and well-rounded hearts. They overwinter better than most other lettuce, and are usually pale green or yellow in colour, with some interesting exceptions.

Cos are tall, thinner-leaved and usually dark green, but with some nicely different colours now becoming available. They do best in slightly warmer conditions and, although normally grown for hearts, many varieties perform well as leaf lettuce.

Batavian have thick, crunchy leaves of variable colour. If allowed to heart, they are pale and crisp, while some can be grown as leaf lettuce.

Iceberg / Crisp make light green hearts of smooth, watery leaves. They are relatively susceptible to tipburn.

Leaf Lettuce are the most suitable for regular picking of leaves as they grow, or for cutting as baby leaves when very small. Some will heart up if allowed to, most will simply make a larger and larger mass of small leaves at their centre. Since many of the cos and Batavian lettuces can also be treated as leaf lettuce and picked over for a regular supply of leaves, this expands the repertoire to a wide range of shapes, colours and flavours.

LEAF LETTUCE

Season of harvest: May-October
Follow with: it depends when they finish – French beans, leeks, kale, oriental leaves are all possible

Variety	Character *Special qualities*	Sow	Spacing (cm) *Harvest*
GRENOBLE RED	Hardy, attractive For leaves or heart, slug-resistant	Mar-Sep	Min. 20x20 May-Oct
REDINA / BIJOU	Vibrant dark red Tasty and ornamental, slug-resistant	Mar-Aug	Min. 20x20 May-Sep
BERGAMO	Vigorous, bright green Attractive, long-lived	Mar-Aug	Min. 20x20 May-Oct

For other varieties see below.

Sowing

A fair rule of thumb in sowing generally is to cover seeds with as much compost as the seed is thick. Lettuce seed is small and fine, and grows best if covered with very little or even no compost at all. I find most success with greenhouse sowings into modules: I just drop lettuce seed on the surface of well-wetted compost, and do not cover it at all. In soil outdoors, draw a shallow drill and sow at the rate of about ten seeds per 50mm.

One special thing to remember when sowing lettuce is that it is not supposed to germinate in hot weather. In practice, I have almost always had excellent germination in high temperatures. Keeping a newly-sown seed tray in the shade is a wise precaution in high summer, until small leaves are visible after three or four days.

If you have sown seed in a row outside, there is a choice to be made after about three weeks: either to crop the plants as baby leaves where they are, or to space them out more widely and either pick leaves off them for a longer time, or wait for a heart to develop. Seed packets often come with advice that promotes the idea of 'regular cutting', as opposed to careful picking of leaves. In fact this leads to plants' untimely demise and the need to re-sow.

I strongly recommend the longer term use of fewer plants, and looking after them more carefully. Above all, they need to be given room to develop a worthwhile root system. If you have raised or bought thirty to forty

---

CHARLES DOWDING'S LETTUCE METHOD

Between two to four weeks after setting out plants, depending on the season (less in summer), the larger outer leaves can be carefully picked off to leave the plant looking quite denuded, but always with no less than four of its youngest leaves at the centre. These will quickly re-grow to provide more medium-sized leaves for salad. Some of the first picking will be slug-eaten or a little mouldy, but thereafter leaf quality should be very good.

In this way, a steady stream of lettuce leaves can be picked off a small area, with much less need than usual to re-sow. The same plants are repeatedly cropped, always leaving the growing central rosette of baby leaves and never using a knife. A miserly three sowings of lettuce can provide leaves for the whole season from late April to early November, depending somewhat on timing of the last and first frosts at either end. You will not see this recommended on any seed packet, as it is very economical with the contents!

The repeated picking of leaves makes the plant want to grow more, and more, and more, because it needs a certain volume of root and leaf before it feels ready to rise to seed. Hence the life and productivity of each plant is considerably increased.

plants – a good number to provide leaves for a family over at least two months – dib holes about 250-300mm apart. Place each plant firmly in its hole, so that the top of its root system is just covered by soil, and then give a little water to each so that its roots are moistened and helped to make contact with the soil all around.

Growing

After about two months of picking, some plants will start to make a notice-able central stem, with their leaves becoming smaller and a flower bud appearing. Few worthwhile leaves will be produced after this happens, so the plant is best removed by twisting it out of the soil, tapping the roots clean of soil lumps and removing it to the compost heap.

If weed seedlings come up thickly among the lettuce, they can be hoed off carefully after any thorough picking, which will have made it easier to pass a hoe between plants. Or you can scrape amongst the plants with a trowel, or hand weed when there are just a few weeds. Keeping the soil clean is highly worthwhile in order to prevent any weeds from flowering, and to provide fewer habitats for slugs.

The lettuce season can be extended by laying fleece over early plantings in late March or April, to keep cold winds at bay and afford some protec-tion on cold nights. This is optional, as the plants will grow without it and sometimes fleece can afford shelter to slugs, in very wet weather. I mostly use it for my very early plantings of lettuce that have been raised in gentle heat from sowings in mid January. They are ready to plant by mid March and usually survive all sorts of inclement weather under fleece, which is stretched out on top of the plants, touching them all, and held down by stones on all sides, one every metre or so. As the plants grow, they firmly push the fleece up and it looks like a tight skin on top of the bed. It is bet-ter tight than loose, so as not to flap around in the wind.

Even without fleece, young lettuce plants resist gentle freezing, enabling a longer season of growth than is commonly appreciated. And over this long stretch of time, lettuce enjoys a 'season within its season', from May to July, when leaf quality is especially high and mildew on leaves is almost absent.

Compared to oriental greens and rocket, lettuce leaves are often pure and unblemished, especially when grown in a compost-rich soil. The com-post is less for nutrients, more for water retention and a certain vitality that is imparted to the plants. For even more healthy vigour, an occasional spraying of liquid seaweed, or prior application of volcanic rock dust can make a difference.

Lettuce leaves are mostly water, and in dry weather they will certainly ben-efit from a good sprinkling every two or three days – not every day, or slugs will enjoy themselves too much. A thorough wetting of the soil once a week is the best method, particularly when plants are being left to form a heart.

Varieties

Here are some commonly available varieties, with my observations of their behaviour in Somerset.

All except Webbs Wonderful can be treated as a leaf lettuce, with frequent picking of outer leaves. Some will make hearts if left unpicked.

Aruba A thin but vigorous oak leaf, red but not deep red, more a matt cherry colour. Susceptible to mildew in the autumn.

Amorina A slightly larger and light cherry-coloured version of Bergamo, one of the prettiest to grow and it adorns any flower bed. Like Bergamo it is slow to flower, so you can enjoy a long season of picking; it also grows well in the darker days of autumn.

Bergamo A bright green, deeply crinkled 'Lollo Biondi' (as opposed to 'Lollo Rosso') type that grows steadily for a long period. If sown in April it should keep cropping, when regularly picked over, until late July, being one of the slowest to rise to seed. The first leaves are a little tricky to pick as they lie close to the soil.

Cardinale Extremely pretty orange-green leaves, quite small and very round. Will make a coloured 'Little Gem' heart if allowed to.

Catalogna Vigorous mid green Italian lettuce with long serrated (oak-shaped) leaves, a top cultivar for early sowings as its speed of growth through April is second to none.

Chartwell A new dark green cos, suitable for both picking of leaves and to make a sweet heart.

Cocarde Like a bronze version of Catalogna, almost equally vigorous but a little quicker to flower. Easier to pick than many oak leaf varieties because there is a little more space between each leaf, allowing access to the fingers.

Freckles Exactly as its name suggests, small spots of dark red to brown on light green leaves. Some plants have disappointingly few freckles, some have a lot and they produce over a long season. I have picked Freckles' leaves from the same plants between mid April and mid July – three whole months.

Grenoble Red or Rouge Grenobloise Firm, crisp, green and bronzed shiny leaves. My favourite for its winter hardiness and ability to resist slugs and mildew. Normally sold as a hearting lettuce, with a pale crisp heart not unlike a crinkly iceberg, but I have found it suitable for cropping as a leaf lettuce, and regular picking of leaves can make it remarkably long-living. For example, my last sowing of the year is in very early September, for planting in a polytunnel in early October. A few leaves are picked in November and a very few from December to mid February. Then production increases, reaching a long peak in May and June. When the plants rise to flower in late June, they are ten months old and have yielded about one hundred leaves each. I grow Grenoble Red less in the summer, since so many other cultivars come into their own then, and in high summer, if allowed to grow a heart, it is prone to tipburn.

Little Gem Probably the most well known, small and sweet cos type, takes two to three months to develop a heart. Its outer leaves may look old and diseased by then but when they are peeled away, a fine, crunchy heart is revealed. Space closer at 150mm.

Lobjoits Like a much larger Little Gem and with smoother leaves. Can be pleasantly sweet in well-blanched hearts but prone to tipburn.

Marvel of Four Seasons A fine butterhead with waxy and attractively mottled leaves, bronze on light green. As the name suggests, it is hardy and can be sown late summer for an attempt at overwintering.

New Red Fire Popular and deservedly so, frilled but not frilly bronze to red leaves that produce over a long season.

Redina, Bijou Two of the darkest red cultivars whose depth of colour will enliven the garden, especially if contrasted against some lighter green lettuce or other vegetables. They crop steadily but at a slower rate than green lettuces. A rule of thumb is that the darker the leaf, the slower its growth. The intensity of colour more than compensates. Some Redina plants grow deeply frilled, similar to Lollo Rossa, but more vigorous and longer lasting.

Roger, Kamalia High yielding Batavian varieties with thick, crunchy, bronzed leaves. Again long-lasting.

Salad Bowl Found in all seed catalogues, green or red oak leaf.

Webbs Wonderful The original crisp lettuce, making a large crunchy heart. Leaves are a little more crinkly than those of a true iceberg such as Saladin, which are brittle, thin and glassy.

Harvesting lettuce (see box 'Charles Dowding's Lettuce Method', page 54)

The regular harvest of leaf lettuce can continue outdoors from May to late October, unless a frost arrives earlier. First harvests of hearts are usually Little Gem in June, others in July and continuing until first frost. Cutting a lettuce heart is more terminal for the plant, although some re-growth will usually happen and it may be worth waiting for the small new shoots if you have no other lettuce available.

Problems

Slugs are the number one pest of lettuce. Here are some tips to lessen their numbers, also applicable to all slug-tender crops, including most other salads.

- Keep soil clear of weeds.
- Grow or buy strong, healthy lettuce plants.
- If sowing directly in soil, you will need to re-sow if nothing is visible after a fortnight because slugs must have eaten the baby seedlings. Setting out plants is more reliable.
- Do not plant too close to walls or areas of long grass and thick vegetation where slugs will be abundant.
- Regular picking of larger leaves, with bare soil between plants, definitely keeps slug numbers down. It also keeps mildew at bay: in damper autumn days especially, many of lettuces' lower and older leaves can be covered on their undersides by this white powdery fungus that saps their goodness and turns them yellow.
- In patio pots, a strip of copper around the outside top rim of the pot can prevent arrival of marauding slugs.
- Collecting slugs and snails by torchlight is a highly effective way of reducing their numbers.

The critical moment is always sowing or planting time. Baby seedlings and newly set out plants are highly attractive to slugs, so lessening their numbers by having soil bare for at least a week beforehand will always help. Planting under fleece in cold weather can enable young lettuce to establish more strongly and resist slug attack.

When slug numbers are correct, there is always a little damage to a few older leaves, but some damage to younger leaves will occur if their numbers are allowed to increase too much. One can never relax too much where slugs are concerned, and growing more resistant lettuce varieties, such as Grenoble Red, is another option. A fair rule of thumb is that the redder the leaf, the less slugs eat of it.

Some summers there may be invasions of lettuce root aphid, which is apparent when plants of any size suddenly wilt and die quite quickly. Once

---

LETTUCE HEARTS

These take two to three months from sowing to maturing. As they firm up, watering is important in dry weather to avoid rotting of leaf ends (tipburn) and to help the heart grow to a good size. Hearts often break out into a flower stem quite quickly, so grow just a few from each sowing. Heart leaves are sweeter and paler than outside leaves, because they have 'self-blanched' as the heart expands.

arrived, the aphids travel only within soil but unfortunately can spread easily to adjacent plants, and I know of no organic remedy at present. They are not supposed to survive the winter, but may do so in milder areas.

One other problem can be tipburn, a browning of leaves' outer margins, but this only happens to certain hearting lettuce in hot dry conditions, when their roots are unable to supply sufficient moisture to all of every leaf. Regular and ample watering of large, hearting plants is important. Smaller plants, regularly picked over, do not suffer tipburn.

Salade composée

Take an attractive selection of salad leaves – some endive, radicchio, lettuce, and parsley. Cut a couple of rashers of bacon into fine strips, and fry them until crispy and set aside. Next make some croutons – cut some stale (or fresh!) bread into cubes and fry them in the pan with the bacon fat and some olive oil till crisp, chop some garlic and add it to the pan. Allow to cool. Make a vinaigrette in the bottom of your salad bowl:

1 teaspoon wholegrain mustard, a couple of grinds of a salt mill, 2 tablespoons of vinegar, 6 tablespoons of olive oil. Dissolve the mustard and salt in the vinegar, then add the oil. It is now ready to receive the leaves. Put the croutons and bacon on top of the leaves to serve, and toss well at the table. Variations can include walnuts, and cubes of cheese; in fact the possibilities are endless.

ORIENTAL LEAVES

Season of harvest: August-November
Follow with: n/a

Species	Character *Special considerations*	Sow	Spacing (cm) *First harvest*
MIZUNA / MIBUNA	Long mild-tasting leaves Rapid growth, pick regularly	Jul-Sep	3x25 or 20x20 3-4 weeks
MUSTARDS	Hot, spicy leaves Few plants needed, many varieties	Jul-Sep	3x25 or 20x20 3-4 weeks
PAK CHOI	Crunchy stems Needs slug-free environment	Jul-Sep	Min 10x10 6 weeks

Pest damage reduced by sowing later

Oriental leaves are tender, fast-growing members of the cabbage family (brassicas) that best expand the range of salad flavours after midsummer. They are easiest to grow as autumn, winter and early spring leaves, in which seasons they make larger, healthier leaves which are less prone to insect attack. Results from sowings in springtime are usually disappointing, because the plants often rise to flower quite quickly and suffer badly from flea beetles. Myriads of these small black insects hop around on most brassica leaves in spring and early summer, eating small round holes in them, which become larger as the leaves grow.

Various organic remedies for flea beetles have been suggested and the most effective is to cover any susceptible crop with fine fleece or mesh so that the beetles are excluded. Even then a few will always do some damage, and the best solution is to sow susceptible plants in late July and August, by which time flea beetles are much less common. August sowings of rocket, for example, provide some of the best rocket leaves of the year – from September through to April in mild areas. Rocket is not strictly an oriental leaf, but is similar in its pattern of growth because it belongs to the same family of plants (brassicas). Chapter 14 (pages 133-148) has further information on the difficulties and rewards of growing them.

As a rule, the later the sowing the cleaner will be the leaves, up to about the middle of August, by which time there are just enough growing days left for outdoor plants to make a worthwhile size before winter, except in polytunnels. Two sowings in July and one in early August will provide a range of interesting flavours for much of the late summer and autumn. As with lettuce, sowing seed thickly will provide many small leaves, or thinning down to plants at 200-250mm apart will provide larger leaves and thicker stems over a longer period, suitable for stir fries as well as salad.

Chinese Cabbage Usually grown for hearts, sown in July and harvested in early autumn before any notable frost. One heart can provide a number of salads, and since they store well I describe them fully in the next chapter on winter salads.

Komatsuna Extra fast growth, so good for late sowings in September. Reasonably mild flavour, not dissimilar to pak choi, and equally popular with slugs: leaves often have holes in.

Mizuna Probably the fastest and most productive salad plant of all, with long feathery leaves, thin white stems and a mild but spicy flavour. Best kept for winter but if you like it in summer too, and don't mind some holes from flea beetles, regular small sowings after mid July will provide abundant leaves. An abundance of leaves from each plant makes it suitable for cutting, within a month of sowing and about 3cm above soil level. Second and third cuttings may be had at ten day or two week intervals. If left to grow large, the leaves become rather long with spindly stems. Kyoto is a good variety for leaves that are less spindly.

Mibuna Long, thin, dark green, smooth leaves have an appealing mild taste, possibly the least peppery of all oriental leaves. No varietal distinctions; sow as for Mizuna.

Mustard Comes in red, green and golden colours, with quite long and more or less serrated leaves. The common attribute is a hot, pungent flavour and fast growth; so regular picking of small leaves is definitely a good idea. Any larger leaves can be added to stir fries, in moderation. Best sown in August for picking from late August, Golden Streaks and Ruby Streaks are good varieties for autumn leaves.

Pak Choi An increasing number of varieties is now being offered. For summer salads, green-stemmed pak choi is worthwhile because it tends to make more, smaller leaves than the white-stemmed kinds. I find that any sowings before August are prone to flower quite quickly, except for Joi Choi (see page 81). Pak Choi's mild and succulent taste is unfortunately appreciated enormously by slugs, the large outer leaves especially. So once again, pick small leaves regularly and also carefully because pak choi grows so fast that it has a very fragile root system which can be uprooted if leaves are pulled off too roughly.

Shugiku Also called chop suey greens, a member of the chrysanthemum family with no named varieties on offer. Its pungent flavour is quite different to anything else and if you like it, keep picking the vigorous new shoots before they flower, over quite a long period.

OTHER LEAF FLAVOURS

Season of harvest: Apr-Nov, depending on type of vegetable or herb
Follow with: it depends on crop chosen

Vegetable / Herb	Character / Special care	Sow	Spacing (cm) / First harvest
BASIL	Great range of flavours / Keep warm and on the dry side	Apr-Jun	25x25 / 12 weeks
BROAD BEANS	Bean taste in leaves / Pinch out growing points at flowering	Nov-Apr	10x20 / 25 / 16-20 weeks
CHARDS red, yellow, white	Vibrant colour / Darker colours less vigorous	Mar-Jul	Variable / 8 weeks
DILL	Fresh clean flavour / Keep picking leaves and flowers	Mar-Jul	20x20 / 8-10 weeks
ENDIVES / CHICORIES	Bitter taste, rich colours / Late summer crop	Jun-Jul	25x25 / 6-12 weeks
PARSLEY	Rich flavour, vitamins / Long lasting esp. curly parsley	Feb-Jul	25x25 / 10-12 weeks

Vegetable / Herb	Character	Sow	Spacing (cm)
	Special care		First harvest
PEAS, many varieties	Leaves have fine flavour	Feb-May	5x20 or 20x20
	Keep picking growing points		6-10 weeks
PURSLANE,	Succulent fleshy leaves	May-Jul	8x25
Green or Golden	Sow direct, green lasts longest		6-8 weeks
ROCKET,	Peppery taste	Aug-Sep	8x25
many kinds	Small leaves are milder, flowers taste good		4-6 weeks
SPINACH	Deep green	Feb-Jul	20x20 or 5x30
	Keep picking small leaves		6-8 weeks

Lettuces grow fast between May and September so, from not many plants, you should have enough leaves. To add extra interest, flavours and appeal to summer salads, try leaves from any of the following.

Basil The ultimate taste of summer, ready to pick by about mid July from April sowings indoors, continuing until late summer, or longer if nights stay warm (see Herbs chapter, pages 176-185, for more details). Basil is really a Mediterranean plant, and grows best in steady warmth and strong sun, with not too much moisture on its leaves. Best results are always in the greenhouse or polytunnel, or in pots on a sheltered sunny patio. If planted in an open garden, it just needs a long hot summer.

The standard bush basil is productive and good for making pesto; keep picking its larger leaves and any shoots with flower buds. There are many other worthwhile varieties, some of which are less quick to flower: Greek basil is a favourite of mine, providing a steady flow of small-leaved shoots over a long period. It will grow into a fair-sized bush of bright green leaves, and its outermost stems can be trimmed with a knife, similar to pruning box or privet. Lemon and lime basil are true to their names, offering green leaves with a pungent citrus aroma and taste. Sweet Thai has small leaves streaked with dark red and a strong taste of aniseed. Red basils of various names have no special flavour but deep rich colour. Certain catalogues list an even more extensive range, and it is fun to discover what they all taste like.

Broad Beans Less tender than peas and with a stronger flavour; pinch out the very topmost cluster of leaves. This is best done when flowers are appearing on the stem, to encourage filling of the bean pods. Almost any variety will serve this purpose, sown either in November or from February to April. Grow as for beans to eat as described in Chapter 11 (pages 83-97) because pinching out the tops of bean plants that you are growing for broad beans will encourage them to pod up a little earlier.

Chard Leaves of chard in salad are best if they are small. Some salad growers even use them as a large proportion of their leaf mix, sown thickly and harvested as babies. Or you can raise plants in groups of three to five and set them out about 300mm apart, then pick individual leaves as they grow rapidly through many months. Sow from March to June, for harvesting six to eight weeks later. Rainbow Mix Chard or Bright Lights are two mixtures of different coloured chards that are commonly available. For summer salad leaves I recommend using only the red and yellow, because white and pink stemmed plants grow almost too fast and big. In this respect it works well to sow four or five seeds per 3cm module, then to remove the colours you do not want as they grow. Alternatively buy packets of one-colour chard, or even of Bulls' Blood Beet, whose leaves are ruby red, with the bonus of an edible beetroot by the end of summer. Chapter 13 (pages 113-132) has more tips on chard and spinach.

Dill Gives a lovely fresh zest and aroma to early summer salad. Sow as early as March, either direct or with four seeds per 3cm module. Dill makes a stem up to 90cm high and rises to flower quite fast, especially from later sowings, so you may want to sow again in May and as late as July. Keep picking the lower leaves and any flower buds that form; they are edible and tasty. If allowed to set seed, dill can become a native of the garden, popping up here and there. There are few named varieties of dill, although 30cm high Bouquet is an interesting option for small gardens or containers.

Endive or Chicory Strictly speaking these are better in autumn, but can be sown in early June to provide some strong, bitter tastes through the summer. Try Bianca Riccia da Taglio endive for some deeply serrated leaves; if sown in late June and July there is the option of allowing it to heart up (see next chapter). A new variety, Frenzy, has thin deeply-cut leaves and can be sown as early as late May for cutting every week or ten days right through the summer. For leaves of chicory, Treviso Red is reliable but its leaves are mostly green in summer conditions, turning red as temperatures drop in the autumn. Regular picking or cutting will keep leaves small and often more healthy. Palla Rossa radicchio (a kind of chicory) sown in early June will make beautiful deep red hearts by August, which can be dissembled into a bowl of mixed salad for extra luminosity and crunchiness. See next chapter for advice on growing these into hearts and in winter months (pages 66-67).

Orache and Amaranth Neither of these has a taste to marvel at, but their intensity of dark red colouring is remarkable, especially on the undersides of all leaves. Orache – often of no named variety – is a spring plant, best sown from February to April, and regular picking of its many leaves and shoots continues until early July, by which time it will be keener to set seed than to make leaves. Amaranth (try Garnet Red) is a summer plant, best sown late May to July, and its leaves are best picked small. If allowed to grow large, it will send up attractive flower stems with tiny edible seeds.

Parsley Normally listed as a herb, I treat it as a vegetable for its deep green flavour and high vitamin C content. Pick whole stems rather than fragments of them, to encourage new growth and to avoid unattractive yellowing older leaves.

Curled The most common kind in Britain, slow to germinate and slow to develop: it is sometimes said that only the head of the household can get parsley to grow. One sowing in March or April should last the season, another one in July should give plants that have a fair chance of surviving the winter in milder areas. *Moss Curled* is the standard variety and hard to improve upon.

Flat More common in mainland Europe, some people prefer its flavour to the curled. It grows more quickly at first and rises to seed more rapidly as well, so a sowing in March wants to be followed by a sowing in May. Overwintering is possible from a July sowing but not guaranteed. It is often sold as plain-leaved or French, while Italian is not vastly different!

Parsley

Keep a pot by the kitchen door so you can run out to pick some before dishing up. A bit of chopped parsley and garlic will cheer up any plainly cooked vegetable.

Parcel A new variation: celery-flavoured parsley: more suitable for soups and stews as the flavour is strong, almost metallic. Nonetheless, a useful way to introduce a little celery flavour to salads.

Peas Sow these thickly in March to mid May, to provide delicious edible shoots from May to July. Later sowings run the risk of having mildew on their leaves. About six to eight weeks from sowing you need to pinch out the plant's main growing point, or top 6-10cm of stem, which has a fine taste of pea. Several new shoots should then appear, and the successive harvests of these new growing points can last for up to two months, by which time there may well be some peas as well. Many cultivars are suitable, I fancy the tall growing ones do best as they make more vigorous, longer and easier-to-gather shoots. Try Tall Sugar Snap or Alderman.

Purslane Purslane's unusual round and fleshy leaves make it stand out in any salad. Do not sow before May as it thrives in warmth and tolerates dry soil, within reason. See Chapter 17 (pages 176-185) for more details, also winter purslane in next chapter.

September – all second crops

Sugarloaf chicory in September

Red Spinach Bordeaux in September

Green Purslane in June

Blood-veined Sorrel in June

Golden Purslane in June

Chard in June

Leek plants – Autumn Mammoth, six weeks after sowing

Kohlrabi Superschmeltz early November

Kohlrabi Purple Danube in late May

Fennel Montebianco in late September

Beetroot – Boltardy

Rocket There are many different leaf shapes, sizes and flavours. Ordinary salad rocket has larger leaves and a higher yield than wild rocket, whose leaves are thinner, more serrated and with a particularly strong taste that is appreciated by rocket connoisseurs. Wild rocket flowers more readily, with yellow flowers as opposed to white ones on salad rocket. Until recently there were few named varieties available, but now one can buy interesting large-leaved ones such as Apollo and Astro, or Skyrocket which combines different qualities of both wild and salad kinds.

All rocket leaves are dark green and quite peppery to eat, especially in summer, so be sparing with how much you sow. You will get best results from sowings in August, by which time flea beetles are disappearing. Also, more leaves and less flower stems are produced from late summer sowings. Home grown rocket tends to have more bite than the bought kind, which has probably been grown very fast with plenty of water and fertiliser. Usually home-grown rocket crops for about six weeks before rising to seed, at which point pinching out the flowering stem will encourage more, smaller leaves to grow. The flowers are edible and a beautiful ornament to any salad.

Spinach (for Spinach Beet, see pages 70-71) A valuable addition to any salad, especially as it grows rapidly in the spring and early summer. Delicious dark green leaves are reckoned by some to be most nutritious raw, because the iron is more available. Spinach plants resist moderate frost so can be sown in late summer, before about mid August, to over-winter outdoors. I find Medania reliable in this respect: about half my plants usually survive and produce large pickings of dark green leaves.

For best results, grow different varieties at different times, because each one excels at a certain time of year. For example, sow Tarpy F1 in February and March, Tetona in April and May, Emilia in June. Whereas Tetona sown in February grows much more slowly than Tarpy F1, Tarpy F1 sown in April rises to flower much more rapidly than Tetona. Leaves are best picked small and frequently for salads, and can be cooked up if they grow too large. See Chapter 15 for more information.

Note that true spinach, more than spinach beet, is adored by slugs and you may need a night patrol to pick them off.

Spinach salad

Another valuable spring addition to the diet. The first leaves we enjoy as a salad with bacon, croutons, and sometimes a crumbled hard-boiled egg.

Chapter 10

Winter Salads

Leaves to lighten the dark months

Although new growth in winter is slow, there are ways around this and it is definitely possible to enjoy fresh salad leaves. The effort involved can sometimes feel disproportionate, but those few tender leaves are so precious and health-giving that eating them always makes it feel worthwhile.

There are four different ways to fill the salad bowl through the coldest months, from November to April. You could try all or some of growing and storing hearts; cropping leaves outdoors; forcing chicory roots indoors; and growing salad in a polytunnel or greenhouse. Each method produces leaves of different taste, colour and texture.

HEARTS

Vegetable	Character Harvest	Sow Storable @ 0-10ºC	Spacing (cm)
RADICCHIO, Palla Rossa types	Many varieties, colours mostly red Sep-Dec*	1-15 July 6-8 weeks	30x30
SUGARLOAF CHICORIES	Heavy hearts, best leaves at centre Sep-Dec*	1-10 July 6-8 weeks	30x30
CHINESE CABBAGE	Loved by insects, fleece advisable Sep-Nov*	15-30 July 3-4 weeks	30x30
ENDIVE, Scarole types	Rots if too advanced! Sep-Nov*	20-30 July 2-3 weeks	30x30

*frost permitting

Through late autumn and the beginning of winter, we can enjoy hearts of chicories and Chinese cabbage that have been gathered and stored. Timing of sowing is vitally important so that they mature firmly in late October and early November, to be in good condition for keeping over a couple of months. In areas of only mild frost, some may be left growing until mid-winter and harvested fresh.

They need sowing in high summer to have had time to grow into substantial plants with masses of firm, blanched leaves that will keep fresh over a long period. Salad hearts are not frost hardy (much less so than many loose leaves), so they must be picked before any frost of more than about –2°C is expected.

RADICCHIO

These are the red members of the chicory family – hardy and deep rooting plants that offer many kinds of leaves for winter salad. Their often bitter flavour is significantly moderated by allowing them to develop tightly folded hearts, whose blanched leaves take on a slightly sweet taste to offset the residual bitterness, creating a delicious tension between the two.

Northern Italians have had the sense to breed a fine selection of beautifully coloured, crunchy and fresh tasting radicchios of many shapes and shades, whose luminosity alone will brighten plates and hearts in winter. In northern Italy they are eaten as a cooked vegetable, braised in butter or oil for example. I learn more about growing and eating them every winter and become steadily more intrigued. Here I offer the story as I currently know it.

Much of the seed I use is from Franchi or 'Seeds of Italy', and I have asked them why they do not translate the valuable information on their seed packets into English. The reply was that they plan to, after the current stock of many million packets is used up.

Even if there was a translation of the language, the techniques for successful growing of radicchio also need translating to British conditions. Some parts of Britain are actually milder in winter than northern Italy, but are also darker and damper. Leaves can sometimes rot with little provocation. I suspect that Italians have more possibilities than us for growing new leaves in winter, so I concentrate here on radicchio hearts.

Varieties

One or two specially bred varieties can be sown as early as late May to make a worthwhile heart in early autumn: an F1 hybrid called Rialto is extremely reliable in this respect. But mostly we are looking at sowing after the longest day to reduce any risk of premature seeding rather than hearting, and any of the Palla Rossa (red heart in English – but of intriguingly varied colouring) varieties will do, although some are designed to mature a little earlier and some a little later.

Sowing

Sowing in modules is definitely easier than sowing direct, because slugs are partial to young chicory seedlings, and to baby plants as well. A good time to sow is the first half of July, before about 10th to be sure of a fair-sized heart. Sowing later, say in the third week of July can see nice hearts form by November if it is a mild autumn, but they will usually be somewhat smaller, and it is rare to have good hearts from sowings in late July or beyond.

Growing

Clear the growing space of all previous crop residues and weeds, preferably a week or so ahead of planting. As plantings are in late July and up to mid August, they can follow any of peas, broad beans, onions, spring salad, early potatoes, beetroot and so on. It is best if the previous crop was composted, as fresh compost before planting radicchios can encourage slugs. Some watering will be beneficial in dry summers, especially in September as growth becomes substantial.

Hearting Up

Many catalogues offer seed of unspecified Palla Rossa which makes the familiar round red hearts, while Franchi offer varieties such as Agena and Marzatica, with round but white-streaked hearts, and Lusia which is more green than red. The first two have especially thick and crunchy leaves, whereas Lusia's are softer.

By September you should have quite large plants, having given them a little more space than lettuce – at least 300mm in all directions. Then hearts will start to develop, at variable rates, becoming tighter and firmer until. . . . a few of them start to rot. Yes, I am sorry to say that radicchio hearts do not just sit patiently waiting to be gathered, although some will last well. This is why timing of the sowing is important: if too early, they mature before needed; if too late, they barely make a worthwhile heart. You may have a few failures before discovering the best dates for your soil and climate. It will be worth the effort. Lusia has shown some promise in hearting as late as December, as long as the weather stays mild.

Harvesting

When a heart is firm to the touch, slip a knife underneath it, leaving the outer leaves, whose taste will be bitter. The heart may contain up to forty or fifty leaves and they can be unpacked one by one, sometimes chipping away at the stem to release them. Or quarter the whole head if you are feeling extravagant, to make a fine starter or accompaniment to any meal, raw or cooked.

When cutting hearts to store, cut the plant lower to keep a few outer leaves around it, as a wrapper to help keep moisture in. Pack them in a wooden or cardboard box lined with plastic, ideally at any temperature between freezing and about 10°C. If this can be achieved, the inner leaves should stay in fair condition until after Christmas.

Hearts which are loose and still developing at first frost can be left to continue growing; covering with fleece on frosty nights is a way of giving them more time to mature. Some may survive the winter outdoors in milder regions. Once harvested, remove all leaves to the compost heap, and any weeds, in order to enjoy new spring leaves from the same roots (see below).

SUGARLOAF CHICORY

Potentially a large and solid plant, with hearts weighing up to 2kg. I know of only two varieties – ordinary Sugarloaf which is often over 30cm (12") long, and Bianca di Milano which makes a rounder heart with shorter, somewhat crisper leaves.

Sowing

Sow from late June to mid July, bearing in mind that later plantings will be smaller and less solid.

Growing

Similar to radicchio excerpt that it needs extra watering in dry weather.

Harvesting

By early October the hearts should be tightly folded, their interior leaves a pale cream colour, still slightly bitter. They can be kept, in cool dampness, for up to two months, except that the outer leaves will dry and rot a little. The flavour and texture are less interesting than radicchio, but easier growing and storage makes sugarloaf a reliable base for winter salad.

CHINESE CABBAGE

Sowing

Check the details on the seed packet to make sure that you have a hearting variety such as Yuki F1, Wa Wa Sai F1 or Green Rocket F1. Resist the temptation to sow before July, whatever the instructions say. Best sowing dates are even a little later than for chicories, up to early August; beyond that and the plant will grow alright, but with a much lighter, looser heart.

Growing

Although extremely fast growing, chinese cabbage is vulnerable to almost every pest in the garden: caterpillars, flea beetles, pigeons and slugs. By midsummer there are less of some of these, but it is definitely worth the effort to cover a clump of plants with a piece of fine mesh or fleece: rain and light come in, insects stay out. Expensive mesh is supposed to be strong and useable for a few years – or a few days if dogs and cats run across it! Fleece is cheaper but warmer and generally easier to use. Even though one hole is enough to admit enough butterflies to cause significant damage, it is still worthwhile for chinese cabbage.

Harvesting

Harvest around Hallowe'en, before slugs make too many holes, and store as for chicories. A lot of outer leaves will need to be trimmed off, leaving a tight white heart, if all has gone well! The leaves are a great asset to late autumn salad for their texture alone – firm and crunchy. By December however, unless kept in a fridge, they will start to grow mouldy.

ENDIVE

Hearts of endive are really delicious but they do not keep for a long time. I find the broad-leaved kind ('Scarole') easier to grow for hearts, and Bubikopf and Avance are two good varieties. Frizzy-leaved endives, sometimes called 'Frisée', often rot within a week of achieving a nice pale heart.

Sowing

Small sowings through July and even into early August will provide a succession of self-blanched leaves, as late as December if there is no hard frost.

Growing

Growth is rapid after planting out in early to mid August. One hoeing may suffice, and some watering can be necessary in a dry September.

Harvesting

As with chicories, the plant can sometimes look brown and desolate, yet with a small undamaged heart in the middle. Finding such leaves in December is rather exciting! But more salad will be had from harvesting an undamaged plant just before serious frost. Trim off all imperfect leaves and keep as cool as possible, which should give you two to three weeks of eating nice hearts.

NEW LEAVES OUTDOORS

Vegetable	Character Spacing cm	Sow Harvest
CHARD & SPINACH BEET	Keep picking small leaves 4x20 or 12x12	Jun-Aug Mostly spring, Mar-May

Vegetable	Character Spacing cm	Sow Harvest
CORN SALAD (lambs lettuce)	Best leaves from regular picking 6x30 or 15x15	Aug-Sep Oct-Apr
KALE red / green / red russian	Young leaves for salad 20x50 or 35x35	Jul-Aug Feb-May, new shoots
ORIENTAL VEGETABLES	Only good in mild winter variable	late Jul-Sep Feb-May
RADICCHIO	New rosettes after heart is gone 30x30	Jul (as above) Mar-May
ROCKET	Abundant growth in mild winters 6x30 or 20x20	late Jul-Sep New growth from Mar
SORREL	Fresh flavoured baby leaves 30x30	Apr-Jun Mar onwards
SPINACH	New spring leaves are sweet 30x30	Jul-early Aug Mar-May

In the middle of winter, if we are to rely only on freshly gathered leaves, the options are somewhat restricted, especially in frosty weather. It must also be said, if you have not done it before, that it is not much fun to pick small amounts of cold, wet leaves on cold, windy days. However, these outdoor plants are worth tending carefully as they will spring into life with the first relaxing of winter's grip.

There are actually two separate and quite short seasons for outdoor winter leaves: late autumn and early spring. Sandwiched between them is a midwinter lull of dormancy, whose duration will vary every year and from place to place. In Somerset it can be just two weeks of frosty weather over New Year, or three months starting in early December. One never knows in advance, and there is nothing to lose in being prepared for a mild winter by making a few extra sowings in late summer and early autumn.

CHARD AND SPINACH BEET

Varieties

Plants of Chard and Spinach Beet that survive the winter can be a good source of small salad leaves in April, when they surge back to life. The flavour is rather acid, less appealing than true spinach, but in April one is glad for any new leaves. Red and yellow chard are less frost hardy than white chard, while perpetual spinach/spinach beet survives best of all.

Sowing

To be in peak condition at the start of winter, a July sowing is probably best, although anytime between May and August is alright. Either sow lines across a bed, 30cm apart and thin plants to 6-8cm, or sow four seeds in modules planted 30cm apart in all directions.

Growing

Any leaves that grow too large for salad can be picked for cooking, and the first proper frost may damage larger leaves, but hopefully not the new central growth. Plants often look half-dead over winter and some may die, but new growth should appear in early spring.

Harvesting

Trim off frost-damaged leaves and keep picking new growth until flower-stems predominate sometime in May, when a spade may be needed to dig out the main beet-like root (not edible); small feeder roots can be left to decompose *in situ*.

CORN SALAD (LAMBS LETTUCE)

Varieties

Probably the hardiest of all salad plants, and possessed of the greatest ability to recover from frost with spurts of new growth. However, new leaves are mostly small and fiddly to pick, and unlikely to fill a salad bowl unless you have some long rows or beds of plants. Seed companies are now offering greater choice, and the best one I have tried so far is D'Orlanda, whose leaves are larger and easier to gather than, for example, the darker green Vit, whose strong point is more hardiness than size. Favor is a fair trade-off with medium-size dark green leaves, but still on the small side.

Sowing

Seed is best sown direct from late July to early September, bearing in mind that it is slow growing and may be overtaken by weeds if your soil is not too clean. A good average date for sowing in southern Britain is the third or fourth week of August, to have a first picking before Christmas and several more before Easter, when plants will start to produce small, pretty pale blue flowers.

As with rocket, seed catalogues and packets claim that sowing is possible "from March or April". I beg to differ, finding that spring and early summer sowings offer only small yields of mildew-prone leaves before flowering. Even July or early August sowings will attract mildew if it is a warm autumn. Avoid late mildew by more frequent picking (see below).

Growing

If you have kept the soil clean of weeds for the preceding crop, success is more likely. Chickweed, for example, can swamp low-growing lambs lettuce. Hoe in September when dry enough, hand weed thereafter. Roots are very superficial and make a thick mat on top of the soil.

Harvesting

Leaves are best cut, not individually but as small rosettes of six to eight leaves. The first cut will be about 10mm above soil level, leaving some outer leaves and stem below the cut, whence several new rosettes will regrow. In a mild winter, one plant with about 150mm of space around it can grow to fill most of that and produce a good number of small, succulent pickings. Leaves are glossy, waxy and vibrant, a great tonic for the middle of winter.

KALE

Varieties

If you do not like the strong taste of raw kale in salad, try Red Russian.

Sowing

Best sown in modules in early to mid July, two seeds per module as germination is often about 60%, and thin to one plant after about a fortnight.

Growing

Plant at 30x30cm (12" apart). You can cover with mesh or fleece to protect the crop from pigeons and autumn caterpillars, but kale is quite hardy and should survive well, even if many leaves are full of holes. This does not matter because the most edible leaves appear in spring when insects are not around to eat them. However, through the winter you may need to protect the plants with netting against pigeons

Harvesting

Remove most of the old and rotting leaves in early February to make picking easier. In February or March new shoots will appear with beautiful pale red, deeply serrated and extremely tasty leaves. Picking of both these leaves and new stems should be possible until early May, when new growth becomes thinner and more stringy with less leaf and more flower bud. Pull plants out and chop into 20cm lengths with a spade before composting.

ORIENTAL GREENS

Varieties

I find that few of these are likely to survive outdoors through a whole winter, but some do well from a very early sowing in the greenhouse, to be planted out in March under fleece. Mizuna is probably the most worthwhile for its ability to grow at a time when most plants are dormant. Komatsuna is another rapid grower, but less able to defend itself against slugs than Mizuna.

Sowing, growing and harvesting

Sow about six seeds per module in late January, plant them in March at a spacing of 200mm, cover with fleece and keep fleece on throughout, and cut three worthwhile handfuls of leaves from each clump through April, before the plants flower in early May. Later sowings will give a later and smaller harvest because spring is flowering time for all oriental leaves.

RADICCHIO

(See Radicchio above for general growing method)

Long-leaved Trevisos are not intended for hearting, and their leaves of deep red colours become more intense as the temperature drops. They can be cut in one harvest or picked individually through some of the winter, although not in hard frost. Before March it is good to finish picking and to remove all leaf debris, to allow clean new growth in spring, when the same roots send out new baby hearts, rather like a forced chicory but growing outdoors. All kinds of radicchio will do this, to varying extents.

Keep picking or cutting the small new shoots as they develop over, potentially, two or three months until May. By then they will transform into stems more than leaves and the old radicchio root can be removed with a trowel.

Another variety called Grumola offers the chance of overwintering quite large plants from an August sowing, which make small hearts in early spring. There is a green variety Verde, and a red one Rosso, and their flowering shoots are also edible.

ROCKET

Sowing

Sow 4-8 seeds in 2-3cm modules or direct in rows about 20cm apart. From a sowing in late August or even early September there is a fair chance of some plants surviving to produce new leaves in any milder periods, and quite a few leaves in early spring. Ordinary salad rocket is probably the most worthwhile, for its higher yield of leaves.

Growing

Growth should be rapid and insect-free until the first real frost, which may damage some of the larger leaves. Only severe frost kills the plant itself.

Harvesting

Either cut all leaves from a few plants or clumps of plants at a time, about 2cm above soil level, or keep picking larger leaves from the whole patch. New growth will be occasional through midwinter, but significant re-growth in March and April should precede flowering, and flower stems can also be eaten.

SORREL

There is a great choice of interesting leaves here: French/Broad-leaved sorrel has good-sized light green leaves, Buckler sorrel grows in clumps of small round leaves, and Blood-veined sorrel boasts strikingly red veins across its long leaves. Sorrel is perennial and possessed of large enough roots to produce quite a number of new leaves in late winter and early spring. They have a zippy bite, reminiscent of lemon juice, a great taste for clearing away some winter cobwebs.

Sowing

Sow any time from March to June, aiming for a spacing of about 30cm (12") in all directions.

Harvesting

Clear away old leaves (and slugs!) before winter, so that any new growth from late winter is easily visible. Slugs can do some damage, so keep the soil around plants free of weeds and mulch. Regular picking of small leaves will spice up the salad bowl for a couple of months or longer (see pages 174-5 for more details).

SPINACH

Sowing

Certain varieties seem to almost like really cold weather. Two I will mention are Giant Winter for large leaves and Medania for small leaves. There may be others as hardy, and you have nothing to lose by sowing a few rows in late

July or August (preferably before about the 20th) so that plants have time to reach a size where they can grow away from damage by frost and slugs.

Harvesting

Much depends on the winter: for example, in the frosts of 2005-6, about two-thirds of my late July sowing of Medania died. But the third that survived went on to produce masses of new leaves from about mid March, with regular pickings of a delicious taste for eating raw. By May there was even an abundance of large leaves for cooking. Medania's leaves are of high quality – dark green, glossy and slightly sweet, especially in springtime, when they always taste especially good. A cold, dry winter is better for spinach than a wet, mild and slug-infested one.

INDOOR GROWN / FORCED LEAVES

A third possibility is to grow leaves indoors from chicory roots which have been dug up in November, and brought into some part of the house, shed or garage that is dark and frost-free. Yellow chicons will grow out of these, crunchy and bittersweet, and the roots can keep producing them for much of the winter. There is little tradition for this technique in Britain, perhaps because our climate is milder than continental Europe, but I find it a reliable source of crisp, yellow, mildly bitter leaves. Note that chicons require darkness, because too much light on forcing roots will encourage florets of open, pale green leaves.

Varieties

Make sure that the chicory you sow is for forcing: usually it will be called Witloof, possibly Lightning or Yellora F1. Many radicchio roots can also be forced indoors, with less regular chicons.

Sowing

Sow either one seed per 3cm module indoors, or direct in the soil in May, or as late as early July for smaller roots. Module-grown roots will be more branched but this does not matter for forcing, except that they may leave more root fragments in the soil after harvest, and these will grow as vigorous weeds in the following year.

Growing

Give plants about 300mm of room to make fair-sized roots. Plants should make plenty of leaf and you need to prevent too much weed growth, and make sure no weeds are going to seed underneath. Watering is rarely necessary.

Harvesting

Use a spade to lever out the main roots in November. Aim to dig out all roots thicker than your finger.

Forcing

Harvested roots can be placed in pots of moist compost in an outbuilding or garage, preferably frost-free, or wrapped in a polythene bag and brought into a warm dark part of the house for more rapid production, in as little as three weeks. Soon you should see small yellow buds around the top of each root: rub out a few if you want large chicons or leave them all for smaller heads and leaves.

After a few weeks, depending on temperature, some pointy hearts will be growing and can be cut or snapped off when a little firm, taking care to remove all their leaves, allowing room for more chicons to appear.

If roots are kept moist and allowed to develop new roots in pots of compost, they will keep sending out chicons until mid spring, of smaller size and with more pointed leaves. Their bright colour and crunchy texture are a good contrast to the softness of most other fresh winter leaves.

Protected cropping of new leaves

Vegetable	Character	Sow
	Spacing (cm)*	Harvest
CHARD	White chard best for new midwinter leaves	Aug
	4x20 or 12x12	Oct-May
CHERVIL, CORIANDER	Long season of richly flavoured leaves	Sep
	25x25	Nov-May
'DANDELION'	Red-ribbed has vigorous, attractive leaves	Sep
	10x30 or 25x25	Oct-May
ENDIVE	Choice of scarole or frizzy, pick as leaf lettuce	Sep-Oct
	20x20	Nov-May
LAND CRESS	Low-growing, leaves of powerful flavour	Sep-Oct
	20x20	Nov-Apr
LEAF RADISH	Remarkably rapid growth of hairless leaves	Jan-Mar
	20x20 or 5x30	Feb-May
LETTUCE	Pick new larger leaves for 8 months, same plant	Mid Aug to Sep
	25x25	Nov-Jun
MIBUNA	Long leaves, liked by slugs, edible flowers	Sep-Oct
	20x20 or 10x30	Oct-May
MUSTARD	Keep picking small leaves, very spicy	Sep-Oct
	20x20 or 10x30	Nov-May
MIZUNA	Extremely fast growth, becomes ragged	Sep-Oct
	20x20 or 10x30	Nov-Apr

Vegetable	Character Spacing (cm)*	Sow Harvest
PAK CHOI	Less frost- and slug-hardy, crunchy leaves 25x25 or 10x30	Late Aug-Sep Oct-Apr
PARSLEY	The hardiest herb 25x25	Jul Oct-May
ROCKET	Many leaves, flowers in April 20x20 or 6x30	Sep-Oct Nov-Apr
SPINACH	Dark green leaves but liked by slugs, pick regularly 25x25 or 10x30	Aug-Sep Oct-May
TATSOI	Small round leaves, early flowering 20x20 or 10x30	Sep-Oct Nov-Apr
WINTER PURSLANE	Unusual round leaves, thrives in cold 25x25 or 15x30	Sep-Oct Nov-Apr
ORIENTAL MIXES	Entirely depends on seed company rows of 30cm	Sep-Oct Nov-Apr

*the first figure is for module-sown plants: all 4-6 seeds, except one seed for lettuce and endive

A fourth source of leaves is from plants that can be grown in protected spaces, such as conservatories, greenhouses, polytunnels and even under cloches, right through winter and into spring. It is not necessary to keep out all frost since the plants mentioned are frost hardy to -6^0C or more, as long as they have shelter from the combined forces of cold rain, wind, frost and cold raw days.

In a polytunnel, cloche and greenhouse, night time temperatures are often as low as outside, but with a little sun by day the relatively dry soil and calm air can warm up enough to allow a little growth. Even when plants are not growing, they are at least surviving and keeping ready to benefit from any milder spells. Even in a very small garden, a well-managed small greenhouse can provide surprising amounts of leaves to bring health and colour through wintertime, and especially as the days lengthen in early spring, when better light levels bring a noticeable increase in leaf quality.

March and April can be highly productive if winter salad plants have been well looked after, and I include this time of year in the winter section because by then most other winter vegetables such as cabbage, celeriac and carrots are running short. In the middle of winter they are a fair alternative to fresh leaves, grated in coleslaw to bulk up the few leaves available, but by early spring there is not much left from the previous season

Another option is if you have a greenhouse with staging, pots or boxes can be filled with compost and planted up to grow leaves at waist height – simple for picking.

Many of the most suitable plants have already been mentioned, but I will deal with them all again to explain the different sowing dates and altered patterns of growth under cover. Check the table carefully for sowing dates, bearing in mind that these are based on my experience in southern England, and other regions may be a little different.

CHARD

No other plant reflects the winter more vividly than ruby chard. Sow in late August to have a few leaves before Christmas, then with frost the luminous green of the leaves between red veins changes to a dull, very dark green, almost crimson, although some growth can continue. But towards the end of February, a wonderful change occurs as the fresh green colour reappears and leaves become fuller and fleshier. When this happens I always feel that spring is around the corner.

White or yellow chard is less affected colour-wise, and is more vigorous through cold conditions.

DANDELION

When you can find some seed 'Red-ribbed dandelion' (actually a member of the chicory family) will grow fast from a September sowing, offering worthwhile numbers of leaves by November. The long stem carries a worthwhile amount of bitter green leaf – another flavour for the winter salad.

ENDIVE

You can have attractive leaves over a long period from an early autumn sowing of a variety such as Bubikopf, a broad-leaved scarole type, or Markant, with longer frizzy leaves. Lower leaves can be picked off from November to early May, as for leaf lettuce. The flavour is a little bitter and pleasantly different from everything else at that time.

LAND CRESS

The dark round leaves of this very hardy plant have the same iron-rich taste as watercress, and a few leaves will add zest to any salad. Two or three plants may suffice; keep picking larger leaves once they are established, although they hug the soil and are not easy to pick. Variegated land cress has attractive mottled leaves. Beware: pigeons love land cress!

LEAF RADISH

Leaf radish grows as fast as root radish, and is similar except that its leaves are pale green and only slightly hairy, with a fine, mild flavour that is just recognisable as relating to radish. It should over-winter from an October sowing, or can be sown in January / February to crop in March and April for four to six weeks, before the leaves are suddenly replaced by a briefly edible stem with white flowers.

LETTUCE

Grenoble Red, of Alpine origin, will survive most frost from a late August or early September sowing. Keep picking the larger leaves as for summer lettuce, starting in November, less frequently between Christmas and late February, then with increasing regularity, as the leaves become larger and more prolific. First pickings in the autumn can be difficult as the plant is small and tender and holds its leaves right at ground level. Treat plants carefully and by March leaves become much easier to twist off, each plant having the capacity, in well composted soil, to produce a hundred or more leaves by time it flowers in mid to late June.

Other leaf lettuce varieties can also be sown through autumn and winter to make later crops and to fill any gaps. Many such as Cocarde will survive a surprising amount of frost, but one can never be too certain and I would not recommend cos varieties for winter.

Other winter lettuce varieties are mostly Butterheads, for example Arctic King or May Queen, which make hearts in early spring from September and October sowing.

MIBUNA

A fast grower and long-stemmed like Mizuna, but with darker green and non-serrated leaves. Through midwinter it is more productive to pick individual larger leaves rather than cutting everything. Keep plants tidy to reduce slug habitat and enjoy the flowers in spring, as with all oriental vegetables.

MIZUNA

Mizuna is salad speed champion, so one sowing will not cover the whole winter. You can sow in late September to crop before and over Christmas, late October for the New Year, and December to February for the spring. There is always a choice between cutting small leaves frequently and allowing a larger plant to grow with the long white stems. Larger leaves are more susceptible to damage by frost and from mildew. Production of new leaves is less vigorous after three cuttings, when you are more likely to see flowers which are also extremely tasty.

MUSTARD

A few plants will probably suffice, as the occasional mustard leaf in a salad is enough for most people. The main varieties are Red Giant, Green in the Snow and Golden Streaks. Their names tell it all, and their vigour means that regular picking is worthwhile, except in the coldest weather.

PAK CHOI

The top winter variety to grow is Joi Choi F1 for its resistance to frost, and steady production of white-stemmed, dark green leaves over a long period. Cutting leaves carefully rather than trying to pull or break them off is vital, in order not to dislodge or uproot the whole plant, whose roots are thin and fragile. Regular picking of small leaves will help to keep on top of slugs, which are always attracted to pak choi; remove any that you see hiding in the leaves.

PARSLEY

It is definitely worth having an odd corner of parsley, curly or flat from a July sowing, to be well established by winter. I prefer curly parsley for its better health and vigour, also for its longevity – it lasts about a month longer than the flat, until mid May on average. Pick leaves carefully and sparingly in cold weather to allow enough leaves to nourish the roots and help new growth.

ROCKET

As well as growing fast, rocket tends to flower quickly, even in the middle of winter. Keep removing the stems: new leaves will be smaller but they should keep coming until mid to late April and there will be no flea beetle holes. Most kinds of rocket that I have grown are winter-hardy, such as ordinary salad rocket.

SPINACH

Although a favourite of our slimy friends, regular picking will help to keep their numbers down. August sowings can be grown indoors for larger or very plentiful leaves through the autumn, otherwise the early September sowing in 3cm modules is good for small salad leaves through winter. Plants will be ready to go in after removal of tomatoes and other summer crops in early to mid October. First pickings may be there in December, otherwise a lot of leaves should be produced from late February to early May, depending on variety. I find that Medania and Fuji F1 work well.

TATSOI

Smaller, more crinkly leaves than pak choi, slightly harder to pick. The variety Yukina looks like savoy cabbage but is much more tender and keenly appreciated by slugs, so pick off all damaged leaves and keep soil around it very clean. It thrives in cool conditions and sometimes flowers as early as March, after producing leaves in deepest winter when few other plants are doing much. As with pak choi, the flowering stems are edible and of good flavour.

WINTER PURSLANE

Also known as Claytonia and with a very different growth habit to summer purslane, although the leaves are equally juicy and succulent.

Like Mizuna it is most feasible to harvest with a knife around the plants' edges, not across the top, when there are leaves falling downwards at the sides. Aim to have a few clumps and cut them in turn, until white flowers start to appear in late March and April. These are edible but will herald a stiffening of the stems and reduced numbers of new leaves, so there may be little left to eat by mid April.

ORIENTAL SALADS / SALAD MIXES

Packets of mixed seed can be a cheap and simple way of growing many different flavours, but one never knows exactly what will come up and in what proportions. Saladini means small salad leaves, often cut from rows of young plants. Harvesting in this way does not usually allow plants to live as long as when they are more carefully looked after as individuals, so extra sowings are required. I recommend using commercial seed mixes for fun and interest, to see how different plants grow, and for when you are unsure about exactly what you do want to grow.

Pests

Slugs are undoubtedly the chief pest of winter leaves. Bare soil around plants with no weeds will help, as will removing any slugs you see. An occasional night-time foray with a torch may be invaluable, especially at planting time in autumn when one slug can destroy a lot of potential harvests.

It is best in greenhouses and polytunnels to spread compost annually and on the surface in springtime, before tomatoes etc, so that it has mostly been taken in by autumn, leaving a barer soil and less habitat for slugs.

Mildew on older leaves can be a problem, but regular picking of smaller leaves for salads usually prevents it because there are no old leaves on plants.

Chapter 11

Alliums

Magnificent flavours for all times of year

Alliums are staple vegetables – onions, salad onions, leeks, garlic, shallots – which are some of the easiest and most reliable to grow. They are scarcely bothered by slugs or low temperatures, mature at different times of the growing year, and offer reliable additions to many meals.

Alliums and weeds

Alliums' thin and mostly vertical leaves mean that weeds can thrive all around them. In the case of onions especially, weeds are difficult to hoe or pull out by early summer, when their leaves start to fall over a little. So use any fine day in April and May to hoe off any weed seedlings, and every time you do so the soil is becoming cleaner because more weed seeds have germinated and then died without creating new seeds. In this sense, alliums are a good cleaning crop (see also potatoes, on pages 109-111).

BULB ONIONS

Onions are the basis of almost every soup, appear in possibly more recipes than any other vegetable, and are a fine vegetable to grow as well as to eat. The sight of their long round leaves, noticeably longer and stronger every day in the spring, always gives me a lift; an upright habit of growth makes them stand out and is somehow strangely inspiring.

YELLOW ONIONS FROM SPRING-PLANTED SETS

Season of harvest: July-September, use until April
Follow with: autumn / winter salads

Variety	Character Height (cm)	Planting date	Spacing (cm) First ready
STURON	Globe shape 35	Equinox	5-10x30 July

Variety	Character	Planting date	Spacing (cm)
	Height		First ready
TURBO	Longer neck	Equinox	5-10x30
	35		July
STUTTGART GIANT	Flat bulbs keep well	Equinox	5-10x30
	35		July

Planting

The easiest way to grow onions is by planting immature baby ones called sets. These will have been sown late enough the previous summer to make immature onions no bigger than cherries, which on being re-planted will carry on growing for another whole season, into full-sized adults. At planting time they have enough food reserves to propel themselves into more rapid growth than onions grown from seed.

However, if onion sets are planted too early in the year, many of them will 'bolt' rather than make a bigger onion. Exposure to any length of significant frost makes them register that winter has happened, instead of which we want them to believe that they are simply carrying on growing from the year before – so be patient at planting time! Then you may benefit from their potential to grow large bulbs.

In Somerset I find that the equinox around March 21st is a good time to plant sets, giving almost no bolters and a good yield of onions by the middle of summer. Any time between the equinox and mid April will be alright; any later, and some growing time is lost, meaning smaller onions.

There is no golden rule about how to space them. The more room they have, the larger they grow, so it all depends what you want. I give them 60-70cm (2-3") between sets, in rows across the beds which are about 30cm (12") apart. This provides a bountiful harvest of medium-sized bulbs, as long as the soil is in good heart. It is best to have spread some compost by midwinter, to ensure a reasonable tilth for planting time.

Make sure you put them in with the little rooty end going down, the pointy end upwards. Sometimes you can be guided by a small green shoot already appearing out of sets' tops, although it is better that most of them are still dormant at planting time.

Growing

Weeding may keep you busy: if weeds are regularly hoed or pulled up, so that none are allowed to set seed, it will be much easier to grow winter salads, or any other crop, after the onions have gone.

Harvesting

Onions can be gently pulled out of the ground or levered from below with a trowel, once their tops are more yellow than green and start to fall over

– usually from mid July to mid August. Once lifted, bend their necks hard and lie them root-down on the soil to dry for a few days or longer, depending on the weather and if you have space indoors – see page 90 for more ideas.

Problems

See *Salad Onions and Shallots* below.

YELLOW ONIONS FROM SEED

Season of harvest: August-September, use until April
Follow with: corn salad or autumn-sown broad beans, for example

Variety	Character Height (cm)	Sow First ready	Spacing (cm)
STURON	Resists bolting 30	Feb-Mar August	25x25* or 5-10x30
GIANT ZITTAU	Good keeper 30	Feb-Mar August	25x25* or 5-10x30
KELSAE	Huge bulbs 40	Jan August	25x25*

*25x25 spacing is for multi-sown modules

Sowing

Starting from seed is a less easy way to grow onions, but is rewarded with bulbs of superior quality, which may also keep better, especially as their thinner necks often dry more thoroughly.

A tricky aspect is the two months it takes for seed to grow into plants that are large enough to set out. In a greenhouse they can be sown in February or early March, for planting mid April to early May. If 3cm modules are used, six or seven seeds can be sown in each one, for planting and growing together in a clump. Outdoor sowings have to wait until March, close together in a line to make lots of small plants for later planting out.

Growing

Final planting distance is the same as for sets, except for multi-sown modules (see table above). There must be sufficient room for a hoe to pass, unless a thick mulch is used. Personally I prefer a thin mulch of well-rotted compost, through which a hoe can pass, to leave the soil in perfect condition for autumn salad.

To make champion-size onions, sow the variety Kelsae by early January, to have maximum growing time. They grow surprisingly fast: I tried some out of curiosity, mainly to see how they tasted, and was pleasantly surprised at both their enormity and the mild yet rich flavour.

OVERWINTERED ONIONS

(also sometimes called Japanese onions, as they were the first to develop viable varieties)

Season of harvest: May-June, use by Christmas
Follow with: any late summer or autumn vegetable

Variety	Character Height	Sow / Plant Special care	Spacing (cm) First ready
RADAR	From sets 30	Sep-Oct Clean soil	5-10x30 late May
SENSHYU SEMI- GLOBE YELLOW	From seed 30	Late Aug Clean soil	5-10x30 late May

A third option when growing onions is to sow seed or plant sets of certain adapted varieties in late summer or autumn, to grow into small plants for over-wintering. Onions are amazingly hardy, and although the leaves will go quite yellow and shrivelled at the tips in hard frost, come spring they will shoot away and make bulbs by late May or early June. The idea is to have onions at a time when they, and other vegetables, are otherwise scarce.

Planting

From sets, there is a fair planting period of about a month from mid September. Only try it if you have reasonably clean soil, because hoeing is near impossible for much of the winter and small onion leaves can easily become overgrown. Well done if you manage it: fine early onions should justify the effort.

Sowing

From seed it is vital to sow in late August, but not before about 23rd, or the plants will bolt in May. Sowing can't be delayed much beyond the month's end, or plants may be too small to survive a cold winter. I use 3cm modules with seven or eight seeds in each, planted out in late September after French beans or salad.

Harvesting

Some can be used as spring onions from late March. Bulbs are fully formed by about mid June.

YELLOW ONIONS

Season of harvest: July-September
Follow with: autumn salad

Variety	Character Height	Plant / Sow	Spacing (cm) First ready
RED BARON	Fine colour, good keeper 30	April	5-10x30 Jul
ELECTRIC	Autumn planted 30	Sep-Oct	5-10x30 May
LONG RED FLORENCE	Long bulbs, mild flavour 40	Feb-Apr	5-10x30 Jul
PURPLETTE	Small bulbs, many uses 25	Feb-May	5x20 Jun

Definitely more tricky than yellow onions, red bulb onions show less vigour and more inclination to bolt. They seem to prefer hot summers, but I find them maddeningly inconsistent in many ways, although definitely worth growing a few for the rich flavour, sweetness and medicinal quality of successful bulbs.

Planting

Probably the simplest method is to plant sets which have been 'heat-treated', so that bolting is reduced. Usually they are available later than ordinary sets, in about mid April. Planting, growing and harvesting are as for yellow onions.

Recently some over-wintering red onion sets have become available, usually Electric, and I had one year's superb crop, followed by another year's poor one. They are something of a gamble, depending on weather above all.

Sowing

Growing from seed is also possible, with the same caveats as yellow onions of early sowing and slightly later maturity. Red Baron is available in both seed and sets and is an excellent variety. Purplette can be left in its seedbed and selectively pulled as salad onions, with the remaining plants left to make small pretty bulbs, suitable for pickling.

Harvesting and storing

These are the same as for yellow onions.

WHITE BULB ONIONS

These are onions of continental style, sweeter even than other onions and more tender, with thin pale skins, so they are not for storing. Grow and harvest in the same way, just eat more quickly. Paris Silverskin can be sown like salad onions (below) and used quite small, for pickling as well. Walla Walla has the interesting quality of great mildness, for those who like raw onion, and it will make a large onion if given the space of ordinary bulb onions. Note that salad onions such as White Lisbon will also turn into white bulb onions if allowed to grow on.

Onion soup

If one of us feels a cold coming on we make a 10-minute onion soup. Slice a couple of onions (1 per person) and soften in butter, add a bit of chopped garlic for extra medicinal effect, stir in a wooden spoon- ful of flour, and add stock or yeast extract. Simmer for as long as you are prepared to wait, then pour into bowls and inhale the steam before eating / drinking!

SALAD ONIONS

Season of harvest: April-November
Follow with: depends on time of harvest, say with French beans after a June harvest

Variety	Character Height	Sow Special care	Spacing (cm) First ready
WINTER HARDY WHITE LISBON	Autumn sown 30	Aug-early Sep Diligent weeding	1x25 Apr
WHITE LISBON	Stem and bulb 30	Jan-Jul	1x25 Jun
RAMROD	Does not bulb up 40	Jan-early Sep	1x25 Jun

Salad onions are really just immature or still-leafy onion plants, of varieties that have been bred to make a strong stem with firm leaves. Their common name of Spring Onion reveals how they are at their best in spring, before leaf diseases appear, and because they were often the only onion available in spring, between the old and new crops. That was before over-wintered onion bulbs became possible to grow, in Britain at least.

Sowing

Imagine delicious fresh green onion leaves and stems as early as April – a fine way to enliven early salads, soups and many other dishes. You need to sow a salad onion variety such as White Lisbon Winter Hardy in mid to late August. Spring-sown onions, sown February to April, will not be ready until May at the earliest, more likely June, depending how large you want them to grow.

White Lisbon and other old varieties will gradually develop bulbs if left to grow. They are still tasty as larger raw salad onions, or cooked. But if you prefer a thick stem and no bulb, try any derivative of the tall Japanese salad onions, such as Ishikura, whose energy keeps on going into leaf and stem, rather than bulb. A drawback is their tendency to orange spots of rust on the leaves, usually in dry weather, lessened by regular watering.

Sowings in May to July will give salad onions through the summer and into autumn, if you want them then. Remember that they are more prone to rust in summer and autumn, and you will need them less at a time when there are so many other salad options. It is also possible to pinch a green leaf or two from bulb onions for your salad bowl.

Red salad onions

In many varieties on offer, the red colouration does not continue into their stem, apart from a dark outer sheath which is usually too tough to eat. So one ends up with a normal white spring onion. One way round this may be to sow a row of red bulb onions such as North Holland Blood Red and eat them when small, then if there are too many for salad the rest can grow into bulb onions.

Problems with all onions (see also page 91)

Birds An early hazard to growth may be birds pulling sets out of the ground as they start growing, not to eat them but perhaps in search of worms underneath, because worms like allium roots. So it may be necessary to lay some netting on top of the soil for a month, until there is about 75cm (3") of leaf growth, indicating that roots are sufficiently developed to hold the set in place if a bird pulls on it.

Mildew Onion mildew is a grey mould that develops on leaves from about early June onwards. It can happen in both wet and dry years, when mould spores arrive out of nearby infected soil. They will eventually cover all leaves in black sootiness, and subsequent growth is usually poor. The best solution is to lift mildew-infected onions early, before all green-ness disappears, then to leave them on top of the soil for as long as it takes the tops to become thoroughly dry. At this stage they can be stored in shallow boxes, taking care not to damage their skins or necks, which might allow fungus to infect the inside of the onion. The aim is to keep any mildew spores on the dry skin's surface. Official advice is to burn infected leaves, and to grow next year's onions as far away as is practical.

White rot See after shallots.

STORING ONIONS

Any warm, sunny days after lifting will dry skins and tops, leaving a pleasant golden or red ball, round or squashed, depending on variety. When dry and crinkly they can be stacked in boxes or nets or hung on string, and should keep until the following spring.

Should it be wet at harvest time, with the tops staying rather green, an option is to gather up bunches for hanging in a dry airy place or in the house. Or make a rope: hang a stout string at head height, tie about four onions to its bottom by looping and tying the string securely around their necks, then drop onions one by one from on top, held in place by one loop of their necks around the string. Finally cut off all the tops that are sticking out, and hang the heavy rope in dry warmth until needed.

SHALLOTS

Season of harvest: July-August
Follow with: late brassicas, autumn salad

Variety	Character Height (cm)	Sow / Plant First ready	Spacing (cm)
RED SUN	Round, reddish brown 30	Bulbs: Mar Jul	10x30
BANANA SHALLOT	Long, large, thin pink skin 30	Seed: Feb-Mar Jul	5x25
GRISE/GRISELLE	Small dark bulbs, fine flavour 30	Bulbs: Oct-Dec Jul	10x30

A few decades ago, most vegetable gardens included a row of shallots, but now they are rare. Is it because they are smaller than onions and take longer to prepare? Surely we need to remember them in our vegetable plantings, for an extra range of cooking qualities and flavours that are especially apparent in many interesting sauces.

Planting and sowing

As with onions, either seed or bulbs are the starting point. One seed makes one new bulb, while one bulb makes a clump of at least six new bulbs. Traditionally, in Somerset at least, a few of the previous year's shallots were set out at Christmas time. The old saw ran: "Plant on the shortest day, harvest on the longest."

The Banana Shallot is intriguing for an elongated shape and large size, making it sought after in many kitchens. It has a milder flavour and is fast growing, best sown before mid March and only available as seed at the moment. Jermor is a large elongated shallot that can be purchased as a bulb for planting.

Look at the three varieties above and notice how they all have different sowing or planting dates for best results. Red Sun is a standard British shallot, essentially round and quite dark in colour, but it does have a tendency to bolt if planted too early, hence the wait until March. Echalote Grise, also sold as Griselle, deeply esteemed by chefs in France, is best planted in late autumn and matures a little earlier.

Growing

Grow as for onions; regular weeding is the most important job.

Harvesting and storing

Watch for the leaves falling over: harvesting is best done as soon as this happens for best keeping qualities, especially Echalote Grise. Lift them carefully, shake soil out of the roots and leave bulbs on top of the soil for an initial drying. They can then be tied into bunches and hung in a shed or your kitchen, whatever is most convenient. At room temperature they should keep well until spring, but separate any larger bulbs for re-planting.

Problems

White Rot A significant potential problem for all alliums is white rot, a pale fungus which weakens and then kills the stem base and roots. Become suspicious if you see yellowing leaves too early: gently pull on the plant, which may come out easily and reveal its roots succumbing to a white fungus. It exists in odd places in my garden, and I am never too clear how it arrives – possibly from my spreading of infected compost, after inadvertently putting some infected onion or leek on the compost heap. Once it is in a patch of ground, the fungus lies dormant for up to seven years, ready to infect the next onion, leek or garlic.

The common solution is to grow alliums in clean parts of the garden while waiting seven years before next growing them in soil that is infected. However, the white rot fungus is weakened (not killed) by brassicas, so growing any of them in the months before alliums can make it possible to grow onions, leek, garlic and shallots in infected soil.

LEEKS

Season of harvest: August-May
Follow with: any of root vegetables, brassicas, salads etc the following year

Variety	Character Height (cm)	Sow / Plant First ready	Spacing (cm)
KING RICHARD	Earliest, longest, dislikes frost 50	Mar-Jun Aug	10x30
AUTUMN MAMMOTH	Reliable, best before Xmas 40	Apr-Jun Sep	10x30
MUSSELBURGH	Shorter, hardy, dark flag 30	Apr-Jul Nov	10x30
ATLANTA	Hardy, long, late to flower 40	Apr-Jul Mar	10x30

As summer cedes to autumn, leeks are quietly growing and then suddenly appear prominent in the garden, as summer crops fade. They have sweet white stems, and sometimes also offer the only fresh green leaves in frosty winter weather. Their season of maturity lasts for nine months, and best results come from sowing the right variety to harvest in the four seasons within this time.

Varieties for the four seasons

Note that some varieties make short stems (Musselburgh) and some make very long ones. There is a leek for eating in summer called King Richard, whose stems are magnificent, but it is now rarely found in mainstream catalogues. Startrack is similar if you can find it, while most autumn Mammoth varieties are consistent croppers from September to Christmas, and resist some frost. The choice of variety for autumn is considerable, as this is main season for leeks. Besides Autumn Mammoth, of different strains such as Tornado and Goliath, I have had good results with Porvite, Jolant and The Lyon.

Any long stems above ground are most vulnerable to any hard frost: hence the shorter winter and spring varieties such as Musselburgh, although they elongate by late March and through April. At some point in early to mid spring they will form a flower stem inside, which soon becomes too hard to eat, so harvest any remaining leeks if you see small flower buds appearing. St Victor is a spring variety whose pretty violet coloured leaves look nice at a bleak time of year.

Sowing

Leeks grow quite slowly from seed with thin, grassy stems. Do not sow before late March, and around mid April is often better. Aim to sow about forty seeds in rows across a 1.2m bed, to provide about thirty plants per row. Many seed packets contain enough for about four such rows, but leek seed shows its age, and occasionally I have had poor germination from seed that was past its prime.

Planting

By June the young leeks should be nearly as thick as a pencil and ready to be planted out. In dry weather it can helpful to water the seedbed before carefully loosening the roots with a trowel and lifting clumps of plants. Divide them up, discarding any tiddlers, and set each one in a dibbed hole about 12cm (4") deep, then water them in so that wet soil covers the roots. Depth of hole will affect the length of white stem (the sweetest part), but if planted too deep they grow less strongly and are more difficult to harvest. Stems can be earthed up if you want more white on them.

Spacing of leeks will have an effect on their final size, although summer rainfall and soil quality are equally important. I plant at about 8x30cm (3x12"); having them in rows, even on beds, makes hoeing and watering easier.

Growing

Leeks are responsive to thick dressings of manure or compost, both for nutrients and for moisture retention. Moisture is necessary: this must be one reason for leeks to be celebrated in Wales, with its higher rainfall than England. Undoubtedly they grow bigger in wet summers, and with less rust on their leaves.

Harvesting

If grown in well-composted soil, leeks can often be pulled gently out of the ground, their roots cut off and flag trimmed. Push the disturbed soil back down with your boot. If they are too firmly embedded, a spade will be necessary to loosen some roots before lifting.

Summer / Early Autumn Leeks Most will want harvesting before the first severe frost of about −6⁰C, this may be in late November or after Christmas. Frost damage will not be apparent for a little while, and usually reveals itself by plants leaning over as their stems start to rot. Harvest as soon as possible if you see this.

Winter Leeks Although resistant to severe frost, leeks are difficult to extricate from frozen soil. In eastern Europe leeks are harvested before winter sets in, sometimes then rooted in moist sand in an outbuilding. I mention this to make the point that in cold weather, harvested leeks keep for a long time and can be gathered in large batches, to save going out in bitter conditions.

Spring Leeks Some varieties (as above: Atlanta, St Victor) carry on into early May and are then most welcome at a time when few other vegetables are available. They are also growing fast through April, so yields increase rapidly, and quite a few worthwhile meals may be had from a small patch.

Problems

Leeks are affected by **white rot** as much as onions, see above.

Rust is not pretty but nor is it too serious; watering usually helps.

A new pest in southern England is the **leek moth** which lay eggs deep inside young leeks in high summer, leading to maggots eating all baby leaves which stops most growth. The only remedy I know is almost too drastic: chop the leek off about 30cm above ground, compost all debris, maggots included, and wait for re-growth.

SAVING LEEK SEED

Seed can be saved by allowing a good plant to flower in its second summer, then gathering the whole dry head in early autumn. Hang it upside down by its stem in a dry place and knock out the seeds when it feels dry and crisp to touch.

Gratin of leeks

5 or 6 leeks
3 or 4 slices of ham (optional)
20g butter, 20g flour, a teaspoon wholegrain mustard, 250ml creamy milk or single cream nutmeg, salt & pepper
150g cheese

Lightly steam the leeks for about 5 minutes. Drain, reserving the water if any is left. Make a white sauce, mixing the mustard into the flour and butter, add the milk, and if the sauce is too thick add some cooking water from the leeks. Oil a gratin dish; cut the leeks into finger lengths and wrap in ham if you are using it. Lay the leeks in the dish and smother with sauce. Grate the cheese over the top, and bake in a hot oven (180°C) for about 20mins till the top is brown and bubbling.

GARLIC

Season of harvest: June-July, then store until spring
Follow with: French beans, late brassicas, autumn salads

Variety	Character		Flavour	Sow-Plant
	Spacing (cm)	Height (cm)	Special care	Harvest
GERMIDOUR	No stalk, purple skins		Average	Oct-Dec
	15x15 or 10x25	40		Late Jun/Jul
OSWEGO WHITE	No stalk, large white bulb		Average	Oct-Dec
	15x15 or 10x25	40		Late Jun/Jul
SPANISH ROJA	Stalk, av. bulb, thin skin		Strong	Oct-Feb
	15x15 or 10x25	40	Cut stalk when 15cm	Jul
ELEPHANT	Stalk, huge bulbs		Mild	Oct-Nov
GARLIC	30x30	80	Lift before flowering	Jul

Garlic is relatively easy to grow, and with usually impressive results. The best thing about home-grown garlic is its rich and pungent flavour. Less is needed because the sulphurs and aromas are much stronger. Half a clove may be enough for breakfast instead of a whole clove.

There is a fascinatingly broad range of growing styles and flavours, some of which are shown in the chart. Outside the kitchen, garlic has impressive abilities to lower blood pressure and cholesterol, and is an anti-septic. To grow it, consider these three essential pieces of information.

• Young garlic is extremely hardy, and will come through very cold win-ter weather. Plant cloves in the autumn, and see how much bigger the bulbs grow by July.
• Garlic fits well with other vegetables because much of its time in the ground is when they are out of season. Plant cloves when summer crops finish, then after lifting bulbs in July, there is still time to plant French beans, beetroot and winter cabbages, or to sow winter salads.
• It is fun and interesting to try different varieties, but I have enjoyed as much success, in terms of yield, from planting the greengrocer's eating gar-lic as from planting named varieties that are virus-free and certified. My best results are often from garlic bought in the grocer's shop, years before, replanted every year.

Different types

Hardneck garlic grows a flower-stalk between its cloves. Cutting this in mid spring when about 10-15cm (4-6") high will encourage more growing of bulbs, while these tender stems (also known as 'scapes') are delicious raw or cooked. Hardneck varieties often keep better and have a stronger and different flavour to more common softnecks.

Softnecks do not make stems and flowers, are milder in taste and usually start to sprout by the end of the year, and they do need re-planting in autumn for best results.

Elephant garlic is akin to a giant hardneck crossed with a leek and has enormous, mild-tasting cloves. It is tasty as a roasted accompaniment to meat or vegetables, on a kebab or to chew on raw. It needs more space, about 30cm (12") in all directions, looks like a medium-sized leek when growing, and produces a large flower-bud by early July, on average. This is harvest time, before the sheath breaks to reveal hundreds of pale blue flower buds.

Planting

A rule of thumb planting date is early to mid October, after any summer crop has finished. Buy nice-looking bulbs from a shop or catalogue, then break them up into cloves. Most shop garlic is higher yielding 'softneck', and will not flower.

Largest bulbs grow from largest cloves, usually those forming an outer ring around the interior cluster of smaller cloves. Keep the inner ones for cooking. Use a dibber to make holes 5cm (2") deep, at a similar spacing to leeks, and push the cloves in firmly, with their pointy end upwards.

It is good to have some soil covering the clove tops and hiding them from curious birds, who may pull them out. Also if cloves are planted too shallow, they may later be lifted almost out of the ground by frosts which cause topsoil to lift and loosen. Compost can be spread on the soil before or after planting, or even in spring between the rows of leaves.

Growing

By Christmas there may be a few centimetres of spiky green leaf to reassure you that all is well. Any mild spells in winter will see this leaf grow and multiply, or in a cold winter it will simply sit there, although new roots will be forming, ready for a surge of growth in spring.

Any winter weeds need removing by early April to leave the soil clear for garlic's main season of growth. This is normally trouble-free, and your plants, by early June, should have the appearance of small leeks. If the weather is turning dry, rust can now turn the leaves yellow and bring maturity forward. Good garlic weather is plenty of moisture until mid June, then drier towards harvest time. Usually this is early to mid July.

Harvesting

Keep watching however: poke under the soil in late June to see if bulbs are well swollen. Bad cases of rust can make it better to pull bulbs out then, after loosening the soil with a trowel or spade. Handle them carefully because they bruise easily and may then rot, rather than keeping until

Radicchio Rialto in September

Onions Centurion drying in early August

12 Cloves from each bulb ready for planting in October

Chioggia, sown 29 June, photographed November.
Each ring is one lunar month

Pea flower

Radicchio Agena in December (usually hearts up, but this one did not)

Yellow Courgette Parador F1 in July

Summer Squash – Yellow Crookneck

Sweet Orange Baby in pot in greenhouse in mid-September

Tomato – Supersteak F1 in tunnel in October

Squash – Butternut, Uchiki Kuri (red one at back), Snake Gourd,
Buttercup, Blue Ballet in November

Christmas or beyond. Shake all soil out of their tenacious and numerous roots, revealing indented bulbs with the shapes of its cloves under layers of white or purple skin.

Bulbs for storing should not be beautified, but when needed for table an outer layer or two of skin can be carefully peeled off and the roots trimmed to reveal beautiful, shiny new bulbs.

The outer sheath of thin skins will gradually rot if bulbs are left in the ground for too long after maturity. Their cloves are still alright to eat, but bulbs look less attractive and may sprout sooner rather than later.

Storage

Remember that most garlic is ready for re-planting in October, so storage in warm, dry conditions can fool it into thinking that summer is going on, and there is no need to sprout just yet. Bulbs can be kept hung up in bunches, or trimmed off once their leaves are dry.

Set the best bulbs on one side for replanting, since large healthy cloves make larger healthy bulbs. If for some reason you do not manage to plant in October, or even November, cloves can still go in as late as March, but the harvest will definitely be smaller. There is a risk that late plantings give insufficient exposure to cold weather for bulbs to properly develop, i.e. the new bulb may have very few cloves.

Problems

For white rot see under shallots, for rust see the text above.

Charles' mayonnaise

You may not believe the amount of garlic in this recipe, and might like to try using less garlic the first time you follow it. You will notice that garlic is stronger at different times of the year; freshly harvested, it packs a powerful punch.

2 whole eggs
10 cloves of garlic
3 teaspoons wholegrain mustard
1 cupful vinegar
1½ teaspoons salt
pepper
4 – 6 cupfuls olive oil
We use a hand-held blender to whizz together all the ingredients except for the olive oil. Add this gradually.
As a variation you can make green mayonnaise by adding herbs from the garden – tarragon or basil and parsley.

Chapter 12

Choice of Roots

An exploration of amazing flavours

Visitors to my garden, when looking at healthy crops in undug soil, are often surprised that the carrot and parsnip beds have not been 'aerated' or loosened in any way. We have been indoctrinated to believe that roots need man-loosened soil to descend!

I garden on clay soil which is very sticky in springtime, although just on top there is a crumbly tilth, thanks to compost and winter frosts. Seeds can be sown into this frost tilth and tiny seedlings are happy to push straight through it and into the clay below. Carrots and parsnips grow straight and long with very little forking. Only potatoes are sometimes challenging for a no-digger, because they do prefer loose soil, and benefit above all from being earthed up.

Like all other vegetables, roots have seasons, but such long ones that we barely notice them. Last year's potatoes and carrots are barely finished when this year's are beginning. But the taste of a new-season root, freshly harvested, is a remarkable experience for the gardener and is always an exciting event. Beetroot for example, is usually in the background as a kind of plodding vegetable, always there and much the same, even pickled. Yet the first ones in June are utterly gorgeous, a reminder to winter-jaded palates of fresh, sweet flavours which somehow always impress, as if discovered for the first time ever.

BEETROOT

How to grow such a fine flavour? The soil, the seed, timing . . .

Season of harvest: June onwards
Follow with: depends on harvest date, e.g. autumn salad after early Boltardy

Variety	Character	Sow Harvest	Height (cm) Spacing (cm)
BOLTARDY	For earliest sowings, sweet flavour	Feb-Jul Jun-Nov	30 5x30 or 30x30*

Variety	Character	Sow	Height (cm)
		Harvest	*Spacing(cm)*
CHIOGGIA BARABIETOLA	Pink 'moon rings' on white flesh	Apr-Jul	30
		Jul-Nov	5x30 or 30x30*
CYLINDRA OR FORONO	Long and sweet, vulnerable to frost	Apr-Jul	40
		Jul-Nov	5x30 or 30x30*
GOLDEN	Yellow, fine flavour	Apr-Jul	30
		Jul-Nov	5x30 or 30x30*

*5x30 when sown direct, or 30x30 if planted in modules

EARLY BEETROOT

For the very earliest, Boltardy is excellent, to have sweet beets by late spring. It was bred so as not to bolt when sown in the cold of late winter. Fortunately it tastes good as well.

Sowing

First sowings are most successful indoors. I sow three or four beetroot seed into 4cm modules of a tray of forty, but variable numbers of seedlings germinate from each seed, so thin them to four or five per module when still small.

Timing of the sowing depends on your facilities. I have 'electric sand' in the greenhouse, a thermostatically controlled cable running through wet sand underneath all the module and seed trays. Set at 20°C, this allows beetroot to be sown by mid February, planted out in early April as clumps of seedlings, and a few golf-ball-sized roots to be harvested by early June, one of the first fresh vegetables of the season.

Alternatively sow in modules in March in a cold greenhouse, or outdoors in late March or early April, depending on the weather.

Growing

Growth of the scarcely visible dark leaves will be slow at first, but the leaves are not too sought-after by slugs and ought to survive; fleece can be used to bring the harvest forward a week or two. Remember that fleece makes weeds grow faster too!

Harvesting

Beetroot in modular clumps always grows at different speeds, so individual larger roots can be gently twisted out as you need them, leaving the three or four remaining beets to grow on. In this way a small, well-weeded and well-composted patch can be producing over a long period, for two months or more.

There is also the possibility of eating beetroot leaves, in a similar way to spinach beet (pages 70-71), as long as they have not grown tough with age.

AUTUMN AND WINTER BEETROOT

From the table above, you can see that there is a long season of sowing and harvesting. Sown as late as early July, there is still time for a medium-sized, tender root to develop before winter arrives, and the wide range of shapes, colours and flavours makes it interesting to try new possibilities every year.

Storing

In mild areas and winters, roots often keep best in the ground. But in seriously frosty weather they risk freezing right through and then rotting, so you have to make an assessment in mid autumn. Round varieties with less protruding roots are less damaged by frost. On balance, I pull most roots and store them in paper sacks in an outbuilding. Larger ones dry out less. Salads of grated raw beetroot are valuable live food in the winter, with a much earthier flavour than cooked beetroot.

MOON RINGS

All beetroots have rings, but Chioggia's pink ones on white flesh, like tree rings but more vivid, are highly visible when cutting roots both horizontally and vertically. By working back from picking date to sowing date, I find that there is usually a ring for each lunar month. Here is a good example of the importance of moon cycles to plant growth (see Chapter 8, pages 49-51). In red beetroot the rings are faintly present, but scarcely visible.

Beetroot, carrot and apple salad

People are sometimes confused about the length of time beetroot needs to cook. Young spring beetroot need no more than 20 minutes, while an older winter root might need up to an hour in a slow oven. This recipe avoids the problem by using raw beetroot.

1 or 2 beetroot, depending on size
1 or 2 carrots
1 apple
parsley
a handful of walnuts
dressing: either vinaigrette or yoghurt

Grate the beetroot, carrot and apple, chop the parsley and stir in the walnuts and dressing

CARROTS

Season of harvest: June to November
Follow with: depends on date of harvest, e.g. late beetroot after early carrots

Variety	Character Height (cm)	Sow Harvest	Spacing (cm)
AMSTERDAM FORCING	Early, long and thin, deep rooting 25	Mar-May May-Jul	1x25 or less
EARLY NANTES	Early, round ended, easy to pull 40	Mar-Jul May-Nov	1x30
BERLICUM	Maincrop, round end, high yielding 40	May-Jun Sep-Nov	2x30
ROTHILD	Maincrop, extra sweet, deep orange 40	May-Jun Sep-Nov	2x30
RAINBOW MIX	Colourful, range of flavours & vigour 40	Apr-Jun Jun-Oct	1x30

One of the tastiest vegetables you will grow, and one of the most difficult to establish. Once growing, there is a mouth-watering range of flavours to anticipate. Both sweetness and earthy aroma are enhanced in freshly pulled carrots. They express the 'taste of your soil' almost more than any other vegetable.

Sowing

Early sowings from about late March are the riskiest: about half of mine are eaten by slugs as soon as they emerge in damp springs. But I persevere! (see below).

Carrots sown in the relative warmth of May and June will usually (not always!) manage to grow away successfully. Rows can be along or across a bed, about 30cm (12") apart. In dry years, draw out a drill and then carefully water it before sowing, so that only the U- or V-shaped hollow is wet, not the soil on either side of it. After sowing, fill in with the dry soil and firm gently with feet or a spade. Do not water again for two weeks at least.

To sow the seed, I firstly shake seed into cupped fingers and then dribble seed from these into the drill. I rub backwards and forwards with my thumb against the first two or three fingers, as my hand moves steadily over the drill. Aim for about four seeds per centimetre; if in doubt, sow a little more thickly. In a month's time any excess seedlings can be thinned by careful pulling, depending on how well they have come up.

Growing

Weeding is important throughout, especially so that weeds do not smother baby seedlings. Use hands, trowel or hoe, whatever is most comfortable. Later sowings are easier because you will have had time to hoe off the first germinations of weed seedlings and are thus sowing into cleaner soil.

Harvesting

First baby roots are ready in about eight weeks, when a little investigation at surface level should reveal shoulders of small carrots. Larger ones can usually be eased out to leave more room for remaining roots to grow. The long variety Amsterdam, and others in dry soil, may need a trowel to gently lever them out.

After about ten weeks, less in summer, the whole row may be of edible size, depending how large you want them. There is a wide range of possibilities, according to season, variety of carrot, success of sowings and their thickness, spacing within and between rows, soil type, soil fertility and so on.

Too-thick sowings will look good initially but ultimately tend to grow more leaf than root, so thinning to recommended spacing is always worthwhile, above all for autumn harvests. Larger roots keep better than small ones, and involve less cleaning as well.

Carrots resist some frost but are damaged after about mid November in temperatures below about -5°C. Also there will be increasing amounts of slug and maggot holes as growth slows in late autumn, so a mid October harvest is late enough in most areas of Britain. A spade may be needed to gently loosen roots, avoiding wet weather if possible. Shake or scrape off most soil, leaving some to help carrots keep moist in a paper or hessian sack. Ideal conditions for storage are a damp 0-7°C.

Problems

Weeds, slugs and carrot root fly are the three challenges to deal with. Not digging is a first step in reducing germination of new weed seeds, as well as in conserving moisture. Bare soil in the vicinity of carrot seedbeds is vital in keeping slug numbers down. Damage from root fly maggots is harder to prevent, but some suggestions are made below.

Slugs The first month of a carrot's life is always tricky. Small carrot seeds beget tiny seedlings that can easily be devoured overnight in damp weather, should there be just one slug on the prowl. But after the first true leaf appears, the plants become stronger and grow away more readily from occasional nibbles. Here are three suggestions.

Think ahead. Prepare the carrot bed before winter by clearing and keeping clear both the bed and a fair area around it. Slugs live in weedy areas and will happily forage outwards from these to your newly sown carrot seedlings.

Do not sow too early. A fair guide is to wait until the first small weed seedlings appear on any bare soil, indicating sufficient warmth to germinate early crops. These can be hoed off before sowing, making a cleaner seedbed. Mid April is a fair estimate, but if it is continually wet you will do better to wait longer. Carrots always start best in dry springs. An alternative option is to cover the carrot bed with a cloche in mid March, an artificial way of ensuring dry, warm soil.

Do not water the seedbed or baby seedlings: 'Sow in dust, grow they must'. Keeping the soil surface dry will help it to warm up and deter slugs.

In some springs it rains regularly enough for slugs to predominate. Sowing again is the only solution. If one knew of a wet spring in advance, cloches would be worth the trouble, but are extra work in dry or normal conditions and can occasionally make the soil too dry.

Carrot Fly After slugs, the maggots of small carrot flies are a most troublesome pest. Flies are on the wing from mid spring, usually in two or three batches until October.

Certain weather and soil conditions at certain unknowable times are more or less favourable to the descent of maggots' eggs into soil, so one never knows in advance if damage will be mild or severe. Sheltered gardens with a long history of vegetable growing are most at risk, compared to windy hillsides, which are likely to escape attack, because flies suffer in wind.

Damage shows as dark tunnels at the bottom end of growing or maturing roots, which can sometimes be cut off to leave plenty of good carrot. Occasionally almost the whole root is damaged, and this will be the result in late winter if some damage is seen at lifting time in October, because the maggots carry on eating and tunnelling until spring. They do the same in parsnips and celeriac, but with less dramatic effect because their tunnels are on the surface of much larger roots.

Covering young carrots about six weeks after sowing with a fine netting is worthwhile if you want to be sure of totally healthy roots. A vertical 60cm (24") polythene 'wall' around the whole bed, to keep out low-flying pests, is a little less effective but easier for weeding and picking.

I hope that you feel more aware of the challenges and encouraged to grow carrots. A successful crop is never assured, but when achieved is a sign of no little gardening skill.

Carrot salad

Grated carrot, juice of a lemon, olive oil, 1 teaspoon coriander seeds crushed, salt & pepper

CELERIAC

Season of harvest: October to November, store until April
Follow with: spring sowings or plantings

Variety	Sow	Plant	Spacing (cm)	Height (cm)
	Special care		Harvest	
PRINZ	Mid Mar to Apr	May-Jun	35x35	40
	Needs thick compost and moist soil		Oct-Nov & store	
GIANT PRAGUE	Mid Mar to Apr	May-Jun	35x35	40
	Needs thick compost and moist soil		Oct-Nov & store	

Turnip-rooted celery is a strong-tasting root, bringing the flavour of earth and celery to soups, stews and salads in winter and early spring. Celeriac loves to grow in well-composted soil offering moist conditions, and benefits from some extra watering in a dry summer. Its roots are fibrous and mostly superficial.

I have grown many varieties and noticed few significant differences.

Sowing and planting

Decent-sized roots require a long growing season, so seed is usually sown under cover between late March and early May, for planting out by mid June. The seeds are tiny and should not be covered with any compost, so a sheet of glass over the seed tray or modules is beneficial. Nothing will appear for up to three weeks, maybe when you are just about to give up!

The tiny seedlings should be pricked out into 3-4cm modules, until about 7-8cm (3") high, then hardened off and planted after any risk of late frost, which would weaken but probably not kill them.

Growing

Regular hoeing or hand-weeding will probably be necessary until about August. By then, especially if you have planted 'on the square' at about 35x35cm (14x14"), there should be leaves covering all bare soil and preventing much new weed growth.

A thick surface dressing of compost always benefits celeriac immensely, both for a gentle supply of nutrients over its long season, and for retention of moisture in dry weather. Roots grow larger in wet summers.

Harvesting and storing

By September there should be a fair-sized root, mostly above soil level. Some gardeners like to remove all lower leaves, supposedly to help roots to swell. I find this of little benefit growth-wise, but it makes the plants very attractive!

Lifting in mid autumn, and before any severe frost, is about right. Masses of fleshy roots make a spade or trowel helpful, together with a knife to sever roots as or after the plant is eased upwards. With the celeriac in hand, trimming of leaves and excess soil should reveal some hints of white flesh, but trim sparingly if you are harvesting to store the roots, in similar conditions to carrots, because a thin layer of soil always helps to keep roots moist and firm – say in a box or sack in shed or garage, free of significant frost.

Problems

Carrot Root Fly When preparing celeriac to eat, you may see lines of brown across and into its bottom end. These are tunnels of carrot root fly maggots, but as with parsnips the large bulk of the roots means that damage is rarely of major consequence.

Frost is a hazard because so much of the root is above ground and exposed to cold air.

Holes inside the roots can be from dry spells or varietal traits, slug holes are more significant, often inhabited by woodlice, and many slugs may make an earlier harvest worthwhile.

Celeriac

Celeriac adds an interesting flavour to stews and roast root vegetables with carrot, parsnip and potato. It is also very good mashed with potato – about ⅔ potato to ⅓ celeriac.

FLORENCE FENNEL

Season of harvest: June to November
Follow with: depends on harvest date e.g. beetroot / French bean after early Finale

Variety	Character *Special Care*	Sow *Harvest*	Spacing (cm)	Height (cm)
FINALE	Resistant to bolting	May-Jul Late Jun-Oct	30x30	40-50
ROMANESCO	Large bulbs Do not sow early	mid Jun-Jul Sep-Oct	35x35	50-60

Florence Fennel is not well known in Britain, and deserves to be more widely grown. It is an umbellifer, of the same family as carrot, parsnip and celeriac. Eaten raw, the sweet aniseed flavour is refreshing in summer and lends character to salads of all kinds. Gentle cooking brings out a soft, creamy quality which is delicious in soups, ratatouille or just on its own. The feathery leaves can also be eaten, with a mild dill-like flavour, although they are a little chewy.

Sowing

The difficulty in growing fennel has always been its tendency to send up a flowering stem before forming a worthwhile bulb. New varieties such as Finale help to overcome this, but I still recommend sowing after mid April and May, as it is more reliable. Sow direct or in 3cm modules. Sow Romanesco up to mid July for some larger bulbs in autumn.

Growing

If there is too little moisture, bulbs will be smaller and less juicy, so a 50cm (2") dressing of compost is especially worthwhile, preferably spread a couple of months before the fennel is sown or planted.

Harvesting

Bulbs will start to swell on the surface after about six weeks, and if all goes well they will fatten up to over 500g. Any bolting tendency will initially show as a notable elongation of small bulbs, at which point they may as well be eaten, since they are unlikely to grow any fleshier. Trim off all leaves and any tough, sinewy stem to enjoy some unusual and rich flavours. Harvest bulbs before any frost and they may keep until about Christmas time.

Problems

Remove any plants that are becoming stemmy while remembering to sow that variety later in the season next year. After swelling, bulbs may show signs of rot on their lower sheaths; harvest as soon as you see this as the main bulb will grow no more. Any new growth will be of mini-bulbs inside the increasingly fibrous outer sheaths – these are very tasty however!

Roasted fennel

1 onion, 3 or 4 heads of fennel
3 or 4 tomatoes, 2 cloves garlic
1 glass cider or white wine (optional)

Heat a roasting tin with a thin layer of olive oil. Slice an onion into rings. If the bulbs of fennel are large, slice them horizontally into rings; if small, they can be quartered vertically. Put into the roasting tin and cook in a hot oven c.180°C for about 20 minutes. Meanwhile chop some tomatoes and a couple of cloves of garlic. When the fennel looks quite well cooked, add the tomatoes and garlic and return to the oven for another 10 minutes or so. If you now have a rather messy pan you can transfer the fennel mixture to a serving dish and clean up the roasting tin by pouring a wine-glassful of cider or wine into the pan and returning it to the oven for 5 minutes. Then scrape it all out and pour over the fennel.

JERUSALEM ARTICHOKES

See Chapter 16, pages 168-9

PARSNIPS

Season of harvest: September to April
Follow with: nothing that year, e.g. onions the next year

Variety	Character Height (cm)	Sow	Spacing (cm) First ready
WHITE GEM	Reliable to grow, gorgeous to eat 60	Mar-May	2-10x30 Oct or after frost
GLADIATOR F1	As above + resistant to canker 60	Mar-May	2-10x30 Oct or after frost

The three most important things to know are:
- Home-grown parsnips are incredibly sweet and delicious, most notably after frost.
- Always use fresh seed.
- Parsnip seed takes a long time to germinate.

Sowing

It will be difficult to keep the tiny seedlings clear of weeds, unless you have clean soil to sow them in. For best crops I recommend sowing late March to mid April, but if a lot of weed seeds are expected to germinate, I advise waiting until they do and then hoeing them off before sowing parsnips in May.

This can however lead to problems. Sowing later has the disadvantage of a slightly smaller crop, and also of the slowly germinating seed running into a week's dry spring sunshine, which may crisp it up before any root has travelled down to moister zones. It can often be a month between sowing and first leaves appearing, so one is unsure whether they will emerge for a long time. A few radish can be sown in the drill to mark it out at least, and they will be half-ready before the parsnip seedlings appear.

I sow either three or four rows along a 1.2m bed. Squashes or courgettes are good preceding crops if you kept them well weeded, because that will have cleaned the soil and they will have been heavily composted. Most of that compost will have been taken in by worms, leaving a fine tilth for sowing the parsnips, once any debris (dead stems etc) of preceding crops has been raked off.

Growing

By the time each parsnip plant has two or three true leaves, it may be worth thinning them, depending whether you like small or large roots. Bear in mind that, when harvesting, it can be a lot of work to scrape the mud off small roots and you may wish at that point to have thinned them out, to about 7-10cm (3-4") apart.

Young parsnip seedlings will not thrive in recently spread compost, unless it is of top quality, so I sometimes spread compost between the rows of larger parsnip plants in June.

After that, occasional weeding is the only requirement. Keep checking for weeds so that none are seeding, keeping the next crop (onions maybe) in mind. Such thoughts should forever be in the back of your mind when gardening – the long term improvement of your soil, and maintaining it clean of weeds so that subsequent crops are much easier to grow.

Harvesting

Loosening with a fork should be enough, until the tap root snaps, without turning the soil over. The grand moment of first digging is exciting because one is never too sure what may be there. Roots will come out beautifully white in dry autumn weather, but normally they will need at least a gentle scrape before use.

Parsnips are one of the few vegetables that can safely be left in the garden all winter. Their flavour improves significantly with cold weather as starches turn to sugars, so frost is actually beneficial. By March some leaves will start to grow out of any remaining roots: the row becomes visible again, and the last roots want digging by about mid April. By June, if left in the soil, they would be making seed heads which resemble cows' parsley (also an umbellifer). Planting a parsnip root amongst the flowers can make a striking statement!

Frost will have knocked the lumpiness out of any clods brought up when digging parsnips. Knock these to a tilth with fork or rake, to be ready for sowing or planting next spring.

Problems

Canker In wet winters and in heavy soils the root tops may succumb to canker, a brown fungal rot. Even if this happens, there is usually plenty of good root below. When you grow your own vegetables, grading out the bad bits soon becomes second nature and one never discards something which is even half good.

Carrot root fly will also probably have visited your parsnips, and its tiny maggots usually crawl around the outside of roots. Their damage can be trimmed off unless roots are very small – make a note to thin seedling parsnips next year, so they grow bigger. Also crops will improve every year if you apply 50cm of compost annually.

Poor germination after a month of waiting is almost certainly because of old seed. Buy some more and sow again immediately.

Parsnip soufflé

500g parsnips
300 ml milk
5 eggs
100g cheddar cheese, grated
Cut up the parsnips and steam or boil till tender. Make a white sauce starting with a generous knob of butter, a large spoonful of flour (we use our own home-ground wholemeal). Start by sautéing an onion in the butter before making the sauce. At this point you can add some wholegrain mustard if you wish. Add the milk and when you have a nice creamy sauce add the cheese, leaving enough to sprinkle on the surface of the soufflé. Now separate the eggs, beating the yolks into the sauce (waiting for it to cool a little so you don't end up with scrambled eggs). Drain the parsnips, and purée them. Season with salt, pepper, nutmeg to taste, and mix into the sauce. Add a pinch of salt to the egg whites, and whisk them. Carefully fold the sauce into the whites and pour into a buttered soufflé dish. Sprinkle the remaining grated cheese on top and bake for 30 minutes at 200°C. Sometimes when we cook this for the family we put the mixture in a shallow, oval 'plat sabot' so it will cook more quickly.

POTATOES

Season of harvest: late May-October and then from store
Follow with: leeks, kale, salad (after first and second earlies mostly)

Variety	Character		Plant	Spacing (cm)
	Height (cm)	Special care		First ready
SPRINT	Exceptionally early		Mar	30x30
	35	Lift as soon as leaves yellow	May	
CHARLOTTE	Waxy salad potato, 2nd early		Mar-Apr	30x40
	40	Watch for blight	Jun	
REMARKA	Waxy, deep yellow maincrop		Apr	45x45
	50	Watch for blight	Aug	
SARPO MIRA	Blight resistant maincrop, red skin		Apr	45x45
	70	Tall leaves may need support	Sep	

Far be it from me, a potato amateur, to give extensive advice on this popular crop. I will limit myself to a few observations on general principles, worthwhile varieties I have grown, and on the scope of potato growing in a no-dig garden.

How they grow

Potatoes are classified according to how quickly they mature. First earlies have the shortest life, second earlies grow a month or two longer, maincrop carry on into the autumn, offering higher yields and usually larger potatoes.

As a potato plant grows, new tubers (potatoes) form both below and near the soil surface. If left uncovered, surfaces of potatoes exposed to light turn green and poisonous – hence the need to ridge or earth-up around their stems. I have used thick wedges of straw to this end, and also have grown potatoes under black polythene for the same reason. Both tended to encourage too many slugs, and even without mulch slugs are a major problem. Most potato farms use slug pellets, especially in wet autumns, whereas I recommend digging any maincrop by late September. They should also be less muddy at this time.

Note that maincrop potatoes take up a fair amount of space and are scarcely viable in small gardens.

First earlies

Most gardeners will do better to grow early potatoes, which are ready from late spring, because the extra flavour of freshly dug potatoes is more apparent in 'first earlies'. Also there is time to plant other vegetables after them, and less need to earth them up since they make less tubers.

Choosing potato varieties

Regarding which variety to grow, the choice is almost daunting, and you will need to consider season of maturity, flavour, and blight resistance. Read catalogues carefully and study the small print! I like Sprint for its incredible earliness, Estima and Wilja (second earlies) and Remarka for their waxy salad potato quality, and any of the Sarpa's for their ability to resist blight. Pink Fir Apple is the classic salad potato maincrop, but has a little more risk of succumbing to blight.

Buying tubers

Potatoes grow most easily from last season's tubers, rather than from seed. Often they are sold in 3kg lots of about thirty tubers, which may be too much for a small garden, so consider sharing an order with friends or neighbours. Smaller packs of 1kg are increasingly available.

You can save money by using some of your harvest – including any green ones – for next year's planting, but avoid doing this if the crop has been infected by blight (see next page).

Planting

I simply make a hole about 10cm (4") into the soil with a trowel and pop seed tubers in, without any digging. Then I spread 50-100cm (2-4") of compost or well-rotted manure. Fleece can help bring on early growth, from a March planting, and prevent frost from damaging leaves too much.

Harvesting

By late May, depending on variety, there may be flowers atop the plant and its leaves may even be yellowing. Both indicate maturity of tubers – any extra growth is limited when leaves start to die off.

Slip a trowel under the plant, about 15cm away from the stems, pulling on them gently at the same time. As the plant rises up from soil level, a cluster of new potatoes should become visible. Most are near to the stem; sometimes you will see white roots leading to potatoes further away. There will also be the original seed potato, now ugly and rotten.

Eating your tubers on that same day will reveal fine fresh potato flavours that are difficult to buy with the groceries. A gentle brushing will prepare them for the pot as there is no skin to peel off, and a little mint in the saucepan will add to the wonderful feeling of summer.

Problems

Frost Potatoes are of the same plant family as tomatoes and aubergines, and are equally sensitive to frost. But if leaves are frozen and blackened by late spring frosts, don't despair because the unfrozen roots will quickly send up new shoots and leaves.

Blight appears in wet or damp summers, between June and September depending on the weather. Once any leaves have turned brown and wilted, it can take as little as two weeks for the whole plant to die and by then many roots may be infected, meaning they will rot if stored, as happened in the 1840s Irish potato famine.

So it is best to harvest any crop as soon as blight is spotted, or to cut all stems just above ground level to stop passage of the fungus into potatoes, through the plants' sap. Then dig the roots as needed.

Another possibility is to grow blight-resistant varieties; the best ones I have grown are Sarpa Mira or Sarpa Axona, from Hungary. They are extremely vigorous, with fair-tasting pink tubers that are more floury than waxy. The stems are vigorous and long, so allow space and perhaps run a string around the row or bed to stop leaves falling over nearby plants. They keep growing vigorously in autumn, but there is a suspicion that their potatoes become more dry and floury if dug from early October onwards, partly depending on weather.

Gratin Dauphinoise

1kg potatoes, peeled and thinly sliced
3 shallots sliced, 4 cloves garlic chopped
250ml full cream milk, 250ml Jersey cream
150g cheddar cheese, grated; salt, pepper, nutmeg

Parboil the potatoes for 5 minutes. Butter a large gratin dish. Build up alternate layers of potatoes and shallots. Mix together the cream, milk and seasoning and pour over the potatoes. Top with grated cheese. Bake at about 180°C for an hour.

ROOTING AROUND

There are other flavours to explore in winter root harvests. I cover them briefly because they are not for everybody, for various reasons.

SALSIFY AND SCORZONERA

These are often mentioned together, perhaps because they are equally fiddly to harvest and clean. They have quite thin roots – scorzonera's are black-skinned, and salsify's are creamy in colour – so edible yields are often small. They are delicacies, not staples. Salsify is reckoned by some people to have a taste of oyster – worth a try if you enjoy something different.

Sowing

Sow directly from April to June. Later sowings may produce smaller roots but perhaps with less forking. Scorzonera is inclined to bolt from sowing too early, wait until May at least.

Growing

Thin plants to about 15cm (6") in rows of 30-35cm.

Harvesting

Sandy soils are most suited to the fiddly work of cleaning soil off thin and tender roots, which snap easily. Leaves will die off before winter but the roots resist most frost. They can be lifted and stored in boxes or sacks in cold areas. Any roots left behind will grow pretty flowers the next spring.

SWEDE, TURNIP AND RADISH

A final mention for swede, turnip and radish. These roots are all members of the brassica (cabbage) family, and I explain their growing in Chapter 14 (pages 133-148) since brassicas all have common requirements.

Chapter 13

Savouring Summer

Vegetables with fruits and seeds

Most fruiting vegetables are killed by frost and require summer warmth to grow. Wait until mid or end May before planting them. The exceptions are peas and broad beans, whose harvest is often the first real taste of summer, after all the leaves of springtime.

BROAD BEANS

Season of harvest: June-August
Follow with: leeks, beetroot, fennel, salad, kale, purple sprouting broccoli

Variety	Character Height (cm)	Sow Harvest	Spacing (cm)
AQUADULCE CLAUDIA	Most frost-hardy 120	Nov-Mar mid Jun to Jul	45x10
MASTERPIECE GREEN LONGPOD	Green Beans 150	Feb-Apr Jul to mid Aug	45x10
THE SUTTON	Small-sized plants 75	Feb-Apr Jul to mid Aug	30x10

Sowing

Aquadulce does well from a January sowing in pots or 4cm modules in the greenhouse, or from a February / March sowing outside. These dates also work for most other varieties, including green-fruiting beans such as Masterpiece Green Long Pod, whose flavour is appealing and somewhat different.

Sowings made in May or June will crop into late summer and autumn, but yields will be low and aphid attack is more likely. Broad beans do best when sown by early spring.

Certain varieties, chiefly Aquadulce Claudia, are so hardy that they can be sown in the ground in autumn, say the first week in November, to stand the winter as seedlings about 50mm high. They may be killed by extreme frost or waterlogged soil in a wet winter, but the gamble is worthwhile. If still there in March, often rather bedraggled looking, they will suddenly start growing strongly and will flower by mid spring, when their cousins the spring-sown beans are still very small. Soon the whole four or five foot of stem will be covered in sweetly scented flowers, whereupon you can pinch out the tops for eating in salads, or lightly steam them as a spring green.

Growing

The plants grow tall enough to be worth supporting. Before plants are more than a metre high, put stout stakes at each corner of the bed or end of the row and others every 2m (6') or so, then run a couple of strings around them keeping the plants within, to help them stay upright. This is not always necessary; in years of quiet weather they look after themselves very well; also there are dwarf varieties listed in many catalogues, which do not need support.

Harvesting

The first pods of November-sown beans should be ready by mid June, when there are few other vegetables to eat, and they can be eaten whole if picked when the beans are pea-size. The beans' flavour will change all the time, becoming milder and creamier, eventually starchy if the pods are left until they change in colour from dark to pale green. By the end of July, or later for spring-sown beans, any remaining pods will be black and containing next year's seeds: pick them off, shell out the hard beans and keep them dry until November.

Once the last pods are picked, I recommend cutting the stem at its base, with a knife or spade, rather than pulling up the whole plant. This way, more of the nitrogen nodules fixed by the plant onto its roots will remain in the soil for use by the next crop, which can be planted straightaway – think ahead and have the plants ready! The bean stems are best chopped or cut before composting, so they rot more quickly. This procedure applies to all peas and beans.

Problems

Mice, rooks or **badgers** may eat or pull out seeds and baby seedlings. Netting plants will stop birds and larger animals, mice are best dealt with by sowing in the greenhouse with some kind of mouse trap primed all the time.

Black Aphids Removing the growing point at the top of the plant, when in full flower, helps to prevent arrival of black aphids that occasionally infest the upper stem of broad bean plants. These aphids are more common on spring-sown beans, probably because faster growth has made them softer and more sappy. If aphids do appear, remove the infested parts to the compost heap as soon as you see them.

Chocolate Spot is a fungal invasion, usually restricted to wet years. Yield will be lower but you can still pick the beans, although your hands may be covered in brown mould from undersides of the leaves.

Rooks and Pigeons occasionally peck out fresh beans. Netting such large plants is difficult; try hanging up unwanted compact discs first.

Broad beans in sorrel sauce

Make a white sauce:
20g butter
20g flour
250 ml creamy milk
salt and pepper or nutmeg
500g broad beans (podded)

Melt the butter, stir in the flour, add the milk a bit at a time, stirring it in well before adding more. If it is warm it will mix in more easily. Season.

Chop the sorrel into shreds and stir into the sauce; it will cook with the heat from the sauce.

Lightly steam the broad beans, drain, and stir into the sauce.

Broad beans tops – the topmost leaves – can be very good in a stir fry or lightly steamed.

COURGETTES

Season of harvest: late June-early October
Follow with: nothing in same year; salad, carrots, beans etc following year

Variety	Character	Sow	Spacing (cm)
	Spread (cm)	Days to first pick	
DEFENDER	Early and prolific	May-early Jun	70-90x150
	100-150	60	
PARADOR	Bright yellow courgettes	May-early Jun	70-90x150
	100-150	70	
RONDO DI NIZZA	Round, green courgettes	May-early Jun	70-90x150
	100-150	60	

When you grow courgettes well, the results can be overwhelming. In summer warmth, each plant produces about one new courgette every day, although some round and yellow varieties are less productive.

Varieties

Choose a variety that is bred to make true courgettes: although courgettes are really baby marrows, some varieties of marrow plant, such as All Green Bush, will produce few courgettes, of an unattractive size and shape. It puzzles me why seed companies offer them as 'courgettes'.

Most catalogues offer a bewildering range of varieties; my favourites are an old F1 Early Gem and Parador for yellow courgettes. Most of the pretty round and yellow ones are good for a change of shape and colour, but the flavour is not massively different and yields can be lower. See Summer Squash below for more varied flavours.

Sowing

Seed can be sown in the greenhouse in late April, for planting outside mid May, at which time a covering of fleece will be a great help to the plant for about three weeks, until it is flowering. Large seeds make for rapid growth, about a month from sowing to planting in reasonable warmth.

Growing

Like all plants of the *Cucurbitae* family, including cucumbers and squashes, courgettes have large leaves, long stems and require plenty of room. Their roots will travel a long way in search of moisture and nutrients to keep churning out the daily fruit, so I try and plant them on the edge of the garden, as far as is practical, and the occasional one on a maturing compost heap. Growth will be excellent if you spread plenty of reasonably well-rotted compost where they are to grow, and perhaps some more around their roots in mid summer.

Harvesting

The early flowers are especially dramatic and exciting, usually brilliant yellow, and all *Cucurbitae* flowers are edible. The first courgettes will be small, even misshapen. They are best picked as soon as their flower is dying so as to encourage new and better fruit, and then the daily or every other day picking will continue until early autumn. Let the fruits grow to the size you like; there is more to eat when they are picked larger, but the texture is less firm. Courgettes store better if you harvest by cutting their thin stem, or they can simply be snapped off.

Production will finally stop when a first autumn frost kills the leaves, and the rotting plant can be left as cover for the soil through the winter. By spring, just a few pale fibres will be left of those plants that threatened to take over the garden – they were nearly all water.

Problems

Slugs There are few pests except for the inevitable slugs, which do most damage early and late in the season. A cold wet May is always bad news and will slow down growth to the point where slug holes in the leaves can outweigh new growth. Planting in early June is better if slugs are suspected.

Mildew By August there will be mildew on many of the older leaves, but this will not prevent the continued appearance of new fruit, sometimes hidden under leaves, until the weather cools significantly.

Courgette soup

Water is the great enemy of courgettes when it comes to cooking – so we never steam them, always fry or bake. The first courgettes are delicious lightly fried with onion, garlic and rosemary. As they get bigger, and less of a novelty we start to use other recipes.

600g courgettes, washed & roughly diced
1 onion, 1 teaspoon ground cumin
250 ml milk
200g potatoes, cubed & peeled
2 or 3 chopped garlic cloves
1 teaspoon oil
500 ml chicken stock, salt & pepper

Sweat the courgettes, potatoes, onion, garlic and cumin in the oil. Add the milk and chicken stock. Simmer until all the veg are soft. Blend, and season to taste.

CUCUMBER

Season of harvest: July-October
Follow with: Japanese onions, garlic, broad beans

Variety	Character	Sow	Spacing (cm)
	Spread (cm)	Special care	Harvest
PETITA	Top flavour and yield	April-May	60-80
	300 (height)	Greenhouse	Jun-Oct
LA DIVA	Resists mildew	April-May	80-100
	150 (spread)	Outdoor	Jul-Sep
CUCINO/ROCKY	Baby cucumbers	April-May	60-80
	300 (height)	Greenhouse	Jul-Oct

One of the fastest growing plants, with an interesting range of fruits that are usually best picked young, before seeds develop and the skin becomes too firm. As mature, seedy fruit they can be cooked or pickled.

Varieties

My favourite over many years in polytunnel growing is Petita, for its convenient small size (about 20cm or 8" long), fine sweet flavour and incredible profusion of cucumbers. Otherwise, try a few different ones of various shapes, colours and flavours, and check the details as to whether it is 'outdoor ridge' for trailing over the soil, or 'indoor' for growing vertically in a greenhouse or tunnel. For the latter I definitely recommend all-female varieties, to avoid bitterness (see below).

Both plants and fruit contain more water than almost anything else, so moisture and humidity are constantly necessary, together with warmth. The easiest to grow are outdoor 'ridge' cucumbers with long trailing stems, like a smaller version of squash plants. Keep a lookout for fruits that may be hidden by the profusion of leaves; in hot weather there could well be one new cucumber every second day. Growth will slow markedly in September as the temperature drops, but the presence by then of many small fruit can see cropping maintained at a high level until frost.

Sowing

Outdoor cucumbers are best sown indoors in May. Be sure to handle young plants carefully when potting on or transplanting, because the sappy stem is fragile and liable to snap, and the roots are also fragile. Outdoor sowing should wait until June, and even then only when there have been a few days of summer warmth.

Greenhouse or polytunnel cucumbers are more work to look after, but highly worthwhile for their quality and yield of fruit, over a longer season. Sow late April, plant late May, and some first pickings may arrive by late June. During July and August there is often a serious surplus.

Growing

Greenhouse plants are usually grown up strings or tied to stakes – always be careful with their brittle stems (see Tomatoes, pages 149-155). Side shoots need pinching out, every four or five days at most, leaving only the baby cucumber at each node. Hybrid F1 varieties are easiest because they set no male flowers, whose presence would mean occurrence of pollination and a subsequent bitter flavour to the fruit.

Plants can grow three or four metres long, so when they reach the top of your greenhouse or tunnel the stem can be looped over a wire or support and encouraged to grow down again. Or the growing point can be pinched out, and one or two side shoots at the top allowed to develop into new stems that trail back down.

Outdoor cucumbers require less trimming and training, but can be harder to establish if June is cooler or wetter than usual. Fleece may help initially, but once growing strongly they should flower and fruit profusely.

Harvesting

Greenhouse plants may yield a cucumber every day in hot weather, so don't inspect them weekly! Fruiting outdoors is about half the speed of indoors. Cucumber flavour varies according to maturity of the fruit; more mature means tougher skin and seedy cucumber. 'Middle-aged' cucumbers have, in my view, a fuller and sweeter flavour than very young and tender ones, but as the gardener you can choose for yourself.

Problems

Lack of warmth at sowing or planting time can sometimes diminish growth to the point where slugs may have a chance.

Mildew usually coats the underside of older leaves in late summer and autumn; these leaves can be removed and plants normally carry on fruiting.

Red Spider Mite can sometimes kill greenhouse cucumber plants. It is almost too small to see, but will reveal its presence by a yellowing of lower leaves and faint cobwebbing on the undersides. By this stage it may be too established to deal with, and will probably over-winter in the greenhouse or tunnel, so a predator (phytoseiulus) will need to be bought and introduced just after planting next year. Predators come with some of their prey as well, so they don't starve, and one then hopes the two populations will achieve a stable balance.

Cucumber

As a change from eating cucumber in its natural state, try dicing it and mixing it with yoghurt, a little garlic, and tarragon, mint or chives.

FRENCH BEANS: DWARF

Season of harvest: July-September
Follow with: salad, garlic, onions

Variety	Character Height (cm)	Sow Days to first ready	Spacing (cm)
SLENDERETTE	Classic green bean 40	May-Jul 70-80, long harvest	45x45
SONESTA	Waxy yellow beans, fast cropper 35	May-Jul 60-70, medium harvest	40x40
PURPLE TEEPEE	Purple beans, easy to pick 35	May-Jul 60-70, short harvest	35x35

These are the essence of summer, crunchy in salad, of vibrant colour when lightly steamed and available in green, yellow or purple. The advantage of dwarf bean plants is that no time-consuming supports are needed, and they crop a week or more ahead of climbers. The disadvantage is that their beans hang close to or even touching the soil, so they can be dirtied by storms and holed by slugs. In a dry summer this is not a problem, and they may crop better (with a little watering) than moisture-demanding climbers.

Varieties

There are many good varieties. I especially recommend Sonesta for its rapidity of growth, a slightly waxy taste, and for the relative ease of finding yellow bean pods as opposed to green ones. Purple Teepee has similar advantages but crops for about a week less. Note that purple beans, like broccoli, turn green when boiled.

Sowing

Sowing, even in a greenhouse, should wait until May because, like runner beans and many other plants in this chapter, they simply will not grow when soil temperatures are below summer levels, around 20°C. Sown too early, the seeds may rot. Even if they germinate, growth will be sluggish (!) and prone to slug attacks. Remember that slugs are simply on the prowl for weak and dying vegetation.

Outdoors I recommend sowing no earlier than the end of May, on average, with a second sowing in late June or even early July for a late crop. Sowing in 3-4cm modules on 1 July for example, either inside or out, will see plants ready to go in the ground by mid month where the garlic will just have been harvested.

Growing

I usually do three or four rows of dwarf beans along my beds, about 35 to 45cm apart in every direction (15-18"), leaving a little room for working around the plants at picking time. In dry weather some water after flowering will increase the harvest.

Harvesting

Once the little bean-pods appear, picking will be possible every few days, depending how large you want them to grow. They are quite hard to find, and if missed or left for too long, the pods swell with seeds and become rather tough.

On average, after four to six weeks of picking the yield diminishes noticeably, and thereafter bean quality is less fine as they become scarce. Hence my recommendation of a second sowing by early July, while the first one can be pulled out by mid to late August.

Some varieties are bred for quick development of seed, so that you can let the pods shrivel and then harvest dry beans for cooking in stews. Yields of dry beans are lower than of pods.

Problems

Slugs are keen on both leaves and beans, but can be tolerated in high summer when plants produce more than they can eat. Keep soil clean with no weeds and do not sow too early; indoor sowings are more reliable than outdoors. Respect the spacings given, as planting too close will create more shade for slugs and also result in a shorter harvest, with more leaf than bean.

Salade Niçoise

225g French beans, cooked
4 tomatoes
200g tin tuna or a tin of anchovy fillets
1 small onion – red if you have it
4 hard-boiled eggs
black olives
lettuce leaves can be added if you wish

for the dressing:
2 tablespoons wine vinegar
6 tablespoons olive oil
1 garlic clove chopped
1 tablespoon chopped fresh herbs

Lightly steam the beans and drain and cool them under running water. Quarter the tomatoes and eggs, slice the onion. Toss the leaves and beans in dressing and arrange the other ingredients on top.

FRENCH BEANS: CLIMBING

Season of harvest: late July-September
Follow with: garlic

Variety	Character	Sow	Spacing (cm)
	Height (cm)	Days to first ready	
HELDA	Flat-podded, early cropper	May-Jun	35x50*
	180-250	70-80 short harvest	
NECKARGOLD	Vigorous plants, yellow beans	May-Jun	35x50
180-250		75-85 medium harvest	
BLAUHILDE	Attractive purple flowers & beans	May-Jun	35x50
	180-250	75-85 long harvest	
BORLOTTA	Pretty flat pods, viable for dry seed	May-Jun	35x50
	180-250	70-80 medium harvest	

*35 = distance between plants, 50 = distance between rows

Varieties

There is a wide choice of seed to produce beans of different colours, shapes and maturity – all out of slugs' reach. Four of the many varieties are highlighted in the table.

Borlotta di Lingua Foco is dual-purpose, meaning that the red and cream striped pods can be harvested as a short flat pod, or left to dry on the plant, picked when the pods are crackling and shelled out for a harvest of small freckled beans. Seed of the other varieties, for sowing, can be produced in the same way, all of varied flavour.

Sowing

As for dwarf beans, sowing in 3-4cm modules from late May should be a reliable way of starting growth. Wait until June for outdoor sowing.

Growing

I grow two rows of climbing beans along my 1.2m beds, about 50cm (20") apart with 30cm (12") between the plants. Alternatively one row could be grown up netting on flat ground, or wigwams of 90cm (36") diameter can be created on beds or anywhere with some good, moisture-retentive soil.

The plants will grow to at least two metres, depending how long your supports are: their large size and rapidity of growth are why they need rich soil. Traditionally, a trench is opened out in late winter or early spring to receive large quantities of well-rotted manure or compost. This is optional: I find it works as well to spread manure or compost on the soil surface by about January, giving time for some weathering to make a fair tilth for sowing or planting.

Supports can be put in place before or after sowing/planting. The aim is to have a bamboo or hazel stick about 8cm (3") from each plant, each stick meeting and being tied to another one opposite, for mutual support of heavy plants in all weathers. The climbing stem may need some help to start growing up its nearby stick – some go wandering or fall down at first.

Flowers will take time to appear because initial growth is often slow. Then the excitement begins as little bean pods suddenly appear and proliferate, along with lots more new leaves. By the time some pods are ready, they may be hidden amongst the foliage and need careful picking. Yellow and purple beans stand out more than heavily disguised green ones.

Harvesting

As with most beans, cropping is prolonged by repeated picking of pods before they become seedy, unless you are growing Borlotta or other varieties for their seed. I find that cropping varies from year to year, sometimes continuing for ten or twelve weeks, sometimes half that. Watering in dry weather is especially helpful to such fast-growing plants.

Problems

Early sowings cause some anxieties – cold weather in late spring may cause leaves to turn yellow, but plants will recover in warmth as long as slugs have not eaten them. Dry summers mean that watering will make a huge difference as soon as flowers are open, otherwise only a few will develop into beans.

French beans (haricots verts)

These are very elegant just served with a little chopped garlic and butter. We steam them very little so they are quite crunchy (for a maximum of 6 minutes – sometimes 2 or 3 will do). Once the beans are cooked, add the chopped garlic clove and some butter, and put back on the heat for a minute or two to cook the garlic.

PEAS

Season of harvest: June-July
Follow with: leeks, beetroot, fennel, salad, kale, purple sprouting

Variety	Character		Sow	Spacing (cm)
	Height (cm)	Special care		First ready
GREENSHSAFT	Conventional peas		Mar-Apr	150x4 in rows*
	75	Sticks or net for support		80-85 days
ONWARD	Conventional peas		Mar-Apr	150x4 in rows*
	75	Sticks or net for support		90-95 days
TALL SUGAR SNAP	Extra sweet, edible snap-pods		Mar-Apr	150x4 in rows*
	150-200	Tall sticks or posts		85-90 days
NORLI	Mange tout for pod only		Mar-Apr	60x4 in beds
	60	Small sticks		75-85 days

*The rows can be on beds

Varieties

Choice of variety is important, and there are two main types. Earlies such as Feltham First have round seeds, taste less sweet and will crop quickly, say by early June. They can grow without support and will finish cropping after just two or perhaps three weeks. Greenshaft is strictly speaking a second early but is often called an early maincrop, because it has wrinkled seed and is sweeter and taller. Maincrops will yield for up to a month, especially if you keep picking mature, pea-filled pods as soon as you see them – and sometimes they need a little looking for! 'Semi-leafless' varieties such as Ambassador make picking easier, although pea pods are definitely more visible than French beans.

Mange tout and sugar pea

A further two categories of pea are Mange Tout and Sugar Pea. These are sometimes confused but are completely different, as a true mange tout, for example Oregon Sugar Pod or Norli, contains only the very tiniest peas, the idea being to eat just its stringless pod. Sugar Peas, by contrast, are both mange tout and full of sweet peas, best picked when the pods are quite fat for a wonderful mouthful of flavour, especially when gathered straight off the plant and eaten raw. There are dwarf varieties such as Sugar Ann or Sugar Bon, and a tall variety, Sugar Snap, which I find will grow to 250cm or more if sufficiently supported, as well as cropping extremely heavily if in healthy soil and well watered. Note that all tall plants need more moisture to nourish their large number of leaves.

Sowing

I find peas really exciting to grow because they can be so fast, and their crop is so sweet and enjoyed by everybody. Some people advise sowing in November, as with broad beans, but I find that they rarely survive and certainly don't thrive. Sowing from mid March in the greenhouse and from late March in the soil, until early May, will give best results. Early sowings can be fleeced to help them on and you may have to do this to keep pigeons from pecking off their leaves, most common in early spring.

I sow three seeds per 4cm module in mid to late March in the greenhouse, or dib three seeds in holes directly, in two rows about 20 cm apart down the centre of a bed, with about 15 cm between clumps of plants. This affords plenty of room for the roots to develop and for good access to pick the peas, especially if tall maincrop varieties are used (see photo).

Growing

Supporting peas can be done in many ways, the two most common being hazel branches and netting tied to stakes. For the tall Sugar Snaps (see below) I use 2.7m stakes at 1.5m intervals, with stout twine looped between them at intervals of 25-30cm vertically.

Peas

One could never tire of eating peas in a very simple way with butter and a bit of mint, but if you want to do something more elaborate add a bit of chopped onion, bacon, parsley, garlic and cream. This applies to sugar snaps as well as podded peas. Another delicious way to eat them is to shred a lettuce heart and stir it in to the peas with plenty of butter.

Harvesting

Once pea pods are visible, it will probably be ten days to two weeks before they swell out with peas. After that there should be a steady succession of well-filled pods, especially if you water in dry weather.

There is always the choice of picking pods with super sweet baby peas or allowing them to fill out and become slightly mealy.

After cropping, as with broad beans, the plants can be cut to ground level to leave all the nitrogen nodules in the soil, before replanting with a wide range of autumn or winter crops.

Problems

Caterpillars The main pest is a caterpillar inside some pods, munching on the ingredients. The pea moth which lays its eggs does not fly until late spring, so some sowings made by late March may crop before the moths appear, while sowing in late spring can avoid them at the other end of their growth cycle. However, **Mildew** is the other problem: this appears after about the second week of July and can ruin an otherwise fine crop, so late sowings are often much diminished by the white mould covering many leaves. Sow early to minimise mildew!

Pea season is June/July and it really is worth growing them as early as possible, to finish cropping by the end of July, at which time French and runner beans will be starting to develop.

SAVING PEA SEED

Saving pea seed is worthwhile and simple, starting with leaving one or two plants unpicked. They need to stay in the ground about a fortnight after the rest have finished cropping, until their pods have turned yellow and dry to the point of feeling crunchy. Pick them all, then either pod out the hard seed immediately or keep the pods somewhere dry until you have time to deal with them. I find that germination from my home-saved seed is consistent and rapid, while subsequent growth is strong and healthy. Seed of runner and French beans can be saved in the same way.

PUMPKIN

See under Squash, page 130

RUNNER BEANS

Season of harvest: late July-September, occasionally October
Follow with: garlic or leave ground mulched with dead leaves and stems

Variety	Character Height (cm)	Sow Special Care	Spacing (cm) Days to first pick
LADY DI	Long tender pods 200	May to mid Jun Water after flowering	35x50 70-85
PAINTED LADY	Red and white flowers 200	May to mid Jun Water after flowering	35x50 70-85
HESTIA	Dwarf plant can be pot-grown 60	May-Jun Shorter season, sow twice	60x60 60

These are the classic British summer vegetable, and barely known in the rest of Europe. This is partly because runner beans need more moisture to crop than French beans, and struggle in hot, dry summers, which are more common on the Continent. So they certainly benefit from any extra watering through a long heatwave, and flourish in a moist Atlantic summer.

Varieties

A large choice covers flower colour as well as bean quality. Runner beans look marvellous in their clothing of red, white or red-and-white flowers in late July and August. Read the small print in seed catalogues or on the packet to make sure you get the colour you want.

Many older varieties have strings on each side of the pod, which need slicing off, so look for a stringless variety such as Polestar or Lady Di if you want to avoid that. Average pod length is 250-300mm (10-12"); any longer and they can be tough. But you might win a prize – most horticultural shows have a class for longest runner bean that is fun to enter.

Sowing/planting

The methods and timing for sowing and planting of runner beans are identical to those for climbing French beans, see above.

In warm city gardens or allotments it may be worth sowing some runner beans in July to crop in the autumn, because flowers set pods better when nights are not too hot (below about 14°C is good) and less watering will be needed then.

Growing

As with climbing French beans, a thick mulch of well-rotted compost or manure, put out in the winter or early spring so that worms have time to take it in a little, will certainly ensure a better and longer-yielding crop. Once the bean plants are well established and climbing fast, they can be further mulched with good compost, if the soil is prone to dry out quickly.

Harvesting

Picking needs to be regular to encourage continued cropping from about late July until end September, when there will be only a few new beans, and after that the leaves will be killed by any autumn frost. The row of sticks is easiest to dismantle in winter, when only the pale, dry stems are left to disentangle from their supports.

Problems

As with French beans, the chief pest is slugs, but mostly in cool wet weather when the plants are scarcely growing. So be patient; if seeds are sown, or plants are planted in warm conditions they should grow away from the odd nibble. Although slightly later than often recommended, early June is a reliable time to sow or plant, to avoid slug damage.

SQUASH

This section includes pumpkins and gourds, all very closely related. Summer squashes bear fruits that are good to eat when young, tender and rather watery, and strictly speaking they include courgettes. Some summer squashes, such as marrows, will develop hard-skinned fruit if allowed to, and these can be kept into the winter.

Winter squashes bear fruits which develop firm, sweet flesh and hard skins in autumn, to enable keeping them until the following spring. They include pumpkins which are a larger and much more watery version, better for carving and showing than for eating. Gourds are a pretty but inedible kind of winter squash.

SUMMER SQUASH

Season of harvest: July-October
Follow with: late sowings such as broad beans – or parsnips / onions / beans etc next year

Variety	Character	Sow Spread (cm)	Spacing (cm) Harvest
CUSTARD WHITE (PATTY PAN)	Scalloped edges	May-early Jun 150	70-90x150 Jul-Sep
TROMBONCINO ALBENGA	Long curved fruit	May-early Jun 150	70-90x150 Aug-Oct
VEGETABLE SPAGHETTI	Stringy flesh	May-early Jun 150	70-90x150 Aug-Oct

In almost every way, summer squash grow like courgettes; they are mostly trailing bushy plants with long stems.

Varieties and harvesting

Tromboncino fruits are still young when 30cm long and can grow to three times that, but even large ones can lie hidden under the broad leaves. Bigger fruits retain a creamy texture and interesting flavour – less watery than marrows. Patty Pan types can be eaten raw when small, or cooked like courgettes when larger.

Little Gem is a tasty round green ball that matures quickly to a sweeter flavour, more yellow flesh and much harder skin, similar to a winter squash, but harvested in summer. *Vegetable Spaghetti* has long stems and large creamy squashes which, after baking or boiling in their skin, can be scooped out in strands which bear some visible resemblance to pasta, although the taste is closer to marrow!

WINTER SQUASH

Season of harvest: September-November
Follow with: late sowings such as broad beans – or parsnips / onions / beans etc next year

Variety	Character	Sow / Spread (cm)	Spacing (cm) / Harvest
BUTTERNUT	Wonderful flavour	May / up to 300	80-100x150 / Late Sep-Nov
UCHIKI KURI	Fast and reliable	May / up to 300	80-100x150 / Aug-Oct
CROWN PRINCE F1	Large, good keeper	May / up to 300	80-100x150 / Sep-Oct

Rapid, rambling growth through summer and early autumn will create a wide selection of fruits to enjoy through the winter; their colours become vivid as they ripen under the fading leaves. They develop hard skins and dense, often orange flesh that boasts a remarkable sweetness and depth of flavour.

Varieties

Of the many varieties, Butternut is a deserved favourite, like a straight fat banana in shape and matt yellow-brown in colour. It has an intriguing way of putting on a spurt of late growth through September, so that its fruit ripen after most other varieties and benefit from being on the plant until first frost. Easiest sign of ripeness is a shrivelling of the stem that attaches them to the plant, with skins becoming hard and darker. Unripe Butternuts with paler skin have a less rich flavour, more reminiscent of marrow.

Tomato – Santa: Cherry Plum in tunnel in September

Asparagus Connovers Colossal in May

Harvesting Asparagus

Tall Sugar Peas growing fast by late May

Asparagus in July

Rocket in flower in May from February sowing

One Greek Basil plant in tunnel in early October

Basiol Violetto Aromatica and French Marigold in tunnel in early October

Melon Sweetheart F1 in July

Three year old tree – Red Falstaff on M9 in early October

Apple – Blenheim Orange in early October

Top Patch with cow in July

Probably the easiest winter squash is Uchiki Kuri, whose bright red onion-shaped fruits mature much earlier than Butternut. Often the plant has completely died off by late September, making the harvest easier. Musquée de Provence is larger and probably sweeter than most other varieties, Marina di Chioggia has extraordinary warty green skin, and Turks Turban is beautifully true to its name. Also there are exciting new varieties just becoming available, which claim to be so sweet that the squashes can be eaten raw, such as Celebration Mixed F1, a descendant of small Acorn squashes.

Sowing

Winter squash need a whole season to ripen properly, so are best sown in early May inside or late May in the soil.

For greenhouse sowing use 3cm modules at first, then pot into 7-10cm pots when the first leaf is developing. After about a fortnight, depending on weather, harden plants off for a few days outside before planting, remembering that they will be killed by any frost, so wait a little if any unusually cold nights are looming.

Growing

Give water at planting time, then after a fortnight's settling in they should grow rampantly. Weeding is the main consideration: hoe initially, then poke around and under the squash leaves to pull out any weed plants before they seed.

Harvesting

Usually in October and before any air frost, cut squashes carefully, which is not easy as the stem should be hard – if it snaps off where joining the fruit, mould will set in at this damaged point. An easier way to separate fruit from plant is by cutting all stems and leaves away from the stem, to avoid having to cut through the hard stem itself.

Keep ripe squashes as dry and warm as possible: room temperature is better than in a shed. They will serve as nice ornaments to your sitting room until the cook is ready.

Problems

Fruit can be under-ripe, from late planting or lack of sun and heat; use as summer squashes. Mildew on leaves in late summer and autumn is a sign of normal ageing.

Pan-fried Butternut Squash

1 butternut squash
4 cloves garlic
1 lemon

Cube the squash. Heat a mixture of olive oil and butter in a large frying pan that has a lid, but don't put the lid on yet. Add the cubes of squash to the pan, stirring from time to time while you chop up the cloves of garlic. Add the garlic to the pan, stir it all up and put a lid on it. Squeeze half the lemon, and when the squash is cooked add the lemon juice.

PUMPKIN

Season of harvest: September-October
Follow with: garlic, autumn-sown beans or any crop next spring

Variety	Character Height (cm)	Sow Harvest	Spacing (cm)
JACK O' LANTERN	Classic Halloween pumpkin 60	May Oct	100x150
ATLANTIC GIANT	Huge, requires much space 80	May Oct	200x200
BABY BEAR	Small with edible seeds 50	May Oct	90x150

Sowing and growing

This is the same as for other squashes, except to note that all pumpkins make long stems and the more these stems run over bare soil, where they can send down roots, the heavier will be the harvest. So to grow monster pumpkins, you need a large area of bare soil.

Baby Bear is worthwhile for its delicious and nutritious seeds, but their nakedness means they keep less well and may germinate poorly.

Harvest

Harvest as for winter squash, being careful not to break the stem. After carving for Halloween, pumpkin flesh will rot within a fortnight or so, and you may have difficulty eating that much soup!

SWEETCORN

Season of harvest: late July-early October
Follow with: salad (after early crops only)

Variety	Character	Sow	Spacing (cm)
	Height (cm)	Days to first pick	
NORTHERN EXTRA SWEET F1	Early supersweet 100-120	May-Jun 75-80	30x30
SWEET NUGGET F1	Fantastic flavour 150-200	May 90-110	35x35
MINIPOP F1	Baby corn 150-200	May-Jun 65-80	20x20

Surely one of the most rewarding vegetables, adored by children of all ages for a sweetness that is accentuated by eating as soon as possible after picking. Home-grown is far superior every time in comparison to a bought cob that is already relatively old, with some of its sugars turned to starch.

Varieties

Recent plant breeding has developed 'supersweet' varieties that are true to their name and worth a try: I warmly recommend Sweet Nugget for both flavour and reliability. Don't be tempted to grow two or more varieties together, because they often cross-pollinate and share out their different characteristics. This was vividly illustrated when I grew blue maize about twenty metres from some ordinary sweetcorn, whose cobs grew as an extraordinary mish-mash of sweet yellow kernels and blue starchy ones.

Sowing

Mid May is a good average sowing date, or mid April in the greenhouse for early crops. Earlier sowing is risky, because in any cold spell the baby plants will turn yellow from being unable to photosynthesise in cool conditions. Slugs may cause damage as well. Last sowings must be done by about mid June, although much depends on the summer.

Sweetcorn can be harvested in July from early varieties such as Swift F1, but may raise the problem of cross-pollination – unless their flowering is well finished before any later and different varieties grow their tassels. It may be safer to grow one variety from two sowings, say early May and early June, if you want sweetcorn over a long period.

Growing

Sweetcorn grows well on beds because four rows in a 'block' all together, 300-350mm (12-14") apart in all directions, ensure an even fall of pollen from the loping tassels on top of the plants onto the emerging hairs of baby cobs. Each hair is attached to a kernel; the pollen that falls onto it allows proper growth rather than an annoying gap on the cob.

In hot weather the corn grows magically fast and may be ready up to a month earlier than in a cool summer.

Harvesting

Usually there is one good cob per plant and one smaller one, ready to pick when the hairs sticking out of their ends turn brown, although baby corn varieties can produce up to about four immature cobs per plant.

If proper sweetcorn is picked when it is immature, the kernels are creamy in colour, smaller, less sweet and of a delicate flavour not unlike baby corn. Then a week or two later they become bright yellow and richly sweet, while the lapse of another fortnight will see the colour become deep yellow, with some of the sweetness turning to chewy starch, like an African 'mealy'. So you have plenty of choice as to what to harvest.

Cook them very lightly, if at all: fresh sweetcorn from the garden is really tender and tastes good raw. You can slice kernels off raw cobs and add them to tomato salad for example.

The second cob is much smaller and less well developed, unless the plants have been grown at wider spacings.

Once the last cob is harvested, chop the plant off at soil level or just below with a sharp spade, and further chop it into small lengths for better composting. Even then its high cellulose content will see it rot very slowly, and I often find half-rotted stems in the compost heap a few months later. These can be re-composted, or used as a mulch for pathways if they are flicked out of the compost after it is spread.

Problems

Badgers Readers in rural areas may already be aware of sweetcorn's chief pest. The badger often eats his way through large sections of farmers' maize and sweetcorn, and if they notice yours, look out! Only a solid wall or fence buried into the soil will keep them out, and they always seem to arrive just before the cobs are ready for us. It can be a nerve-racking wait for the harvest to sweeten: will the plants be ransacked in the night?

Birds The main other scavenger is small birds, who sometimes perch on ripe cobs and peck away at their kernels, but damage is far less significant.

Slugs Most slug damage occurs in spring when the soil is too cold for proper growth, so later sowings are more reliable for gardens prone to slugs or with cold, heavy soil.

Chapter 14

Brassicas

The considerable cabbage family

This chapter looks at cabbage and its many relatives, the traditional main-stays of older kitchen gardens, and includes many fine winter vegetables such as kale and brussels sprouts. They are less common now – perhaps gardeners venture out less than they used to in winter months, preferring summer crops such as courgettes and French beans. Yet brassicas are well-suited to our damp climate: many resist frost extremely well, and brussels sprouts even taste better in cold weather. Many can be grown as a second crop to follow early vegetables such as broad beans or new potatoes.

Treat yourself of a winter evening to perusing one or preferably more seed catalogues (see Resources), because there are some exciting new brassica varieties. Deep red kale, or purple kale with frilly leaves; cauliflowers round or pointed and green, red or white; crinkly or smooth cabbages for almost any season; purple sprouting for all seasons; unusual radishes for spring and winter; kohlrabi; and all the old mainstays, including swede and turnip, which are also brassicas and covered at the chapter's end.

BRASSICA PESTS

Pests love brassicas. I mention them here for you to know the difficulties, some organic solutions and whether you feel it is still worthwhile. The main problem is all those caterpillars, flea beetles and cabbage root flies, which can't wait for you to grow some nice brassica plants. They can wreak major damage between June and about September, which is most of the growing season. In dry years, when insects and butterflies thrive, plants can be so weakened and diminished by losing much of their leaf area and some root as well, that there is nothing for gardeners to harvest, unless they have used pesticides.

Furthermore, many gardens and allotments are patrolled by pigeons, whose favourite fare is leaves of almost any brassica plant – mostly in winter but increasingly in summer.

Are there viable organic solutions? I cannot say an unequivocal 'yes', so brace yourself for some losses, but there are certainly ways of minimising insect attack, and here are a few to consider.

MINIMISING INSECT ATTACKS ON BRASSICAS

1. SOW EARLY OR LATE

Sowings of early cabbage, calabrese, cauliflower, spring radish and turnips, before about early April, can mature in spring before brassica insects are too numerous.

Kale, late winter cabbage, autumn calabrese, winter radish, turnips and purple sprouting broccoli can all have time to make worthwhile growth from sowings in early July. They are much better started off in a greenhouse because outdoor sowings will lose too much leaf to flea beetles, unless it is a wet summer. Planted outside by early August, there is a good chance of enough healthy growth by winter to ensure a fair crop.

Spring cabbage can be the best of all, maturing in April to June when the coast is relatively clear. But they will almost certainly require covering with a net, held up by wooden posts or cloche hoops, to protect against pigeons.

2. MESH AND FLEECE

Mesh is better than fleece in summer because it has less warming effect, but fleece is easier to work with and damages less easily in my experience. They both come in different grades, some fine enough to exclude flea beetles, although insects will readily pass through any torn areas. They are usually white, not so nice to behold as vegetables, and may need to cover the plants for many months. Animals (dogs above all) can sometimes make a few holes in the covers and render them much less effective; otherwise they will last for many years.

3. BRASSICA COLLARS

These may not be necessary except in gardens or allotments where cabbage root fly is on the wing, laying eggs on soil near brassica stems which are then eaten by maggots, sufficiently for young plants to die. Collars can prevent the maggots from devouring plant roots. Tuck them around the stem of new plants.

MINIMISING INSECT ATTACKS ON BRASSICAS (continued)

4. MAXIMUM FERTILITY

Having soil at full potential, bursting with life and health, gives plants more chance to resist and grow away from attacks by pests. Regular applications of good compost, minimal tillage and careful observation are the essence of good gardening and the basis of vigorous plant growth.

5. MANUAL CONTROL

If all else fails, and caterpillars of the dreaded white butterflies are chomping through your leaves, they can be squashed or picked off into a bucket and buried in the compost heap. Usually they lurk on undersides of leaves so may need a little looking for; any egg clusters can also be rubbed out. Caterpillars that fall off must also be removed, as they will simply climb back. Plants need checking every week or so in the height of summer.

Weather extremes

Just occasionally comes a year of unusual pestilence or weather which is unfavourable to certain vegetables – while helping certain others. Hot, dry summers are difficult for moisture-loving brassicas, under the cosh of huge numbers of flea beetles and caterpillars.

On the other hand, heat and drought are beneficial to tomatoes, cucumbers and courgettes, within reason. Spread the risks of weather extremes by growing a wide range of vegetables, also by sowing some brassicas later than usual.

General tips

It is often said that brassicas like firm soil to anchor their significant bulk or tall stems. I find that undug soil suits them well, with a good dressing of organic matter in winter or spring.

Note that one is usually planting rather than sowing direct, because initial growth is slow and final planting distance is mostly wide, so a small seedbed or a few modules will suffice for quite large areas. Using indoor-raised plants also saves growing time and is important in combating pests, by allowing full use of the year's second half, when they are less numerous. If you have no greenhouse or protected space to raise plants, see if you can co-operate with a friend who has.

BROCCOLI FOR ALL SEASONS
(includes Calabrese)

Season of harvest: July-May
Follow with: autumn salad, depending on final harvest

Variety	Character	Sow	Spacing (cm)
	Special Care	Harvest	Height (cm)
BELSTAR F1	Suitable for early heads	Mar-Jun	35x40
	Fleece for early harvest	Jun-Oct	75
GREEN SPROUTING	Main season all rounder	Apr-May	40x40
	Pinch out caterpillars	Jul-Oct	90
PURPLE SPROUTING	Small-medium shoots in spring	May-Jun	40x40
	Sow late, net in winter	Mar-May	90

There is broccoli and broccoli. What you grow in the garden will probably not be an exact replica of the large, blemish-free supermarket heads. It will come in a range of sizes and colours, with occasional discolourations and probably some caterpillars living inside it – in summer and autumn at least. But the sense of achievement and extra waves of flavour will make it worthwhile.

Varieties

Much depends on the season you are aiming for, so read the small print carefully to be sure of growing a variety which is best adapted to your sowing and harvesting dates. Most calabrese is F1, and they make a larger first head, for instance Belstar and Fiesta. For repeated cropping of smaller shoots, open pollinated varieties such as Green Sprouting are good.

EARLY CALABRESE

Sowing and growing

Early harvests are most feasible with greenhouse sowing. Sow from early March indoors, plant out in April under fleece to provide warmth and keep pigeons at bay. In May the fleece can be replaced with a net if pigeons are still around.

Harvesting

First heads may be ready in late June, hopefully before caterpillars, while secondary heading will depend on the weather, and a wet summer is best. See extra advice on picking on the next page. In hot, dry weather it may be best to remove plants after the first heading, to have time for another crop such as leeks or autumn salad, whose demands for water, although critical, are smaller until about September.

LATE CALABRESE

Sowing

Sow from May to July; the later sowings can yield healthy pickings in autumn.

Growing

Late calabrese is almost more weather-dependent than early crops, and definitely prone to caterpillar damage. Sometimes they live in the heads, completely out of sight and hard to deal with. If plants head up in October, when it may be too wet and windy for butterflies, you can hope for a fair harvest of one large and several smaller heads, until any moderate frost, probably in November. These plants do not survive the winter.

Harvesting early and late calabrese

Watch how the small growing leaves at the plant's centre give way to a small bud, which then develops into a head of up to 400g as the florets increase and a stem elongates. Best time to harvest is before the stem grows too long or the flower buds show any sign of opening. Be careful to make a clean cut and to damage few leaves; then within two to three weeks new heads should appear lower down, similar to the first one but smaller. Cropping can last for about two months, but any drought will decrease the plant's yield and any frost will damage remaining buds in the autumn.

PURPLE SPROUTING

This generic term applies to winter-hardy broccoli, which starts to send out spears in late winter and continues shooting until mid spring. There are varieties for early and late seasons within this time span, such as Early Purple and then Cardinal, also for white spears such as White Eye.

Sowing and growing

Sowing as late as July is possible and advisable. Insects make it difficult to succeed with outdoor sowings, so I recommend sowing two seeds per 3-4cm module under cover, thinning to one plant in each and setting out by mid August, after broad beans or early roots or salad. Note that netting or other protection against birds may be needed.

Harvesting

First shoots are the largest, usually in March but varying according to variety and weather. Later pickings become thinner-stemmed as the plant tries harder and harder to flower. Any mild weather in late winter can trigger growth of first spears and it is exciting to find these – often the only fresh green harvest of that season.

Problems

Autumn caterpillars are not usually too troublesome, but pigeons are another story, because they are often very hungry in spring, just as we also are keenly anticipating some fresh green vegetables. Netting must be thorough and well clear of the plants, I have known fat pigeons land on my net and happily peck through it at leaves and broccoli.

Broccoli and bacon tart

Pastry:
150g plain flour
150g rolled oats
150g butter
1 egg
a pinch of salt

Filling:
250g broccoli
4 rashers bacon, cut into strips
1 onion
30g butter
110g hard cheese (our neighbourhood cheese is Keen's Cheddar)
4 large eggs
300ml full-fat milk or single cream
salt and pepper

Make the pastry, and line a deep 23cm tart tin. For the filling, blanch the broccoli. Fry the bacon and onion in butter until the onion is translucent. Spread over pastry, then add the broccoli and ⅔ of the cheese. Whisk milk/cream with the eggs and season, and pour over the filling. Sprinkle the remaining cheese on top and bake for about 30 mins at 190°C.

BRUSSELS SPROUTS

Season of harvest: October-March

Variety	Character	Sow	Plant	Spacing (cm)
	Height (cm)	Harvest		
IGOR F1	Reliable firm buttons	Apr-May	May-early Jul	60x60
	90	Oct-Jan		

Variety	Character	Sow	Plant	Spacing (cm)
	Height (cm)	Harvest		
NOISETTE	Small, nutty flavour, old variety	Apr-May	May-early Jul	60x60
	70	Oct-Mar		
RED BULL	Red colour, stronger after frost	Apr-May	May-early Jul	60x60
	80	Oct-Mar		

Sprouts are really small heads of cabbage, growing up a long stem and maturing at different dates, according to variety.

Flavour is the goal

Brussels sprouts in our gardens may not look like the impressive photographs in seed catalogues, but I have a feeling they taste better. A freshly picked, organic sprout is a mid winter treat, as nice raw as cooked, in children's eyes as well.

Varieties

The chart above encompasses a range of maturity dates and even of colour. Check the details on seed packets before buying, and bear in mind that more effort has been invested in breeding F1 hybrids, whose buttons are often firmer than many of the current selection of open-pollinated varieties.

Sowing

Early spring sowings give the earliest sprouts, even on 'late' varieties. A fair sowing date is mid spring, from about early April to mid May: early June is possible, but plants will be smaller. Wide spacings at planting time give opportunities to crop lettuce between, and I have found that sprout plants grow better for some company until they are larger and well established.

Harvesting

Growth of tall stems should be fast through the summer and early autumn, then slow as buttons begin to grow and firm up. The bottom few are often poor and best removed; thereafter they can be picked as soon as their accompanying leaves turn yellow. Remove these leaves even if you are not ready to pick sprouts, so they do not dangle down and spoil the harvest as they decay.

By late winter, any remaining sprouts will open out and produce a rapidly elongating flower stem. This is also edible, as is the top of each sprout plant, before or after it begins to flower, as long as pigeons can be kept off. Tall stakes are needed for netting, or something bright and mobile such as childrens' mini-windmills or old CDs.

By May there will be almost nothing left to eat, and the stem can be twisted out of the ground and chopped into lengths before composting.

Problems

Apart from all the suspects considered above, slugs can damage sprouts, especially old ones, hence the advice to pick regularly. Various fungal diseases such as 'black spot' can spoil some outer leaves in wet weather. The cook may well need to do some extra trimming.

There can also be some 'blown sprouts' of open leaves, with no tight button. These are delicious, with a slightly different flavour.

Stir-fried Brussels sprouts

1 onion
500g Brussels sprouts
200g chestnuts
2 rashers bacon
1 clove garlic
soy sauce

The slowest part of this dish is peeling the chestnuts, so start with them. Prepare all the ingredients before you start frying. Chop the onion, slice the bacon into matchsticks, and slice the sprouts finely. Heat some sunflower oil in a wok or large pan. Start with the onion and bacon, then add the sprouts and chestnuts, and finally the garlic. Keep it all moving so the sprouts cook but still remain crunchy. Finally stir in soy sauce to taste.

CAULIFLOWER

Season of harvest: April to November
Follow with: variable, e.g. beans after spring cauliflower

Variety	Character	Sow	Spacing (cm)
	Special care	Harvest	Height (cm)
ALL THE YEAR ROUND	Medium size, hardy	Jan-Jul	45x45
	Fleece helps early crops	Jun-Nov	40
SNOWCAP	Large, late maturity	May-Jun	50x50
	Perhaps fleece in late frost	Nov-Dec	45
PURPLE CAPE	Spring heading, rich colour	Jun-Jul	50x50
	Netting in winter	Apr	40

Consider the following before growing cauliflowers:

- They are large plants, and for a worthwhile head require more space than most other brassicas.
- They like a rich, well-composted soil.

- They are inclined to head up all together – a true feast-or-famine vegetable.
- Once in head, they must be picked and eaten, otherwise the white florets open into stems and flowers.

Varieties and sowing

I recommend a late winter sowing indoors of All the Year Round or the fast Candid Charm F1, to pick in early summer, hopefully before caterpillars arrive. Or try a late spring sowing of Snowcap for heading in late autumn, as it has some frost resistance. Walcheren Winter Pilgrim or Purple Cape are over-wintering cauliflower plants that mature the following spring, from sowing in early summer.

Another variation is mini-cauliflowers – special fast-maturing varieties such as Igloo, which can be planted as close to each other as lettuce, 22x22cm (about 9x9") apart. The last word goes to Romanesco, an Italian broccoli with exquisitely pointed, pale green minarets in a dome-shaped head. Caterpillars love it too, unfortunately.

Harvesting

As harvesting time approaches for the variety you are growing, watch out for tightly curled leaves at the centre which are probably hiding a baby curd. A further week or fortnight should see the larger curd become visible; let it grow until its surface becomes slightly uneven on a longer stem, indicating a change from growing larger to first thoughts of flowering. In warm weather, do not delay picking beyond this point or you will soon have large white sprouting.

KALE

Season of harvest: September-April

Variety	Character / Height (cm)	Sow / Harvest	Spacing (cm)
DWARF GREEN CURLED	Deeply curled, prolific / 60	Jun-Jul / Sep-Apr	45x45
REDBOR F1	Dark red, ornamental / 95	Jun-Jul / Sep-Apr	45x45
RED RUSSIAN	Soft young leaves for salad / 50	June-July / Feb-May	45x45

Kale is fun to grow, and slightly easier than many other brassicas. It used to be looked down on as the greens one had to eat when nothing else was available. This is a clue to its hardiness in winter. Add to this the recent access to a range of different kale varieties offering more flavours, colours and possibilities in the kitchen, and kale becomes a worthy addition to any garden.

Varieties

Red varieties seem less interesting to insects than green ones. Redbor has an especially dark and appealing colour, mostly lost in cooking when its flavour is similar to green curly kales – a little ordinary, but mouth-watering with some garlic and butter.

Red Russian (also called Ragged Jack and Red Winter), more pink than red, has flatter serrated leaves which are milder in flavour and really tasty in salads, mainly in winter and spring when it can be a real star of the garden.

Nero di Toscano (also known as Black Cabbage and Laccinato Blue) has been popular for its long, dark green, indented leaves. They are best eaten small, as otherwise you may need to cut out the sinewy central vein of each leaf.

Sowing

Because of pests, I recommend sowing under cover in early July, for planting by early August. Sowing even later can work, but plants will be smaller. If kale is sown in spring, as recommended on seed packets and in most books, it will grow quite large but may struggle with caterpillars, especially in hot summers.

Harvesting

In any spells of mild winter weather, kale plants will grow a new leaf or two, enough to provide occasional meals. Green kales are more productive than red ones, and should offer small leaves in March and April before and during flowering.

Red Russian comes into its own in the new year, because by March it should be sending out new stems with tender baby leaves – excellent in salad – whose regular picking will encourage more of the same until about early May, when stems elongate and flowering shoots replace most leaves. These are nice to eat at first, but soon become tougher.

SPRING CABBAGE

Season of harvest: April-June
Follow with: almost any other vegetable

Variety	Character Spacing (cm)	Sow Harvest	Plant
APRIL	Small, early pointed hearts 20x30	Aug Apr	Sep-Oct
OFFENHAM FLOWER OF SPRING	Good for greens, later hearts 20x30	Aug Apr-May	Sep-Oct

Variety	Character	Sow	Plant
	Spacing (cm)	*Harvest*	
SPRING HERO F1	Solid round heads	Aug	Sep-Oct
	40x40	May-Jun	
SPRING-SOWN HISPI	Pointed hearts, fast growing	Feb-Mar	Apr
	30x30	Jun	
SPRING-SOWN DERBY DAY	Small round heads	Mar	Apr
	40x40	Jun	

Spring Cabbage was almost obligatory in old kitchen gardens, providing tender green leaves between April and June, well before most other vegetables are ready; likewise in a modern organic garden or allotment, because in addition it grows for table when there are few insects causing trouble.

First attempts may yield some impressive pickings, or suggest better methods for next year. Weather obviously plays a major part and extreme winters can very occasionally kill spring cabbages – but not often.

Sowing

Sowing date is important, the aim being to have plants large enough to deal with winter weather, yet small enough that no heart is attempted before winter, which might cause death by frost and no cabbage in spring. Local knowledge must play a part in deciding on a sowing date between early and late August. Variable autumn weather can make this tricky.

Harvesting

Well-filled rows of small cabbage plants by late October, netted against pigeons, will provide possibilities come early spring of cutting some for 'spring greens'. These are simply leaves of un-hearted cabbage, full of lovely dark chlorophyll that is so welcome at winter's end. Offenham is good for this. Plants left to grow should heart up later, depending on variety. Wait until you see a noticeable round heart (Spring Hero) or pointed heart (other varieties), mostly in May.

Further sowings of Hispi and Derby Day in late winter can yield tender leaves on your plate in June, again at a time of few cabbage pests apart from birds.

WINTER CABBAGE

Season of harvest: December-March
Follow with: next year's vegetables

Variety	Character	Sow	Plant	Spacing (cm)
	Special care		*Harvest*	*Height (cm)*
TUNDRA	Crunchy crinkled heart	May-Jun	Jun-Jul	50x50
	Patrol caterpillars, net against pigeons		Oct-Jan	50

Variety	Character	Sow	Plant	Spacing (cm)
	Special care		Harvest	Height (cm)
JANUARY KING	Red-blushed hardy hearts	May-Jun	Jun-Jul	50x50
	May rot before winter if sown too early		Nov-Feb	50
MARNER	Red cabbage to store	May-Jun	Jun-Jul	50x50
LAGERROT	Cut dense heart in November to store		Nov	50
HOLLAND	White cabbage to store	May-Jun	Jun-Jul	50x50
WINTER WHITE			Nov	50

It is possible to have year-round cabbage, but in summer and autumn there are so many other delicious vegetables that I concentrate here on cabbage for winter.

Varieties and growing

A glance at the table reveals that there are cabbages of varied colour and texture, but all are grown in much the same way. Sowing date is important: May is better for coleslaw cabbages to store, as they need time to form a dense head, while the first two varieties are, within reason, frost hardy and will stand better if still firming up as winter sets in, rather than having a tight, mature head in November.

A solid red heart is harder to achieve than a solid white one, and both need rich soil, sufficient time and steady amounts of moisture. Tundra and January King have less dense heads.

SAVOY CABBAGE

There are also Savoy Cabbages, such as Ormskirk, whose texture is the most crinkled and whose leaves are among the darkest green – even its heads are pale green rather than creamy white. Sometimes without a dense head or with only a small one, the leaves of savoys are a delicious winter – and even spring – green.

Savoys are perhaps the most winter-hardy cabbage, so late sowing can be worthwhile up to July, but a June sowing is better for more chance of good hearts in winter. Keep an eye on them from November because their time of hearting varies a little with different weather. It is a wonderful treat to cut a savoy heart in mid winter.

BRASSICA ROOTS

Some brassicas grow large roots that are a fine addition to winter meals. You may not think of radish, swede and turnip as being closely related to cabbage and broccoli, but they have so much in common that I include them here rather than in the Roots chapter. Above all they share a vulnerability to the same pests, meaning a careful look at sowing dates and the use of fleece will ensure more successful crops.

Problems for brassica roots are explained at the end of this chapter, because the same ones apply equally to all of them.

RADISH

Season of harvest: April-November
Follow with: almost any vegetable after spring radish

Variety	Character Height (cm)	Sow	Spacing (cm) First ready
CHERRY BELLE	Fast, bright red & round 15	Mar-Jul	1x25 40-50 days
FRENCH BREAKFAST	Fast, long red & white 20	Mar-Jul	1x25 40-50 days
CHINA ROSE	Heavy pink winter root 35	Late Jul-Aug Oct-Nov, will store	10x30

Varieties

Radish has declined in popularity recently, but for sheer speed of growth it deserves a small place in gardens, especially in spring. Round red varieties (Cherry Belle or Sparkler) or long pink and white ones (French Breakfast) can be sown late winter to mature by about mid April in some areas. The taste is usually milder in spring, and heats up with the weather.

Winter radish Minnowase grows large, white and cylindrical, and can be used fresh or stored, as can China Rose, which is pink-skinned and rounder. Both are good for grating, pickling or for braising in stir-fries.

Sowing

Sow thinly, direct into the soil. Sowing after May will see more cabbage root fly damage. Winter radish such as Minnowase and China Rose must not be sown before July or they risk bolting.

Harvesting

Spring radish can be pulled as soon as you wish, depending partly on how spicy you like the flavour. Larger radish tend to be hotter. Thickly sown rows can be successively thinned of larger roots to allow growth of small ones, but if left too long, radish become hollow and soft.

SWEDE

Season of harvest: September-December

Variety	Special character Height (cm)	Sow	Spacing (cm) Harvest
MARIAN	Reliable cropper 50	Jun-early Jul	20x40 Sep onwards
MAGRES	Fine yellow flesh 50	Jun-early Jul	20x40 Sep onwards
BRORA	Excellent flavour 50	Jun-early Jul	20x40 Sep onwards

Varieties

I have not noticed a huge difference between the growth and flavour of different swedes.

An ability to resist frost makes them a valuable winter vegetable, if their cabbage-like flavour is to your liking. After frost they become slightly sweet, delicious boiled then mashed with a little butter, salt and pepper.

Sowing

Do not sow before May: June is better, and midsummer's day is about right, due to flea beetles and also to the tendency of early sowings to flower before making a root of any size. Swedes need room to grow, about 20cm (9") distance from their neighbours, so they can either be sown in 3-4cm modules and planted out, or thinned in late summer.

Harvesting

Frost hardiness means they can stay out until April, but if it is more con-venient, pull them and store until spring. Large ones keep best, in boxes or sacks in a cool shed, even in below freezing temperatures.

TURNIP

Season of harvest: May-June and October-December
Follow with: leeks, French beans, beetroot etc after spring turnips

Variety	Character Special care	Sow Harvest	Spacing (cm) Height (cm)
MILAN PURPLE TOP	Reliable early & late, flat Keep thinning, eat before too large	Mar & Aug May & Sep-Nov	5x30 25
PRIMERA F1	Rapid growth Keep thinning, eat before too large	Mar & Aug-Sep May & Sep-Nov	5x25 25
GOLDEN BALL	Globe-shaped, winter root Large roots will store	Aug Oct-Dec	10x30 35

Varieties

The main variation is in root shape and colour. Milan and Primera are both flat with pretty purple and red tops respectively, while Golden Ball is rounder, yellow and grows large with less risk of becoming woody.

Sowing

Turnips grow almost as fast as radish and have two similar dates for successful sowing – see the chart. Late winter sowings, thinned to 3-5cm (1-2") apart, will give baby turnips by mid spring. The young leaves can be used as a welcome green at this time as well, and should be mostly clear of flea beetle. In Somerset I can sow turnip as late as early September, although late August is more reliable, making them a useful catch crop after summer carrots, salads, onions or whatever else finishes in August.

Harvesting

Spring turnips are best eaten by June before pests arrive in force, and they may become woody in heat. Autumn roots will stand some frost, but are best harvested before Christmas and will keep for a few weeks – in a cool shed, for example.

OTHER BRASSICAS

KOHLRABI

Another brassica root (actually a swelling of the plants' stems, just above ground level), with a sweet taste and delicate texture provided it's picked when about the size of a tennis ball. Most of the time, any extra growth results in woodiness. So it is a half-season crop, maturing about ten weeks after sowing.

Sowing and growing

An early sowing in April for cropping in June / July should avoid most brassica pests. Either raise plants in 3cm modules or sow direct and thin to about 25x25cm (10x10"), watering in dry weather to reduce woodiness. For a second sowing, a variety of note is White Superschmelz for its ability to grow large roots without turning woody. It can be sown as late as July, avoiding most pests, and harvested as late as December if nights have not gone below about -3°C.

ORIENTAL LEAVES

These are a large assembly of fast-growing brassicas, best sown late summer to give leaves through autumn and sometimes into winter. Any frost hardiness is offset, however, by quite slow growth in cold, wet soil, and increased levels of slug damage. This is explained more fully in Chapter 10 (pages 66-82), which emphasizes the value of oriental leaves for small salad leaves in winter.

Sowing and growing

To grow them into large leaves for cooking, it is mostly a question of starting at the right time and of allowing extra space between plants. *Pak choi* is one of the best varieties and a mid summer or July sowing, planted at or thinned to 30x30cm (12x12") should produce quite a number of chunky but imperfect leaves until frost arrives. *Joi Choi*, as in winter, is my variety of choice, in this case because it crops for a long time before flowering. Water will be needed in dry summers. Green pak choi has somewhat smaller leaves than white-stemmed varieties.

Like many oriental leaves, they will be imperfect with small flea beetle holes and perhaps some larger pieces eaten by slugs. Most of this damage will be lost in cooking, while the notable flavour will remain.

Kohlrabi with mustard

Kohlrabi tastes something like a cross between a turnip and a cabbage. If it has a coarse skin it may need removing, otherwise cut the kohlrabi into large chunks. Steam in a very little water for about 5 minutes and test with a fork to see when it is soft. If cooked, drain and add a generous knob of butter to the pan so all the cubes are coated, then add a teaspoon or 2 of wholegrain mustard.

PROBLEMS OF BRASSICA ROOTS

Cabbage root fly is sometimes the most damaging pest, its maggots tunnelling around some or all roots. The only sure way to prevent damage is by covering with fleece or mesh, soon after sowing. Another strategy is to grow large roots by respecting the sowing dates, spreading good compost, watering if necessary etc, so that a lot of good flesh remains after cutting away the damaged outer parts.

Flea beetle will devour many late spring and early summer sowings, so the aim is to work either side of this period. You can either harvest a fast-grown crop from an early sowing – especially radish and turnip – or a late autumn crop from sowings after midsummer's day or thereabouts. Again, fleece can be useful.

Caterpillars will almost certainly appear at some point, but by avoiding midsummer growth their damage should be limited and does not affect the part of the plant being eaten.

Chapter 15

Tomatoes, Greenhouse and other Vegetables

Exotic colours and sweet flavours

Even should you be without a sheltered structure, this chapter will be of interest because some of its vegetables can also be grown outside. Perhaps reading about the intriguing possibilities will inspire you to build or buy a shelter.

THE KEY INGREDIENT OF SUCCESS

Spread a good 7cm (3") of compost or well-rotted manure before or just after planting indoor summer crops, whose rapid growth requires a lively soil with plenty of nutrients and moisture-holding ability. See text for advice on minimal supplementary feeding.

TOMATO

Varieties

Choosing the right variety, to suit both your palate and the conditions in your garden, is a key part of successful growing. I recommend reading the whole section on tomatoes before committing yourself. Varietal choice has to be considered alongside growing methods, whether plants are indoors or out, on the ground or tied to a stake.

For most of us, tomatoes are the number one summer crop. I even find them exciting in winter, planning which to grow and imagining their flavours, which we, as gardeners have much better access to than shoppers. We can grow tasty, non-commercial varieties, and use cultural methods that enhance flavour ahead of yield.

Any vote on flavour would currently go well for Sungold (mainly greenhouse but it will grow outside), a relatively recent hybrid with small, orange tomatoes. Its acidity, sweetness, extreme fruitiness and earliness are irresistible, but long stems and a relatively low yield make it non-commercial and it is rarely, if ever, seen for sale.

In a similar vein, large beef tomatoes, so-called for their dense, 'meaty' flesh, nearly all come from abroad because they need more sunshine and heat than is commonly found in Britain. But to make the journey, they need tough skins and an unripe condition. Even when we lived in France, not far from the French tomato headquarters of Marmande, it was difficult to buy good tomatoes at market.

I was then fortunate to find a fruity beef variety growing in an old lady's garden, from which I saved seed. It had soft skin, dense flesh and an unrivalled sweetness, so that I could sell it for twice the price of other growers' standard fruit at market. Although it is difficult to grow that beef variety in British conditions, Super Marmande and Supersteak are good substitutes.

Preparing the soil

I include this extra section on soil preparation because I feel there is some misunderstanding about the perceived need to use proprietary tomato feeds. Tomatoes grow fast and require plenty of nutrients, but in most soils a thick (5-7cm) dressing of good compost or well-rotted manure should provide these, spread any time from winter to just before planting. The resulting plants may not be the biggest, but they have an excellent chance of bearing fine crops and of being healthy.

The nutrients in compost become available as plants ask for them, making for more balanced growth than when artificial, soluble fertiliser is applied. Tomatoes are reckoned to 'need high potash fertiliser or liquid feed'. This may be so, but I feel that the risk of concentrating on any one nutrient is a relative depletion or imbalance of many others. My tomatoes grow steadily and healthily, with the compost helping to ensure nutritious fruit and excellent flavours.

Growbags

Growbags will benefit from some liquid feeding, and they are the easiest solution for paved greenhouses, especially now that organic ones are available. Go for larger sizes because otherwise watering can become a chore, as mature tomato plants will suck small growbags dry in half a day of hot sunshine.

Sowing seed and raising plants

Whichever sort of tomato you grow, the methods are similar. Sow by late winter in gentle heat, about 20°C. Initial growth will be slow and can be in a seed tray on the windowsill, but not for too long or the stems will become lank and flimsy.

After four or five weeks the large seedlings can be carefully pricked or moved into 5cm pots, giving them more compost for roots and daylight for leaves. After another ten days or two weeks, they can be re-potted into 8-10cm pots. Growth is strongest when small plants are successively re-potted to gradually larger pots because it avoids them becoming waterlogged in large ones. Plants do best when they have just a little extra compost and space.

You will know if they are too close together and in need of re-potting because stems will be long and thin, with pale leaves, rather than short and fat stems with broad, dark leaves.

INDOOR TALL TOMATO
(also called 'Cordon' or 'Indeterminate')

Season of harvest: July-October
Follow with: winter salad such as spinach, rocket, mustard, lettuce

Variety	Character	Sow	Spacing (cm)
	Special Care	First ready	Height (cm)
SUNGOLD	Orange, cherry-sized, top flavour	Feb-Mar	50x50
	Give room to grow	Late Jun	250+
GARDENERS	Red, cherry-sized, fine flavour	Feb-Mar	50x50
DELIGHT	Water moderately	Jul	200+
SANTA	Glossy red, small plum, sweet	Feb-Mar	50x50
		Jul	200
ALICANTE	Reliable, red, medium size	Feb-Mar	50x50
		Jul	200
GOLDEN	Yellow, tasty fruits, medium size	Feb-Mar	50x50
SUNRISE		Jul	200
(SUPER)	Large, red, dense, sweet beefsteak	Feb-Mar	50x50
MARMANDE	Loves heat, stop at 3 trusses	Aug	160
SAN MARZANO	Dense red plum for bottling	Feb-Mar	50x50
		Jul	200

All of the above will make a long central stem, sometimes to more than ten metres in commercial greenhouses. They also send out new stems or side shoots all the time, which need removing.

Planting and supporting

Planting holes can be made with a trowel, slightly larger than the rootball and deeper too, especially if the stem is long: new roots will grow out of it below soil level. As support, a cane or stick can be firmly pushed in near to the roots, or a string buried under the rootball at planting time, its other end tied vertically above to a polytunnel bar or greenhouse roof. As plants grow, their main stem is gently twisted around the string, saving the need to keep tying it to a stake.

Side-shooting

If side shoots are not removed, cordon tomato plants become a bushy jungle of leaves with many trusses of small fruits. So watch for any new stem growing between leaves and the main stem: these should be rubbed out or gently snapped off. You need to continue removing side shoots right through the season, as well as pinching off occasional shoots at the end of trusses, where new growing points may emerge, and at the top of plants where they sometimes fork.

Flavour and fruiting in summer

I remove the first truss of flowers because its fruit often sit at soil level and are nibbled by slugs as they ripen. This may happen even at the bottom of the second truss, which can be shortened. In any case, the quality of the earliest fruit can sometimes be poor in cool weather.

Many books advocate artificial pollination but I have never practised it and have always enjoyed plenty of fruit. They swell quickly as the plants elongate rapidly in June and July, but can take a frustrating time to ripen.

Flavour will depend partly on how ripe or over-ripe the fruits are when picked; acidity is increasingly balanced by sweetness, then almost disappears into a mellow softness if fruits are extra-ripe. Under-watering increases depth of flavour and sweetness, but means less fruit. Over-watering, especially on dry soil, can make ripe tomatoes split open. Learning to water for the growth you want can take a year or two of experimenting.

Flavour and fruiting in autumn

With falling temperature and light levels, both growth and ripening will slow. A good remedy is to 'stop' plants in August by pinching out their main growing point, to focus plants' resources into the development and maturing of fruit. Continue pinching out side shoots and water less. Finished trusses and all leaves up to (not above) the lowest fruiting truss can be removed to increase light and air-flow around plants.

By time of the first frost, any trusses with unripe fruit can be cut off and brought into the house to ripen, but flavour will be less impressive. Pull out the plants and cut them into pieces to aid breakdown in a compost heap or bin. Then plant some winter salad, for example from seed you have sown into modules in early September (see Chapter 10, pages 66-82).

Problems

Aphids Compost-grown, correctly watered tomatoes should maintain a healthy state. Planting marigolds nearby is a deterrent to whitefly, which can occasionally be numerous enough to slow growth as they suck plants' sap.

It is possible to buy aphid predators, but they are quite expensive and last only one summer. Spraying with soapy water can reduce aphid numbers; also plants often outgrow them, partly because aphids are most numerous in late spring. Some seasons are simply worse than others.

Potato blight can be more problematic (see Chapter 12, page 111), but only if water has been regularly sprayed on the leaves. After about mid July, aim to water the soil or growbag only, especially in a damp, overcast summer.

OUTDOOR TALL TOMATO

Season of harvest: August-October
Follow with: autumn sown broad beans or mustard green manure

Variety	Character	Sow	Spacing (cm)
	Special Care	*First ready*	*Height (cm)*
ALICANTE	Good cropper, med. red fruit	Mar-early Apr	60x60
	Stop by early Aug	Aug	130
FERLINE F1	Some blight resistance, red fruit	Mar-early Apr	60x60
	Stop by early Aug	Aug	130
SWEET MILLION F1	Small sweet red fruit	Mar-early Apr	60x60
	Best in sheltered spot	Jul/Aug	150

There are several differences between growing tall tomatoes indoors and outdoors. When growing outdoor tomatoes:

- Sow after mid March and plant a month later, at the end of spring, usually in June.
- Use a 2m (6') cane at most, and tie in the growing stem every fortnight or so.
- Grow only varieties recommended for outdoor use.
- Pinch out the main growing point after four to six trusses have appeared, probably in early August. Even then, the top trusses may yield more green than ripe fruit.
- Total yield will be much less than from indoor-grown plants, and more dependent on summer weather.
- In wet or grey summers, blight will affect leaves and cause all fruit to rot. Some varieties claim some blight resistance, but weather is the key factor. Every year is different.
- Sweetness may be lacking in wet summers.

In spite of these drawbacks, it is always fun to try outdoor tomatoes and sometimes the rewards are significant. Ferline has excellent deep colour and good flavour, Sweet Million is a fine cherry tomato but susceptible to blight.

Another possibility, for cool and wet areas especially, is smaller bush tomatoes that can be cloched all summer to keep their leaves dry.

OUTDOOR BUSH TOMATO
(also called 'Determinate')

Season of harvest: July-September
Follow with: as above

Variety	Special character Special care	Sow First ready	Spacing (cm) Height (cm)
SUB-ARCTIC PLENTY	Extremely hardy and early Can be cloched	Mar-Apr Jun	45x45 50
RED ALERT	Early, prolific, tasty Pick off slugs	Mar-Apr Jul	45x45 50
ROMA	Dense plum fruit for cooking Minimal watering	Mar-Apr Mostly Aug-Sep	45x45 50
TUMBLER F1	Compact habit for baskets Regular watering	Mar-Apr Jul/Aug	30

Varieties

These varieties produce quite small fruit at ground level, with no staking or side-shooting. Growing is less work than tall varieties but picking is more work, with fruit often underneath leaves and stems, sometimes damaged by slugs where they lie on the soil.

Success depends on weather above all, with many promising crops lost to blight after late July. Sub-Arctic Plenty is worth trying in cooler or wetter regions, for its ability to set and ripen fruit in cooler early summer weather, even before blight arrives. Red Alert somehow combines early fruiting with a good, sweet flavour. Roma and other plum tomatoes tend to crop a little later, with a dense flesh making them better for cooking and bottling than for eating raw.

Growing

Polythene cloches are extra work and expense, but can repay the effort and will ensure a worthwhile harvest. Fleece will help plants to fruit early but cannot prevent blight later on.

Most bush varieties can be grown in containers as long as they are in a sunny position. Any lack of sun will delay picking and reduce sweetness of the fruit.

Even hanging baskets can be made productive: Tumbler and other basket varieties yield well, and are of good flavour but not top-rate. Avoid over-watering to maintain sweetness, although large plants in small containers need regular watering to survive, let alone grow. These plants will definitely benefit from some liquid feed of comfrey leaves or stinging nettles soaked in water (very smelly) and diluted about twenty to one, or of a proprietary organic liquid feed.

Problems

Slugs can spoil much fruit; tall tomatoes are better in slug-prone areas.
Blight is the main problem – cloches will help.

Tomato soup with apple

This is good for using up the glut of tomatoes at the end of the season when the plants need to come out to make room for the next crop. It is also a time when the apple trees are groaning with fruit. I find the apples add a bit of sweetness and body to the soup. No precise measurements here. Work on the basis of 1 onion and 1 apple to 1 kg tomatoes. Garlic, celery and a good stock help enormously.

Sweat the chopped onion in a large saucepan, add chopped celery, apple and tomatoes, a couple of cloves of garlic, and then add the stock. Bring to the boil then simmer for about 20 minutes. Liquidise, and if you don't like tomato skins, sieve the soup.

AUBERGINE

Season of harvest: July-October
Follow with: winter salad such as spinach, rocket, mustard

Variety	Character Height (cm)	Sow First ready	Spacing (cm)
MONEYMAKER F1	Relatively easy, long black fruit 100	Feb-Mar Jul	50x50
BLACK BEAUTY	Lower yield of shorter, round fruit 100	Feb-Mar Jul	50x50
MINI FINGERS	Clusters of small, thin, dark fruit 80	Feb-Mar Jul	50x50

The keyword for aubergines is heat, so they are most reliably grown indoors. Without sufficient warmth, growth is slow and fruiting inconsequential.

Aubergine fruits come in many shapes, sizes and colours. White or violet ones such as Rosa Bianca are no more difficult to grow than standard dark purple ones, but may yield a little less. Growth of all varieties is significantly slower at temperatures below about 20°C.

Sowing

Sow in February or March, with a temperature of 20°C or higher if possible. Seedlings emerge and grow more slowly than tomatoes; their potting-on requirements are the same. If you have no reliable source of heat in the greenhouse, you could buy small plants to arrive in April or May, then grow them on before planting.

Growing

By planting time in late spring, an already flowering plant about 15cm (6") high will give best chance of a fair crop by mid, rather than late summer.

Although aubergine plants vary in height according to variety, most will benefit from a stout cane near their stem, around which some string can be looped to hold branches up and keep fruit above soil level.

Correct watering makes a big difference. Initial slow growth, above all in grey, cool weather, means care must be taken to avoid drowning the roots. But any hot sun on larger plants will result in rapid evapotranspiration, such that soil or growbags can dry out enough to diminish fruiting. Be generous with water in a hot summer.

Harvesting

Aubergines are best harvested before they become too seedy and bitter. This can be hard to judge and varies according to variety but watch for any dulling of skin colour and any abnormality of shape, such as swelling across the middle, which reveal the end of growth and beginning of seeding.

Some weather conditions encourage so much fruit-set that the harvest, even on large-fruiting varieties, consists of many small aubergines rather than a few large ones. If you want the latter, some thinning of baby fruit will be necessary. This should not be necessary with varieties bred for small fruit, which will thrive in pots on a warm patio, although they will crop later than aubergines under glass or polythene. On outdoor plants I rarely achieve anything to eat before mid August.

By early autumn, plants can be large enough to maintain reasonable growth of fruit for a time, until the first cold nights slow them right down. By the time fruiting is finished and plants are pulled out, their stems are woody and require chopping or shredding to help them rot into compost.

Problems

Slugs enjoy aubergines so it is best to support fruit that touch the soil, with a block of wood perhaps.

Red spider mite can destroy indoor plants, and the predator phytoseiulus is a reliable remedy, as long as it is introduced as soon as or before red spider is suspected. I recommend this if red spider was present the previous year in your greenhouse or polytunnel.

Aphids: as for tomatoes

Garlic aubergines

The idea behind this is to treat the aubergine as if it were garlic bread – the same old butter, parsley and garlic with the odd variation!

Slice the aubergines in half length-wise. Score them with a diagonal criss-cross pattern and lay on a baking tray. In a small bowl, mash together butter, chopped garlic, and a mixture of herbs – basil and parsley are popular. Spread the butter over the aubergine as if buttering bread. Roast in a hot oven (200°C) for about half an hour.

CAPSICUM

Season of harvest: August-October
Follow with: winter salad such as spinach, rocket, mustard

Variety	Character	Sow	Spacing (cm)
	Special care	First ready	Height (cm)
1. Sweet Peppers			
MARCONI ROSSA	Long, pale green then red	Feb/Mar	50x50
	Stake & tie loosely	Jul/Aug	75
SWEET BABY ORANGE	Smaller fruit & plant, sweet	Feb/Mar	50x50
	Suitable for large patio pot	Jul/Aug	60
2. Hot Peppers (Chillies)			
MEEK AND MILD	Mild chilli, vigorous plant	Feb/Mar	50x50
		Jul/Aug	75
HABENERO	Terribly hot small orange chilli	Feb/Mar	50x50
	Eater beware!	Jul/Aug	75

Capsicums include sweet peppers and chillies of all colours. Like aubergines, they are members of the tomato and potato family, *Solanaceae*. Their green fruit is an immature stage to ripening, which involves a colour change and some sweetening or heating of the flesh.

The vastly different flavours of available varieties, both of peppers and chilli, make it difficult to single out any for general recommendation. Those in the chart have worked well for my family, except that many of the Habanero were never eaten, they were so spicy! Meek and Mild lived up to its gentle name, especially the last fruits in October, which had little heat in them. Ultimate choice of variety depends on your requirements and taste.

Sowing and growing

Capsicums have the same requirements as aubergines (see above, pages 155-7). Heat is again the most difficult part in Britain, particularly for seedlings and young plants. So again, it may be worth buying plants rather than seed.

Harvesting

Chilli plants can provide a large number of fruit, so one in a pot may provide sufficient for a few months. When mature (meaning red, orange, yellow or purple according to variety) they can be picked and kept indoors at room temperature to dry. Make sure that they are fully ripe before attempting to keep them; for instance orange chillies of a red variety are immature and may go mouldy. Depth of flavour is often awesome.

Peppers will only be sweet if allowed to develop their ripe colour. But in our climate, this involves waiting two to four weeks beyond when they could have been picked as green peppers; and while they are maturing, plants are forming less new peppers than if green ones had been picked off. So harvests of ripe fruit are later and smaller, but sweeter and more interesting.

Peppers carry on fruiting a little later than aubergines, but the last peppers are extremely slow to ripen and at risk from slugs.

Problems

As for aubergines.

Pepper and goat's cheese tart

2 onions, 3 peppers
2 cloves garlic
200g goat's cheese
rosemary / thyme / basil

dough base:
500g wholemeal flour
1 teaspoon easy-blend yeast
1 teaspoon salt

This is essentially a pizza. Start by making the dough and leave to rise in a warm place. Meanwhile slice the onions into rings, and the peppers into elegant blades. Chop the garlic, and depending on the nature of your goats cheese either crumble it or slice into rounds. Stretch the dough into a round, arrange the topping, and bake in a hot oven c.200°C for about 20 minutes.

CUCUMBER

See Chapter 13, pages 117-9

MELON AND WATERMELON

Season of harvest: August-September
Follow with: winter salad such as spinach, rocket, mustard

Variety	Character	Sow	Spacing (cm)
	Special care	*First ready*	*Height (cm)*
SWEETHEART F1	Prolific crop of early Cantaloupe melons	Apr	50x50
	Regular pinching out	August mostly	up to 200
MINNESOTA MIDGET	Early, small fragrant outdoor melon	Apr	50x50
	Suitable for outdoors	Jul-Aug	30
WATER MELON	Juicy, needs hot summer	Apr	70x70
SUGAR BABY	Water more than melon	Aug-Sep	30

MELON

The melon is another heat-loving plant, similar in appearance and cultural requirements to cucumber. Varietal choice plays a big part here, and there is one, Sweetheart, which seems especially well adapted to British greenhouse temperatures, more than most other varieties I have tried. It bears an early and reliable crop of sweet, succulent orange flesh, inside a pale green skin. When grown under cover, some of its early fruits can weigh up to 1.5kg; later ones are smaller and sometimes less sweet, whereas Minnesota Midget is well adapted to outdoor growing.

Sowing

Sowing is best in early spring with gentle warmth. Two re-pottings may be necessary before planting out as late as early June, by which time there may be a trailing stem and some flowers.

Growing

Vertical or horizontal? Indoor melon plants can either be allowed to ramble across the soil like a squash plant, or be grown up a string or stake like a cucumber. The latter is advantageous for keeping fruit off the ground, where ants, slugs and woodlice can sometimes get to them before the gardener spots they are ripe.

Vertical cultivation I run a re-usable polypropylene string (binder twine) from my polytunnel's crop support bar, straight down to the bottom of a planting hole, just as for tomatoes. The melon plant is gently firmed in, with a knotted end of the string underneath its developing rootball.

Carefully wrap the main stem around the string as it grows. By July it should be lengthening rapidly (up to 7cm daily in hot weather), so twice weekly attention is needed for keeping plants supported.

Baby melons should be seen on all side shoots from the main stem, at the first node of each one, i.e. where their first leaf is growing. Melons grow best with only one on each sideshoot, cutting the rest of the stem off once the first fruit is formed. So while the main stem is growing fast, to 200cm (80") or more, a lot of pinching out is needed of other incipient stems, just after the point where they carry baby melons. Up to seven or eight fruit may develop on one plant, in rich soil and a hot summer, with plenty of water.

It is a good idea to remove the first few melon side shoots altogether, so that the lowest melon hangs just above soil level, clear of all other interested parties there.

Horizontal cultivation Melons grown at soil level are usually smaller and less perfect, but of equally impressive flavour. As with vertical melons, their stems require pinching out, but it is harder to see where. I usually let plants grow about 80cm (30") in one or more directions before pinching out all their growing points, and subsequently all others I see. The growing points are the ends of stems and side shoots, where small new leaves are developing. Baby melons should be visible on plants when you do the first pinching out. The main growing area will now fill up with leaves and fruit, but keep paths clear by pushing errant stems back on top of the plant. This advice applies to both indoor and outdoor melons.

Harvesting

Ripeness is revealed in many ways, the most striking being a wonderful aroma of sweet melon. At the same time, there may be a little cracking or splitting of the skin around its stem. Skin colour will become more yellow and soften.

In Britain, cutting open a ripe melon that you have grown yourself gives a wonderful feeling of achievement, and the flavour is as remarkable as anything one can imagine.

For melons on the ground, small blocks of wood can be placed underneath to keep them clean and make it easier to spot any hint of ripeness.

WATERMELON

Watermelon plants also love heat, but will tolerate cooler conditions than melon, so a sheltered outdoor location in full sun is suitable. No special pruning is required, and most varieties will ramble a long way with some large and heavy fruit, hence my recommendation of Sugar Baby, a more compact variety.

Sowing and growing

As for melon, except to omit pruning.

Harvesting

Ripeness of Sugar Baby's fruit is indicated by a darkening of skin colour to almost black, and fruits can weigh 3-4kg in good soil and with sufficient sun and moisture.

CAPE GOOSEBERRY / TOMATILLO

Season of harvest: August-October
Follow with: winter salad such as spinach, rocket, mustard

| Variety | Character | Sow | Spacing (cm) |
	Special care	First ready	Height (cm)
CAPE GOOSEBERRY	Large plants, tangy fruits	Mar/Apr	70x70
	Stake and tie up bushy plants	Aug	90
PINEAPPLE	Smaller, earlier fruits	Mar/Apr	70x70
	Stake and tie up bushy plants	Jul	60
TOMATILLO VERDE	Fruit for cooking mostly	Feb/Mar	70x70
	Grow upwards like tomato	Aug	150

These are exotic plants of the nightshade family from New Mexico, not too difficult to grow because of their exceptional vigour. Tomatillo fruit are green and up to 4cm across, quite tart and for cooking with. Cape gooseberries are cherry size or smaller, mostly dark yellow and sweet but also acidic, rather citrus-like, more fruit than vegetable and wrapped in a pretty, pointed, parchment-like lantern. Cape gooseberries are also known as Physalis and golden berry, while Chinese Lanterns are an ornamental version with red lanterns (when ripe) and inedible fruit.

Varieties

I have recently enjoyed Pineapple for the unexpected sweetness of small berries that really do taste of pineapple. It is described as 'dwarf', but mine grew to over a metre high and required supporting all around with canes and string to hold the stems up a little, to prevent them covering paths and also to keep lanterns clear of the soil. For small spaces, Little Lantern is worth a try, reckoned to grow no more than 50cm high with a spread of about 80cm.

Tomatillo Verde offers larger and tarter fruits than cape gooseberries, resembling wrapped-up green tomatoes. It is for use in Mexican cooking and not really for eating raw.

Sowing

Sow in March like tomatoes; plant in May inside, or June outside.

Growing

Growing outside will make the harvest smaller, later and perhaps less sweet. But the restriction of growth may be a good thing because, indoors, these plants shoot rampantly in all directions and need staking plus some tying-in. I have not worked out a best way of doing this except for tomatilloes, which can be staked or strung up like tomatoes, with sideshooting.

Harvesting

Cropping indoors may start by late July; watch for a change in colour of cape gooseberry lanterns, from pale green to bright yellow to matt beige. They are edible in all three stages, to cook when unripe and to eat raw or cooked when sweet and yet still tangy, with many powerful flavours.

Fruits picked in colder weather, before frost, should store well in their wrappers, sometimes until Christmas.

Problems

Pest and disease are not a main worry here, but restricting growth to facilitate picking may be – see above.

OTHER VEGETABLES: NON-GREENHOUSE CROPS

I have put these few vegetables here because they are somewhat specialised or of unusual habit, rather like most of the above. They are outdoor crops.

CELERY

Season of harvest: August-October
Follow with: garlic, autumn sown beans

Variety	Character Height (cm)	Sow Harvest	Spacing (cm)
GOLDEN SELF-BLANCHING	Tall yellow stems 40	Apr-May Aug-Nov	25x25
GREEN UTAH	Tall green stems, self-blanch 40	Apr-May Aug-Nov	25x25
CELERY LEAF	Many smaller stems 40	Apr-Jun Regularly	25x25

Varieties

I recommend self-blanching varieties because blanching with ridges of soil usually results in even more slug holes. Celery is better for some blanching to reduce its bitterness. Self-blanching works by close planting, excluding light around stems, with a dense canopy of leaves above them. There is a choice of pale yellow or pale green stems, from the varieties above, and celery leaf for small repeat pickings.

Sowing

Climate-warming has played a part here, because it used to be that the summer was about right for bringing celery to maturity, from sowing in March. Now there are almost two seasons, in southern Britain at least: sow in March for late summer celery, sow in May for late autumn celery.

Raise plants indoors: sow seed on the surface of compost in a seed tray and cover with glass to retain moisture. Water with a fine rose about once a week. Seedlings may take three weeks to germinate and pricking out into 3cm modules can be done after about five weeks.

Growing

All celery is shallow rooting, and grows best where surface moisture is abundant. Frequent watering is better than occasional soaks, and in dry summers it can be difficult to grow well. Use the later sowing date if watering is difficult, so that most rapid growth happens in damper autumn weather.

Harvesting

The nicest stems are usually found soon after the canopy has closed over. Celery will grow on beyond that stage, with outer stems becoming tougher and, often, new side shoots growing out of the base. If the main stem is cut above soil level, there may be time for these to give a small second pick. Harvest before temperatures of about –2°C or lower; celery stalks will keep well in a polythene bag in cool conditions.

Celery leaf takes this a stage further and is picked over regularly by pulling off or cutting larger outside stems, and then larger numbers of small ones as the plant develops.

Problems

It is difficult to grow beautiful celery, but the taste is always strong. Slug-holes tend to spoil the appearance of most outer and some inner leaves, although this is less important for soups and stews. Keep well weeded, harvest on the young side, and trim hard when picking to remove the most damaged leaves.

Celery soup

1 head of celery, chopped
2 onions
500ml chicken stock
500ml full cream milk

Soften the vegetables in butter. Stir in a couple of tablespoons of flour, add the milk and stock. Bring the boil then simmer for 20 minutes or until the celery is soft. Liquidise before serving.

SPINACH, CHARD AND BEET (PERPETUAL SPINACH)

Season of harvest: April-November
Follow with: (spinach only) many vegetables, depending on season of harvest

Variety	Character		Sow	Spacing (cm)
	Height (cm)	Special Care	Harvest	
1. True Spinach				
TETONA	Slow to grow and to bolt, tender		Mar-Aug	5x25
	30	Keep moist	1-2 months per sowing	
MEDANIA	Over-winters well, dark sweet leaves		Jul-Aug	10x30
	40	Keep plants tidy	Autumn and spring	
2. Chard and beet				
PERPETUAL SPINACH	Long season of picking, versatile		Mar-Jul	30x30
	60	Regular picking	Up to ten months	
RAINBOW CHARD	Stems of red, yellow, white, pink		Mar-Jul	30x30
	60	Regular picking	Up to ten months	

Varieties

All spinach is of the beetroot family (*Beta vulgaris*), of which some kinds make more of a beet root than others. True spinach, the least rooty, grows quickly and briefly, for two or three months usually, while the 'perpetual' is regularly picked off the same plant, whose increasingly large root keeps sprouting new leaves. Chard of all colours works in the same way.

TRUE SPINACH

True spinach is extremely useful as a salad plant, in winter and spring above all – see page 65 and pages 75-6 for more detailed descriptions of growing and harvesting as salad leaves. As a cooked green, leaves are simply allowed to grow larger. Slug holes will appear in the process, but conveniently disappear again in cooking! Keep plants clean by removing any yellowing leaves, to afford less habitat for slugs under ground-level foliage.

Slugs and woodlice can make it difficult to grow spinach from direct sowing. I mostly raise plants indoors, about three seeds per 3-4cm module. One tray of forty to sixty module plants should yield substantial pickings.

Best sowing dates are March-April and then July. After mid spring it becomes difficult to grow many leaves before plants run to seed, so I recommend not sowing true spinach from about late May to mid July, depending slightly on weather. Best conditions are dry springs for less slugs and wet summers for abundant leaves.

PERPETUAL SPINACH AND CHARD

These leaves also are useful for salads, picked small – see Chapters 9 & 10 for detailed descriptions of growing and harvesting as salad leaves. A few plants can provide large leaves for many, many meals, but with a different flavour to true spinach – generally more acidic. Chards come in a fine range of colours, and their vivid stems may brighten up the garden as much as the table.

Regular picking obliges plants to keep producing smaller leaves. Chard and leaf beet leaves will grow huge if allowed to, and whilst still edible they are tougher than small leaves. As the weather cools in autumn, growth will gradually slow, then stop during most winters, and any severe frost will kill roots as well. However in milder areas and winters, plants should survive to produce another month or two of leaves in early spring, before sending up highly ornamental coloured stems. Ruby chard is especially striking.

Strawberry Spinach is found in some seed catalogues, but provides few edible leaves. It is more interesting for the bright red, seedy fruits that cling to its stems; they are edible, but nothing like as sweet as strawberries.

Chapter 16

Perennial Vegetables

Regular early harvests every year

'Easy', that over-used word, really does apply here. Perennial vegetables grow again, every year, from roots that survive over winter. There is no need to start again in the spring, and early crops are assured, growing vigorously while newly sown seedlings of annual vegetables are only just underway.

Certain characteristics are common to perennial vegetables:

- Before planting, it is imperative to clean soil of all perennial weeds.
- Most perennial vegetable plants take up a larger space than annual vegetables.
- They crop in spring or early summer.
- After harvest, growth in late summer and autumn is for the benefit of next year's crop.

ARTICHOKE

There are two unrelated kinds of artichoke, sharing only the name. In a way they are both perennial, although Jerusalem artichokes are not supposed to be. It is just that some of their tubers always manage to hide at digging time, to re-grow in the spring into very tall stems with little sunflowers on top in the autumn. The flowers rotate to follow the sun, resulting in their Italian name of *girasole articiocco*, corrupted in English to 'Jerusalem'.

By contrast, globe artichokes (true perennials) are large grey-green bushes of the thistle family that re-grow, even twice a year, with edible flower buds. Their flavour is slightly acidic and deliciously nutty, with nibbles of nuttiness at the bottom of each leaf, around tender hearts of a creamy consistency.

Also included here, to complete the series, are Chinese artichokes which are of a different family again, and are annuals.

GLOBE ARTICHOKE

Season of harvest: June / July, sometimes September

Variety	Character	Sow/Plant	Spacing (cm)
	Special care	*First ready*	*Height (cm)*
GREEN GLOBE	Early medium heads	Mar-May	100x100 or 45x150
	Remove all growth after harvest	Jul	100+
ROMANESCO	Later, smaller purple heads	Mar-May	100x100 or 45x150
	Remove all growth after harvest	Jul	100+

Sowing/planting

From seed, sow into small pots or 3cm modules in early spring and re-pot into 8-10cm pots after six weeks, then plant into weed-free ground in June. Plants can be raised outdoors, but will grow more strongly in a greenhouse; note that mice sometimes eat the seeds. First artichokes may come in September, otherwise should appear the following July.

Alternatively, after an established plant has finished fruiting in summer, use a sharp spade to chop away a piece of root and stem with some leaves, and plant this straight into moist new ground, or into a large pot of compost to grow on before planting the following spring. Either way, fruiting in the first summer will be slight, but should be significant thereafter.

In good soil each plant can produce up to three or four large globes and six or more small ones. This is based on one plant consisting of three or four separate growing points, having been given sufficient room for each one to develop (see table). If you have space, two different varieties can be a good idea to spread the harvest.

Growing

Once all the globes are picked, usually by late July, cut out the old woody stems with a sharp spade, just above soil level, and pull off all old and yellowing leaves. Some new shoots should already be appearing, and once these are about 10-20cm (4-8") high, snap or pull off any excess to leave three or four plants for the next harvest. Larger heads are more likely if this is done. In long warm seasons, small heads are sometimes produced in late summer or early autumn – worth picking, but more of a snack than a meal.

Harvesting

There is scope to vary dates of picking by choosing to eat small, tender heads or larger, more fibrous ones. Young heads cut easily, and their peeled stem is as delicious as any heart – if young enough they can be eaten whole, leaves and all. Older heads are more fibrous, but with more 'meat' at the bottom of each leaf that is peeled off, and their stalk is woody.

Old unpicked heads will eventually transform into vivid clusters of translucent, sky-blue petals which can be dried when cut and hung upside down in an airy spot.

Problems

Frosty winters can make all leaf growth disappear and the plants may appear dead until April when, normally, they shoot again. Slugs and snails like using their older leaves as a base for damaging raids elsewhere, so it really is worth removing all old leaves after harvest.

Artichokes

These are surprisingly popular with our children. Cut the stalks off and steam the heads in a little water for 20-30 minutes. Serve with garlic mayonnaise or vinaigrette or melted butter.

JERUSALEM ARTICHOKE

Season of harvest: November-April

Variety	Character	Sow/Plant	Spacing (cm)
	Special care	*First ready*	*Height (cm)*
FUSEAU	Not too knobbly	Mar-May	60x60 or 45x90
	Dig roots thoroughly	Oct-Nov	250
GERARD	Red, fine flavour	Mar-May	60x60 or 45x90
	Dig roots thoroughly	Oct-Nov	250

Jerusalem artichokes bring a welcome extra dimension of flavour to winter soups and salads. They would surely be better known and more widely used, were it not for their ability to cause gaseous eruptions. Not everybody is so affected, however, and you may be lucky. Some claim that eating them raw can avoid the problem – and their nutty flavour is superb in a grated salad.

They are almost too easy to grow, such that they keep re-growing, because one or two of their tubers can never be found at harvest time, and then quickly re-grow into new plants from April. Bear in mind the height of their woody stems – up to 3m (10').

Some roots are uneven, relatively small and involve a lot of scrubbing to remove soil. If peeled, they discolour quite fast once the flesh is in contact with air.

Planting

Set tubers about 15cm (6") deep in early spring. Great vigour and height of stems make them more feasible to grow in a clump or section of bed, rather than in a row or line, which robs more light from its neighbours. Do not grow them to the south of tomatoes or French beans, for example.

Harvesting

Tubers can be dug out once leaves die off in autumn, and are totally frost hardy, happy to lie in the soil until needed. Last digging is usually in early April, when some new shoots may be visible from undug tubers. To clean the soil completely for a different crop, return to remove any newly shooting tubers every week or two until mid May. By then there should be none left and compost can be spread before planting a new crop.

Problems

Slugs may nibble new growth in spring but plants usually grow away.
Mice may burrow amongst tubers in winter and enjoy many meals; a good cat is probably the only answer.

CHINESE ARTICHOKE

Season of harvest: November-March

Character	Plant	Spacing (cm)
Height (cm)	Special care	First ready
Sweet and nutty flavour	Initially in pots then outside after frost has finished	40x40
50	Dig carefully late autumn, store in sack	Oct/Nov

A final variation is Chinese Artichokes, also called Crosnes, from the town in France where they were first grown in Europe. They are members of the mint family, much esteemed by certain chefs and writers, with a flavour (much of it in the skin) that resembles their Jerusalem 'cousins'. Their tubers are pale and ridged, akin to sections of caterpillars, and are suitable for salads and all kinds of cooking. Note that these are not supposed to be perennial in any sense, because tubers are damaged by frost.

Planting

Tubers will probably need ordering from a specialist catalogue and should arrive in late winter. If you receive them before all risk of frost has passed, plant in pots in a greenhouse before setting them out in late spring. They have slightly hairy dark green leaves and small flowers appreciated by bees.

Harvesting

All top growth is killed by frost and it is best to dig tubers soon after this, to avoid frost and slug damage over the winter. Then store them in a sack or box in a cool but frost-free place. The roots are more frost-hardy than is claimed, and may survive winter to grow again.

ASPARAGUS

Season of harvest: late April-late June, from mature plants only

Variety	Character	Sow/Plant First ready	Spacing (cm) Height (cm)
SEED – CONNOVERS COLOSSAL	Slower	Mar/Jul Small picking after 3 yrs	60x90 200
CROWNS – CONNOVERS COLOSSAL	Quicker	Mar Small picking after 2 yrs	60x90 200

One of the finest tastes in vegetables, and one of the most expensive – two good incentives to grow your own. They are easy to grow, but need plenty of space – rather more in fact than is often recommended, especially as they grow older.

Preparing soil

Make sure you start with clean soil. If you plant into soil with couch grass or bindweed roots, you are simply creating difficulties for yourself over many years, because the weed roots will multiply and can never be cleared out once asparagus crowns have become established. Be patient and do the job thoroughly.

Seed or crowns

The difference between sowing seed and planting crowns is mostly in time to cropping. A year's wait can be saved, but sowing your own is satisfying and should make for healthy plants. On two separate occasions I have sown seed of Connovers Colossal in March, planted it in July, and harvested quite a few spears two springs later, or three years after sowing. Substantial harvests begin about five years from sowing, or four years from planting crowns.

This may sound a long wait, but I assure you it will pass quickly. Then you can enjoy many years of superb meals. There are divided views on the lifetime of an asparagus bed, and anything from ten to twenty years is suggested; I feel the latter is achievable.

Planting

Think ahead: have some ground clean of weeds by late summer if possible. This gives time for any lurking perennial weed roots to be dug out before winter and again at planting time. Asparagus is easy to grow if you are thorough with weed clearing.

Trenches are often recommended, but planting on flat ground works well. Confusion arises because white asparagus used to be grown, rather than green; it was whitened by blanching with soil, hence the ridges and trenches. But tastes and varieties change. Green spears, from most varieties now on offer, are delicious and much easier to grow.

I recommend a bed, block or square of asparagus, easier to look after than one long row. Over the years, many roots spread far into neighbouring soil and the fern-like top growth will grow tall and floppy, benefiting from support, but partly supporting itself if grown all together.

To plant crowns, dig a hole slightly larger than the triffid-like roots, lay them in it with the centre higher than root ends, then cover everything with about 7cm (3") of soil. A good spacing is 60cm (2') between plants and 90cm (3') between rows. Water in if dry, then simply keep clear of weeds with regular hoeing. A 5cm (2") top dressing of compost will help conserve moisture and feed the growing roots. New spears from the crown will rapidly bush out into pretty ferns, with more appearing until early summer and lasting until mid autumn, when they turn yellow and die.

Growing on

My experience suggests that asparagus benefits from a good annual dressing of compost or well-rotted manure, either in winter or as soon as picking has finished. Rich, fertile soil will encourage strong growth, an abundant forest of ferns through each summer and autumn, and plenty of new spears every spring.

Summer growth should, after about three years, resemble a mini-forest about 2m (6') high, dark enough underneath to prevent germination of too many weeds. Any that do appear must be removed before they seed, so that the soil becomes and stays clean, making it easier to maintain.

In late autumn or winter, dying top growth can be cut off and composted, or left to rot on the surface if there are few weeds to hoe in springtime. The most difficult weed can be asparagus itself, from its own fertile berries which drop off or are excreted elsewhere by birds. All-male hybrids such as Jersey Knight F1 mostly have no berries and tend to yield heavier spears, but I cannot vouch for their longevity.

Harvesting

Excitement mounts in April as you scan the plot daily, hoping to see a first spear-head, which should appear, approximately, on St. George's Day (April 23rd), the Summer Solstice being an average end-point to the harvest. Spears can be cut at soil level when 15cm (6") or so, although if left a little longer they snap off easily just above soil level and are less chewy at the bottom.

Growth depends on temperature, so in cool weather, picking may be possible every third or fourth day, while in a heatwave there can be worthwhile new growth every day.

Young plants, to be picked lightly, can either be picked until late May, or part-picked – occasional spears removed – until late June. The former is easier, the latter more suitable for occasional visits to the garden.

Problems

The main difficulty is **asparagus beetle**, about 1cm long, red and black, chewing the leaves and stems as well. I find that well-composted soil imparts enough vigour to plants for them to tolerate some beetles and keep their numbers to manageable levels, with strong and healthy crowns producing vigorous new leaves.

Whilst it takes a long time to tire of eating asparagus lightly steamed and dipped in hollandaise, mayonnaise or poached egg, towards the end of the season we start to cook other dishes with it.

Asparagus gougère

1 Somerset camembert, spring onions, a handful of asparagus, choux pastry mixture (see Spinach gougère recipe – use ½ quantities)

This dish revolves around the camembert, so choose a circular oven-proof dish that will take a camembert with a comfortable margin of about 2 inches all round it.

Lightly steam the asparagus spears. Make the choux pastry. Oil or butter the dish, place the camembert in the middle and spoon the choux mixture around it. Cut deep incisions into the camembert and insert spears of asparagus. Chop the spring onions and sprinkle over the top. Place in a hot oven for about 20mins. The cheese should melt and ooze every where. The Somerset camembert is ideal, as the flavour is not too strong for the asparagus.

RHUBARB

Season of harvest: March to July

Variety	Character	Sow / Plant First ready	Spacing (cm) Height (cm)
GLASKIN'S PERPETUAL	Reliable, early stems	Sow Mar-Apr, plant July Mar	90x90 100+
VICTORIA	Better as maincrop	Sow Mar-Apr, plant July Apr	90x90 100+
TIMPERLEY EARLY	Forcing or maincrop	Plant Nov-Mar Mar	90x90 100+

Rhubarb grows in a similar way to asparagus, but the end product is utterly different, English to the core, an acid, pink harbinger of spring. Adding some cream, sugar and root ginger can transform it into a great delicacy.

Sowing

Sowing adds a year of waiting. Sow seed in pots indoors or out if you choose this option.

Planting

Commencement of the harvesting period depends on variety, so here is a tip to find a good crown for planting. In early spring, look out for a garden or allotment with vigorous new rhubarb appearing. Be cheeky and ask the owner nicely for a piece of root off its side during the following winter. He or she should be happy to oblige, because rhubarb roots or crowns enlarge every year, until they consist of a significant mound of dark knobbiness, mostly above ground. Otherwise, buy crowns or rooted crowns in pots from a catalogue or nursery. Plant so that all new shoots are just above soil level.

Roots are vigorous and feed outwards a long way, which is why rhubarb is often banished to a distant corner of the plot, not to interfere with other vegetables or flowers. A damp corner suits it, whereas dry soil will slow its growth. Plenty of compost or manure will be repaid in long, fleshy stalks.

Some rhubarb makes flower stems from about mid spring. While pretty, they are best cut out because their presence depresses leaf growth and diverts energy to production of seed.

Harvesting

Hold back in rhubarb's first year, so that energy captured by the leaves can go into building up its roots. During the second spring, it should be possible to gather stems for six to eight weeks, and for up to three months a year from then on.

The first leaves and stems seem to take an age as they poke gingerly out of the crown, being singed by late winter frosts. Putting a large terracotta pot or bucket over them can speed up growth a little and will blanch stems to pink instead of red, with a milder flavour. But starving the leaves of light hampers future growth and should not be done every year.

Commercial pink rhubarb is 'forced' in dark sheds, from crowns that are grown in fields and dug up before winter. By the next spring they are exhausted from lack of light and cannot be re-used, unlike garden rhubarb, which often lasts for decades.

Picking is usually done by twisting and pulling larger stems so that they come away from the crown at their base. The large, inedible leaf is cut off and composted. One crown should produce three or more weekly meals for two people, between about late April and early summer. After the middle of summer, both quality and flavour deteriorate. Also it is best for the plant to leave it in peace, as one does for asparagus, to allow it to replenish.

Problems

Rhubarb should grow easily and without fuss, as long as moisture is present. When forcing with pots, check for and remove slugs inside every week or so.

Rhubarb mousse (for 8)

*700g rhubarb, 1 orange, a knob of root ginger about 1 inch
250ml cream (double or Jersey), 4 eggs, 2 sachets gelatine*

Cook the rhubarb with zest and juice of orange and grated ginger. Separate the eggs, whisk the yolks and sugar together until light and frothy. Whip the cream. Strain the rhubarb; mix the gelatine with the hot juice. Whisk egg whites. Mix all together and pour into individual serving cups or a nice glass bowl.

This recipe also works if you leave out the cream but use 1 kg rhubarb.

SORREL

Season of harvest: March to October

Variety	Character	Sow/Plant	Spacing (cm)
	Special Care	First ready	Height (cm)
BROAD LEAVED	Large spinach-like leaves, high yield	Apr-May	30x30
	Remove flowering stems	Feb/Mar	30
BUCKLER LEAVED	Small round leaves, extra flavour	Apr-May	30x30
	Remove flowering stems	Mar/Apr	20
BLOOD VEINED	Medium leaves with deep red veins	Apr-May	30x30
	Remove flowering stems	Mar/Apr	25

Sorrel is a herb, but I include it here because of its versatility and many uses. The table is an indication of the range of sorrels available; all kinds have a refreshing, zesty, acidic, lemon-like flavour, which in tiny quantities enlivens sandwiches and spring salads. Larger leaves are excellent in soups and omelettes, an exciting green addition to winter-jaded palates.

Varieties

Of the three types in the table, Buckler Leaved is best for salad use, for the smallness of its leaves and an extra amount of flavour. It is also generally esteemed for use in cream of sorrel soup. Broad Leaved is most suitable for general cooking, partly because its larger leaves are easier and quicker to pick. Blood veined is similar but with a flatter growth habit, and of striking appearance.

Sowing / planting

Buying plants is an option, but growth from seed is fast and successful. Sow into 3cm modules in early spring in a greenhouse or mid spring outdoors, for planting out by late spring. Two or three plants per module or small pot is feasible, or one plant for larger leaves.

Growing

Some leaves will be ready to gather by mid summer; thereafter, just keep picking. Growth diminishes in autumn; remove all decaying leaves in winter to reduce slug numbers ahead of new tender leaves from February onwards, when it is mild.

Harvesting

Early spring growth is best gathered leaf by leaf, to preserve small growing leaves at the centre of each plant. Later in spring, handfuls of leaves can be cut with a knife, about 3-5cm (1-2") above soil level, and used in many fantastic dishes. Flower stems need to be cut or pulled out when they appear – from May until early autumn.

Problems

Sorrel is of the *Rumex* family, as are docks, and both succumb to frequent attack by small shiny green beetles from mid spring onwards. If these beetles frequent your locality, sorrel may become almost impossible to grow as leaves will be shredded with innumerable holes. Buckler Leaved resists a little better than the other kinds.

Slugs also enjoy sorrel, but should make odd holes rather than devouring all growth. A night patrol with torch may be needed.

Dry weather makes sorrel suffer and even die, so some watering is beneficial in dry summers.

Chapter 17

Herbs and Edible Flowers

Discovering extra dimensions of taste and colour

HERBS

Once you succeed at growing your own vegetables, and then eat them fresh from the garden, your plate will fill with deeply intense flavours in need of little enhancement. You will probably find less need to use seasonings and strong-flavoured additions in cooking.

And yet there are other stimulating tastes in small herb leaves, and vibrant colours in a few flower petals. They inspire the eye, surprise the palate, and make gardening, cooking and eating even more interesting.

Many herbs grow well in containers, sometimes better than in soil where they may grow too rampantly and with less flavour. Containers can be close to the kitchen, and are also good for coping with the spreading roots of mint, the seeding habit of fennel, and for helping keep the roots of French tarragon dry in winter.

Propagating herbs

It is quick and simple to buy plants at a nursery or store, but beware the problem of rapidly grown, fine-looking but 'soft' plants which may struggle in a normal outdoor environment. I found this twice with bought thyme, which died in winter, so then I grew some from seed and it has survived well.

Growing herbs from seed takes longer and may be tricky without a greenhouse, but the results are impressive. Sow into 3cm modules in spring, thin to one seedling per module, pot into small pots after four to six weeks, and plant out two to three months after sowing. Buying a seed packet for each herb is still cheaper than buying plants, and you can have the pleasure of giving spare plants to friends or charity events.

Some herbs are easily raised from plant division, using a sharp spade or trowel to cut into a mature plant, to remove a piece of root and stem from its side. Do this at any time except summer, bedding the off-cut in a pot of moist compost until growing strongly.

Growing

Read carefully the notes on each herb, explaining their relative performance in soil or containers. Differences in vigour make it impractical to grow certain kinds together: sage or lemon balm would smother chives, for example.

I have categorised each herb into four grades, according to its strength of growth, to help you decide where to grow each one, and with what. Grouping them can save time – watering is easier if some are together in a large container, rather than having small individual pots. If growing in a border, the least vigorous herbs will require some bare, clean soil and full sunlight to grow well. Keep plants of the same category together.

CATEGORISATION OF HERBS USED IN THE TABLES

A: Compact annuals which require good soil or compost and regular moisture.

B: Reasonably hardy plants, still needing moist soil or compost, benefiting from room to grow

C: Strong growing perennials which need more space and can grow large. Poor soil suits them.

D: Rampant vigour, best grown on their own and poor soil again is alright.

BASIL (Annual A)

Season of harvest: June-September, best leaves in greenhouse / polytunnel / full sun

Variety	Character	Sow	Spacing (cm)
	Special care	First ready	Height (cm)
GREEK	Small leaves, slow to flower	Mar-May indoors	25x25
	Pick/cut around edges, best indoors	Jun-Jul	25
LEMON	Deeply scented leaves	Mar-May indoors	25x25
	Pick regularly, remove flower stems	Jun-Jul	35
RED	Deeply coloured leaves	Mar-May indoors	25x25
	As for Lemon	Jun-Jul	35
SWEET	Often used for pesto	Mar-May indoors	25x25
GENOVESE	As for Lemon	Jun-Jul	35

I have talked about basil in Chapter 9 (page 62) as an ingredient of summer salad. There is a wide range of flavours to experiment with, for a June to September season of harvest. It is difficult to lengthen this, even in a greenhouse, because basil fades rapidly in poor light and cool nights. Some basils can be overwintered but will grow very little, and it may not be worth the effort since basil flavour is most complementary to summer leaves and vegetables.

Sow and grow in warmth: April or May sowings are early enough. Be careful not to over-water young seedlings, especially in dull weather, and to plant out in full sun or in a greenhouse/conservatory. Pick off larger leaves as needed and all ends of flowering stems as soon as they appear, to encourage more leafy growth.

CHERVIL (Annual A)

Season of harvest: March-June

Variety	Character	Sow	Spacing (cm)
	Special care	First ready	Height (cm)
CURLED CHERVIL	Rich aniseed flavour, hardy	Sep/Mar-Apr	20x20
	Keep moist at all times, grows in shade	Mar	25

Chervil has a particular season – the spring – when it yields some rich, spicy leaves. It is not easy to have leaves at other times because it likes damp soil and is encouraged by light and heat to flower. Autumn chervil may succeed in moist, shady spots.

Because it has some frost hardiness, an early autumn sowing in the greenhouse is possible, with new leaves to harvest throughout a mild winter. Outdoor chervil can be fleeced to encourage extra leaves before flowering stems appear in late spring. Late spring and summer sowings will yield few leaves, except in cool, damp weather.

Regular picking of larger bottom leaves, as with parsley, is good for keeping plants in full production.

CHIVES (Perennial B)

Season of harvest: March-June and autumn

Variety	Character	Sow	Spacing (cm)
	Special care	First ready	Height (cm)
USUALLY UNSPECIFIED	Vigorous, long-lasting, early	Mar/Apr	30x30
	Keep moist, remove dead flowers	Mar	40

Chives can be sown in spring or raised from a divided clump, since chive plants become larger every year. Leaves are like thin and pungent spring onions, and can sometimes be picked in late winter, usually by cutting a small bunch – not the whole clump.

Towards mid spring some flower stems will appear, blossoming into purple pom-poms whose florets make a tasty and pretty garnish: break a flower head apart to reveal its numerous mini-flowers. Leaf production diminishes by summer, unless the roots are kept constantly moist.

After flowering it is worth dead-heading before seeds set and scatter everywhere.

CORIANDER (Annual A)

Season of harvest: May-October

Variety	Character	Sow First ready	Spacing (cm) Height (cm)
CORIANDER (no name)	Large pungent leaves, seeds later	Mar-Jul May/Jun	25x25 50
CONFETTI	Fine serrated leaves, slow to seed	Mar-Jul May/Jun	25x25 30
LEMON CORIANDER	Citrus flavour to leaves	Mar-Jul May/Jun	25x25 50

For leaves Coriander is easy to grow and tolerates frost, but often flowers before many leaves have been harvested, even from varieties which are bred for leaves rather than seeds. Late summer sowings in the greenhouse should overwinter indoors and provide leaves until May; otherwise sow late winter for planting out in early spring.

Leaves suddenly become soft and feathery when a flower stem appears; removing it can prolong leafiness for a while.

For seed The delicate white flowers are ornamental and edible, turning into clusters of small seeds which, when properly dry and brown at the end of summer, can be used as tasty condiment in a pepper mill. I pull up whole plants and hang them in an airy outbuilding until there is time to rub out the seeds. Leafy debris amongst the seeds can be gently blown off.

For coriander in winter, sow in about mid September in 3cm modules or small pots in a greenhouse. Pot-on or plant under cover and harvest occasional leaves when mild spells encourage new growth. Plants may not survive below about -4°C.

DANDELION

Red Ribbed Dandelion (actually of the chicory family) is intriguing, with fleshy leaves similar to some strains of chicory, and a slightly less bitter flavour.

Normal sowing date is springtime, but early autumn is possible, as frost does not kill the roots. Leaves will be less abundant in hot weather, but should be plentiful again in autumn.

DILL (Annual A)

(See also Chapter 9, page 63)

Season of harvest: May-October

Variety	Character	Sow	Spacing (cm)
	Special care	*First ready*	*Height (cm)*
DILL (NO NAME)	Large leaves then flowers	Mar-Jul	20x20
	Keep moist and picked	May	60
BOUQUET	Smaller plant, finer leaves	Mar-Jul	15x15
	Suitable for containers	May	30

Dill for leaves grows best in spring and early summer, whereas it is more inclined to make flower and seed from sowings in June or later. The leaves have a wonderfully sweet and refreshing taste, suitable for flavouring many salads and soups. Normally they have long spindly stems, although Bouquet is more compact and feathery, suitable for growing in restricted spaces.

If seed-heads are left to become brown and dry at the end of summer, cut the stem and shake out seed over newspaper. They can be sown again, used as condiment in a pepper grinder, or added to stews and soups.

FENNEL, COMMON (Perennial C)

Season of harvest: April-October

Variety	Character	Sow	Spacing (cm)
	Special care	*First ready*	*Height (cm)*
COMMON	Vigorous, use leaves and seeds	Mar-Jul	30x30
	Do not allow seeds to spread	Apr	60
BRONZE	Similar but dark bronze leaves	Mar-Jul	30x30
	Do not allow seeds to spread	Apr	60

Be careful here. Unlike Sweet Florence fennel (also called bulb fennel), this perennial is hardy and persistent, and may be invasive if allowed to seed, so I advise careful harvest of the seeds for cooking. They have an aniseed flavour, similar to but stronger than dill, while the leaves are milder and often used in fish dishes.

Sow in spring, and then by summer's end flower stems may be 150cm high. Two colours are available: green and bronze. Both will make large plants that may smother or diminish smaller neighbours, so this fennel is perhaps unsuitable for small gardens.

GARLIC CHIVES (Perennial B)

See chives for details of sowing and growing; named varieties are not usually offered. Growth is similar but leaves are flat and with a pronounced garlic flavour. Clusters of white flowers in August are a bonus, and edible, but beware the vigorous seedlings if seeds are allowed to drop – they can be invasive.

MINT (Perennial D)

Season of harvest: April-October

Variety	Character	Sow	Spacing (cm)
	Special care	*First ready*	*Height (cm)*
APPLE MINT	Large fleshy leaves	Mar-May	30x30
	Grow in contained soil/compost	Apr/May	30
PEPPERMINT	The most common mint	Mar-May	30x30
		Apr/May	30
SPEARMINT	Less pungent than peppermint	Mar-May	30x30
		Apr/May	30

A garden without mint is hard to imagine, yet mint is powerfully invasive, through roots that spread rapidly in all directions. Hence the advice to grow it in pots or containers, with regular watering for its mass of new leaves.

There is a whole world of mint flavours and leaf sizes, from chocolate mint to apple mint to tiny Moroccan mint. Traditional mint, most commonly offered for sale as plants, is spearmint (from its pointed leaves) or peppermint.

Mint is not often sown because it is so easily increased by digging up and potting-on some roots from established plants. New plants can be set out at any time of year, and need watering in dry weather.

By late spring small flower stems appear and leaf production diminishes. Before or after flowering, removing seed heads will encourage some more leaves.

PARCEL (Biennial B)

Parcel grows and looks like parsley and delivers a powerful celery flavour, so it is a useful condiment for soups, lasagne and stews. Grow as for parsley below.

PARSLEY (Biennial B)

Season of harvest: May-November and April-May from same plants

Variety	Character	Sow	Spacing (cm)
	Special care	*First ready*	*Height (cm)*
MOSS CURLED	Densely curled bright green, hardy	Mar-Jul	15x15
	Pick and water regularly	Late May	20
PLAIN LEAVED	Longer stems, faster growing	Mar-Jul	15x15
	Pick and water regularly and remove flowers	Early May	25

Sow in early spring for vitamin-rich leaves all summer. See Chapter 9 (page 64) for extra details. Note that curled parsley produces leaves for longer than flat parsley, which is inclined to flower before season's end, so will require a second sowing in June or July.

PURSLANE (Annual A)

Season of harvest: June-September and March-April

Variety	Character	Sow	Spacing (cm)
	Special care	*First ready*	*Height (cm)*
GREEN PURSLANE	Glowing yellow leaves	May-Jul	7x25
	Tolerates drought, check for flowers	Jun	25
GOLDEN PURSLANE	Many harvests	May-Jul	7x25
	Tolerates drought, check for flowers	Jun	25
WINTER PURSLANE	Hardy plant, tender leaves	Sep-Oct	7x25 or 20x20
(Claytonia)	Survives frost, vigorous in late winter	Feb/Mar	25

Purslane is as much a leaf as a herb, so unusual that it belongs here as well as under leaves (see Chapters 9 & 10), with succulent leaves to add a pleasant bite and notable flavour to salads. Green Purslane lasts longer than Golden Purslane in summer, and its longer stems make picking easier, while Winter Purslane is immensely hardy and brings another dimension to late winter salad.

Summer purslane has an unusual, almost invisible way of flowering and seeding, through small, angular pods that are almost hidden at the ends of its stems. These pods have a bitter flavour and will quickly set and scatter seed, so it is best to look on summer purslane as a quick catch crop, to be cleared between about eight and twelve weeks after sowing, for golden and green purslane respectively.

It is a heat-loving plant, best sown between mid May and late July, and does well in dry conditions. Three or four weeks after sowing, pick off the small rosettes at the end of all stems, then keep picking off new rosettes which grow out of those stems until there are only flowering stems left.

Winter purslane is extremely hardy, excellent in winter salads, and unlike its summer cousin has attractive white flowers on long white stems, nice to eat and slower to set seed.

ROSEMARY (Perennial C)

Rosemary is rarely raised from seed in small gardens, but it does grow well from a spring sowing, preferably in 3cm modules and then potted-on. By the second year you will have a large bush with aromatic, oily leaves and vivacious light blue flowers in early spring. Because it can grow rapidly, cut off most new growth after flowering and again in mid summer, especially in wet seasons. If this is not done, a lot of dry, dead wood will accumulate around the plant's middle and its outer edges will tend to smother other plants.

SAGE (Perennial C)

Like rosemary, rarely grown from seed, but follow the same procedure if you wish to. Sage also profits from hard pruning, mainly in late spring after a vivid blue flowering. *Salvia officinalis* is normal 'herb' sage, but many types of salvia have a hint of sage to their leaves and purple sage is a fine combination of beauty and flavour. By the age of four or five years, plants become woody and bare at their base, so can be worth replacing with young ones.

Tangerine sage is another member of the extended family but is unlikely to survive a British winter. It small scarlet flowers, for a long part of summer and autumn, are both attractive and tasty, with a fine small droplet of sweet nectar in their base.

SORREL (Perennial C)

See Chapter 10 (page 75) and also Chapter 16 (pages 174-5) for details of the different kinds of mouth-filling flavour which sorrel provides.

TARRAGON, FRENCH (Perennial D)

Seed catalogues offer only Russian Tarragon, because French Tarragon cannot be raised from seed and must be propagated by separating and re-potting some root off an existing plant. This can be done in autumn or spring. The two kinds have quite different flavours; French is considered more interesting. Both kinds are vigorous, needing about 60cm of space around them and growing to 90cm when they flower. French tarragon does not tolerate wet soil in winter, thriving best in free-draining soil or even a large pot of three-quarters sand and one quarter compost. Cut all growth to soil level every winter; summer pruning may also be needed to keep it tidy.

THYME (Perennial B)

Season of harvest: Mainly March-October

Variety	Character	Sow	Spacing (cm)
	Special care	*First ready*	*Height (cm)*
COMMON THYME	Tiny fragrant leaves, pretty flowers	Apr	30x30
	Cut back in winter, good in pots	Almost year-round	15
LEMON/ORANGE THYME	Citrus aromas to leaves and flowers	Apr	30x30
	Cut back in winter, good in pots	Almost year-round	15
CREEPING THYME	Larger leaves, hugs the ground	Apr	30x30
	Good for covering paths	Almost year round	5

One of the smallest perennial herbs, and most suited to dry conditions, which promote longer life and intense flavour in its tiny leaves. A tendency to grow long and straggly makes it worthwhile to prune in both summer and winter. Thyme can be fragile and die unexpectedly, but new plants may appear from its seeding and it is worth sowing thyme every three or four years, to have younger, bushy plants.

The chart above gives an idea of some thymes of different flavours and habits. A liking for dry soil makes them suitable for growing in pots, which need only occasional watering in summer.

EDIBLE FLOWERS

Many flowers are edible, more than are commonly used. Even if not eaten, their presence on a plate of salad leaves or cooked food says 'This meal is special'. Here are a few suggestions.

BORAGE flowers, bright blue, are good with salad or to brighten up summer drinks.

CHARD makes tiny flowers on a long stem. Both are pretty and edible, and bitter in flavour.

CHIVE flowers can be broken into small florets of delicate mauve, with a taste of onion.

COURGETTE / SQUASH flowers are usually cooked as a dish in their own right. The classic recipe involves dipping them in batter and then frying. Courgettes in particular will produce flowers all season long; both male (on stems) and female (on fruits) are edible.

DILL flowers, very pale yellow, can be eaten as clusters of small buds.

MARJORAM is covered with pale mauve flowers at the end of summer, attractive to many insects and with a herby taste that adds zest to certain dishes. Sweet marjoram's leaves give oregano flavour.

MIZUNA flowers readily in early summer on succulent stems, which are delicious as long as the stems are tender. See Oriental Vegetables, pages 69-61.

NASTURTIUM flowers of all colours have a strong flavour and bring a vivid lure to table as well. Empress of India is a useful variety, for deep red flowers and dark magenta leaves, all edible.

ORIENTAL VEGETABLES all flower readily, although you may not have wanted them to. They are mostly pale yellow on tender stems and mild in flavour. Purple Choy Sum is grown mostly for its flowering stems, which bring a hint of blue to the salad bowl.

PEA flowers in late spring are an early taste of summer, recognisably 'pea' in taste.

ROCKET flowers are white on salad rocket and yellow on wild rocket. Look closely at the petals to admire some intricate patterns. Their flavour is as spicy and interesting as rocket leaves.

TANGERINE SAGE – see above under sage.

Chapter 18

Tree Fruit

The Garden of Eden at Home

An apricot off your own tree, plums with their delicate bloom, small and large cherries, green and red apples all of different flavour – even small gardens can be home to many of these.

I assure you that home-grown fruit, picked ripe and sweet, tastes outrageously, mouth-wateringly wonderful. But it is not always easy to grow, so read the small print carefully. Then the first successful harvest will have you hooked, and determined to try more.

I have suffered as many failures as I have enjoyed successes with organic fruit, which gives me the experience to offer advice on what really works, and where difficulties may arise.

Think out before plant out

The long-term nature of fruit growing invites careful consideration of what to plant where, with a balancing of desire and practicality. For example, it is possible to grow peaches in most of Britain, but the disease risks are high and may outweigh any good harvests.

Fruit trees are in the same place for a long time, encouraging some build-up of tricky pests, disease and weeds. Good gardening can overcome many of these potential problems, and reduce the rest to a manageable level.

I urge you, if new to fruit, to read the whole of this chapter in order to gain a feel for what is achievable in relation to your garden and your lifestyle. Then you can peruse a catalogue of fruit trees and bushes, or visit a nursery, with much better understanding of what is worth buying and planting. Often it will be rather less than is claimed by the sellers, and a bit of knowledge will save you much time and money.

As an example, consider the season of harvest by imagining when fruit would be of most value to you, or might go to waste. Most plums and gages are ripe in August, when you might be on holiday. Apple varieties ripen at different times: some apples go soft by the end of summer while some can be stored into the following spring, when all fruit is at a premium.

Maximising available space

Size of garden may be a crucial factor. If trees are too crowded, fruit will not set or ripen well. Consider the space-saving options of dwarfing root-stocks, and of growing trees against walls or in containers.

Rootstocks

Most fruiting trees are grafted onto roots of different trees, called root-stocks, whose vigour is usually less than the main tree. Without rootstocks there would be little chance of growing tree fruit in a small garden, and waiting times for fruit after planting would be much longer.

Apples have the most options, and their most dwarfing M27 or M9 rootstocks are suitable for most gardens, often giving apples in the second summer after planting, and rarely growing more than about 3m (10') high or wide. For cherries, Gisela 5 rootstock makes it possible to have a small tree with plenty of fruit which can be netted.

The best approach is to check what rootstock is offered, together with the expected size of its tree. All fruit tree labels or catalogue descriptions should contain this information.

Planting

Planting season for bare-rooted fruit trees is November to May, and the earlier the better. Even in winter, roots can be settling in and drainage water will be packing soil all around them. March and April plantings are more likely to need watering in a dry spring, as will container-grown trees, especially as they can be planted at any time of year, even in summer.

Note that small trees are easier to plant, and establish more rapidly than large trees.

As long as your soil is reasonably dark and crumbly, simply dig a hole a little larger than the rootball, drop it in and firm soil around the roots as you back-fill. A large hole with some added compost is worthwhile for pale clay or ex-building sites, but not fresh manure, which might encourage rapid but less healthy growth.

Damaged roots can be trimmed back with secateurs and thick root-balls of container grown trees can be unwrapped a little so that some roots are free of tangle and ready to grow outwards. Some suppliers offer small containers of mycorrhizae for adding to soil around tree roots, and these will almost certainly enhance growth significantly, depending on your soil's health.

Staking is often necessary, especially for dwarfing rootstocks; again, check instructions supplied with each tree.

Weeding and watering

Keep soil around small trees clear of weeds and grass, so that they are not deprived of moisture and nutrients. A 50cm annual dressing of compost will benefit them, and some water in dry summers can make quite a difference to the size of harvest on dwarf-rootstock trees.

Shaping trees

All trees can be trained to whatever shape and pattern fits best into any garden, always provided the vigour of the rootstock matches the desired size and shape. For example, cordons and espalier apple trees require M9, M26 or MM106 in order of increasing vigour and size of the tree. Any variety can be chosen on these rootstocks. Specialist fruit books go into the details, but common sense is often enough to suggest how to train branches against a wall or along a fence, by tying in or wiring up those growing in the right direction and cutting off ones that are not. All nurseries listed in Resources will offer sound advice, often through their web pages.

Patience is vital, since best results often come from planting small 'maidens' that are simply 1-2m stems, out of whose buds will grow twigs that become branches. A maiden has short, easily transplanted roots and adapts more quickly to a new site than a larger tree, with less risk of drying out in the first summer – and small trees cost less.

Pruning

Q. Why prune, when trees and bushes produce without it?
A. To have better-sized, nicely coloured, easier to pick, more frequent and top quality fruit, through judicious cuts, which stimulate trees into making new and healthy growth.

I used to hate pruning, feeling it an unnatural thing to do. But I have had enough harvests of small, diseased or difficult-to-harvest fruit to make me appreciate the wisdom of cutting out wood or stems at certain times of year. Thinning excess young fruit is another worthwhile little job in the same vein.

APPLES

Apples are well suited to Britain's mild and damp climate, and with cold enough winters to 'vernalise' apple trees and make them flower every spring. Their blossom is a joy in its own right: clusters of pink and white every May, which according to weather and insects will become mature fruit between late August and mid October, depending on region and variety.

They have the largest section of this chapter because they are the easiest and most reliable fruit to grow in most of Britain, with the greatest choice of flavours and culinary possibilities.

Rootstocks

Apples are always propagated from cuttings that are grafted onto rootstocks of varied vigour. This is because self-sown apples do not grow 'true to variety', take a few years to start cropping, and grow much larger than most of us want.

Check carefully which rootstock you are buying: it is as important as the tree variety, and it should always be stated. Note that M9, probably the best choice for small gardens, has weak and brittle roots. A permanent stake or support will therefore lengthen the life of its tree and enable it to fruit better. More vigorous rootstocks can grow without stakes after two or three years of establishing themselves.

The table below outlines some possible tree sizes and planting distances for different rootstocks, for how long they need staking, the number of years after planting a maiden when fruiting begins, and how much fruit a mature tree might yield.

Name	Average height	Spread (metres) Staking	Planting distance (m) Top yield (kg)	First fruit (yrs)
M27	1.5	1.5 Always	1.2x1.8 4-8	2
M9	2.1	2.7 Always	2.5x3.5 8-14	2/3
M26	2.7	3.6 5 yrs	3.0x4.5 12-25	2/3
MM106	3.5	4.0 5yrs	3.6x4.5 16-40	3/4
MM111	4.2	4.5 3yrs	4.5x6.0 25-70	4/5
M25	5.0	6.0 -	6.0x7.5 30-80	5/6

Pollination

Most apple trees fruit best when other varieties are flowering nearby, so that insects 'cross-pollinate' and help fruit to set. Fortunately most varieties flower at about the same time, so as long as you have two or three different ones, there should be no problem. Bramley and Winston are two of a few self-fertile varieties, setting plenty of fruit without other pollen nearby.

EATING APPLES

Choose a good variety for your location, and keep improving your soil after planting with some good compost on the surface or, perhaps best of all, some well-rotted horse manure. By the second autumn, if you have trees on M9 or M27 rootstocks, there will be really good apples to savour. And I mean savour, because I rarely manage to buy apples with a depth of flavour and quality of flesh to compare with my own.

The chart is to help you decide which varieties are most suitable for your garden. It includes varieties that I have succeeded with organically, and which have been recommended to me.

Scab is the worst enemy of eaters because its dark and sometimes large, indented spots can really spoil the appearance of an otherwise good fruit. The chart column headed 'disease resistance' refers mostly to scab, and in areas of high rainfall it is important to plant varieties with good resistance to it. I have not included Cox's Orange Pippin because it is more susceptible to disease than other varieties listed.

Variety	Origin (c.)	Character	
	Disease resistance	Harvest	Keeps until
ASHMEADS KERNEL	1700	Crisp russet, acid, excellent keeper	
	Medium	Oct	Jan/Feb
BLENHEIM ORANGE	1840	Large, slightly conical & russeted, mellow	
	Medium	Late Sep/Oct	Dec, soft by Nov
BRAEBURN HILENA	2000	Crisp, thick skin, keeps well, needs warmth	
	Low	Oct	Jan/Feb
CEVAAL	2000	Like Cox, small red/yellow	
	Good	Sep	Nov
DEVON CRISP	1990	Shiny red early, keeps briefly	
	Good	Aug	Sep
DISCOVERY	1950	Bright red, crisp white flesh, very early	
	Med-Good	Aug	early Sep
EGREMONT RUSSET	1870	Small golden-brown russet, top flavour	
	Med	Sep	Dec
ELLISONS ORANGE	1900	Shiny red/yellow, spicy flavour, vigorous	
	Med	Sep	Oct/Nov
FORTUNE (LAXTONS)	1900	Red, fine flavour & acidity, smallish tree	
	Med	Sep	Dec
HEREFORDSHIRE RUSSET	2003	Small golden russet	
	Good	Sep	Dec
KIDDS ORANGE RED	1920	Small, red, rich flavour, sweet/acid balance	
	Med	Late Sep/Oct	Dec/Jan
LORD LAMBOURNE	1910	Red stripes, steady cropper, smallish tree	
	Med	Sep	Nov

Variety	Origin (c.)	Character	
	Disease resistance	Harvest	Keeps until
PINOVA	2000	Fine flavour, small red/yellow fruit	
	Good	Sep	Dec
RAJKA	1980	Medium red/yellow fruits	
	Med-Good	Oct	Dec
RED FALSTAFF	1965	Fine flavour, high yield, reliable	
	Good	Oct	Jan
SATURN	1980	Large conical, green/red fruit	
	Good	Oct	Dec
SPARTAN	1930	Medium size, crimson skin, white flesh	
	Med-Good	Oct	Jan
SUNSET	1920	Like Cox, heavy cropper, acid then soft	
	Good	Sep	Nov
WINSTON	1920	Small, mostly green/yellow, self-fertile	
	Low-Med	Oct	Feb/Mar

Eaters are sweet to eat, when in season and properly ripe. Each variety has an average maturity date, for example August-September for Discovery, October-November for Sunset and November-January for Kidds Orange. To have apples after that is not so easy, whatever the description may say, because fruits often shrivel a little and, in my experience, ripen earlier than they are meant to. See cooking apples for late eaters.

COOKING APPLES

Variety	Origin	Character	
	Disease resistance	Harvest	Keeps Until
BOUNTIFUL	1960	Heavy cropping, large early cookers & eaters	
	Good	Sep	Dec
BRAMLEY	1820	Large flat deep green fruit, reliable cropper	
	Med-Good	Oct	Mar
EDWARD VII	1900	Late flowering, large round green/red fruit	
	Med	Oct	Mar
NEWTON WONDER	1850	Large green/red fruit, reliable cropper	
	Med-Good	Oct	Mar
REV W WILKS	1900	Early cropping, large yellow fruit, low acidity	
	Med-Good	Late Aug/Sep	Oct

Cooking apples have higher acidity than eaters and are often easier to grow because of better disease resistance. They also crop more heavily.

The classic cooking variety is Bramley, and it deserves its reputation, succeeding both as small trees and as large old ones, which continue to drop vast amounts of dark green apples every year. If picked and stored, they turn more yellow in late winter and can become just sweet enough to eat, if still acidic. Newton Wonder is better as a dual-purpose apple, good to eat in February and March.

Bountiful, an exciting relatively new variety, makes a good companion to Bramley, being ready earlier and becoming edible by November as it ripens. It stays crisper than many eating apples and is often large, especially when thinned out on the tree in summer.

CIDER APPLES

These are more tannic, indicated by how they dry the mouth out, after a briefly pleasing sweetness. Note that eaters and cookers can also be fermented into ciders of contrasting flavours.

CRAB APPLES

Crab apples are small, acidic and tannic, almost inedible but rich in flavour for making jelly. They are also highly ornamental, for blossom and fruit: Golden Hornet has clusters of small bright yellow fruit that stay on the tree until December, and John Downie bears larger red crab apples. Other varieties are available (see Resources, pages 217-8).

Pruning apples

Pruning is more an art than a science because few people agree on all the details. I aim to keep it simple and advise you to think in winter of removing about one third of last season's growth, either by cutting off whole branches or by shortening them. The aim is to have:

- a well spaced framework of main branches
- some fruiting spurs – knobbly protrusions or short twigs
- enough other branches to make leaves for nourishment of present fruit, without shading it too much.

Pruning is mostly done in winter when leaves are absent. If overdone, the tree may make vigorous new stemmy growth in the following season, somewhat at the expense of fruit. Summer pruning, in addition to winter pruning, can spread the load and help in restricting or re-directing growth, without trees making excessive new growth to compensate. Usually it is done from about mid July to early August, and involves shortening new stems by a half or more, especially on trees of special shape. Also remove any leaves which overhang fruit so that sun can ripen its skin to deeper red colours.

Thinning fruit

In years of plentiful fruit, some will fall in June and July (the 'June drop'), but enough may still remain on the tree that apples are too cramped to grow large. I usually cut or carefully twist off one apple of every remaining pair, or two out of every three, as long as I can reach them, by about the middle of July. Larger fruit are then possible, and the tree is spared from supporting a huge harvest, making it more likely to fruit well the following year.

Harvesting

If apples fall they bruise and will eventually rot, so it is important to pick them before they are so ripe as to fall in an autumn gale (cider apples excepted). They mostly need picking before full ripeness is achieved, between mid August and mid October, depending on variety and region. Eaters usually taste both sweet and acidic at picking time, while cookers are mostly firm and green.

Handle apples carefully, laying them out in boxes or trays, preferably store them in a cool but frost-free place, and check to see when they ripen – shown by yellowing of the skin, with their flesh becoming softer and sweeter. Or eat them earlier if you prefer crunchy fruit with more 'bite'.

Problems

Non-organic apple growers and gardeners use a range of toxic sprays, mostly fungicides and some pesticides that contain organophosphates. Your home-grown fruit will be clear of all these poisons but may not avoid the codling moth's maggots, aphid damage to young leaves, or black scab fungal patches on leaves and fruit.

Growing resistant varieties is a good start – for instance, Sunset rather than Cox, which is unfortunately difficult to grow organically. Use the chart to find varieties with good resistance. Correct planting distances and good pruning help to keep air and light around the leaves. Healthy, well-drained soil with some compost or manure, but not over-manured, also helps.

Much depends on how much time and money you want to invest in achieving blemish-free fruit. Codling moth traps hung in trees from May to July, and grease or glue-bands for the trunk from late September are two effective solutions, as long as you remember to apply them at the right times.

The bottom line is that many organic apples are less fine in appearance than chemically grown ones, but are clean of invisible residues – and so is the trees' environment. The choice is ours.

Apple crumble

Our favourite crumble topping is:
100g butter
80g wholemeal flour
50g muscovado sugar
80g porridge oats
1 apple per person

This serves 4-6; I usually double it for Sunday lunch when we have visitors. Peel, core and slice apples. Butter a large shallow dish. Arrange apples and sprinkle with cinnamon or nutmeg. Add a couple of tablespoons of apple juice or water. Rub the butter into the flour, then add the sugar and oats. Sprinkle over the apples and bake in a hot oven c.180°C for 20-25 mins.

APRICOTS

VARIETY	Character e.g Rootstock	Years to fruit Harvest	Height (m) Spread (m)
FLAVORCOT	Large orange fruits Torinel	2/3 mid Aug	3.0-3.5 3.5
LARQUEN	Large orange fruits Torinel	4/5 mid Aug	3.0-3.5 3.5
DOUCOUER	Med, early orange fruits St Julien A	4/5 late Jul	3.5-4.5 4.5

Note that apricot varieties, and many other fruit trees, have named rather than numbered rootstocks. In order of size they are Pixy, Torinel and St. Julien A.

Varieties

There have been amazing breakthroughs in apricot breeding, such that varieties now exist for planting in open ground as far north as Hadrian's Wall (Tomcot). But a sheltered, sunny aspect is nonetheless always recommended!

Apricot trees are vigorous, even in Britain, so where space is limited try Goldcott for a free-standing tree of about 4m, or much less if fan-trained to a wall (see below). Or look for a tree on Pixy rootstock.

Some of the new varieties, such as Flavorcot and Larquen, bear large fruit almost the size of peaches. I harvested fifteen large apricots in Flavorcot's second summer (on rootstock Torinel), planted as a maiden the previous spring. It flowered in early April, later than usual after a cold winter, which just avoided a late frost.

Apricots are one of the first fruit trees to blossom in March or April, and most problems arise from either frost on the flowers or lack of insects for pollination. Tickling flowers lightly with a soft brush may be necessary.

Planting

Because spring frost does more harm to the blossom than cool winds, be sure not to plant in a frost pocket. Even some south-facing walls can be treacherous because their warmth encourages early blossom, but may not keep ice off flowers if the wall is at the bottom end of sloping ground.

Growing

Torinel and St Julien A rootstocks are quite vigorous, and more suitable for an open orchard area than a confined wall space. Little pruning is recommended or necessary, mostly to remove any crossing or obstructing branches, and is best done in late spring. Fan training against a wall is possible, but will require summer pruning to keep growth in check.

Harvesting

Fruits look well coloured and ripe for at least a fortnight before they are soft and sweet. A gentle squeeze every now and then will reveal the gradual change to juicy flesh. When ripe they should come off readily in your hand – a moment to really savour!

CHERRIES

VARIETY	Character Spread (m)	e.g. Rootstock Years to fruit	Height (m) Harvest
SUMMER SUN	Excellent for British weather 3.0-3.5	Gisela 5 3/4	2.5-3.0 Late Jul
STELLA	Excellent for British weather 3.0-3.5	Gisela 5 3/4	2.5-3.0 Late Jul
STARK GOLD	Large yellow fruit 3.0-3.5	Gisela 5 3/4	2.5-3.0 Late Jul
CROWN MORELLO	Cooking cherry for cold spots 4.0-5.5	Colt 3/5	3.0-4.0 Aug

The RHS have excellent information on making the most of dwarf cherries (see Resources). For the keen amateur fruit grower, these are an exciting prospect.

Look out for trees on Gisela 5 rootstock, which is becoming common as it proves its ability to keep growth manageable, whilst allowing a plentiful harvest. Smaller trees also mean that small gardens can accommodate one or more trees, preferably in full sun, except for Morello, which is often grown against north-facing walls.

Pruning

Cherries are susceptible to silverleaf and canker, so do not prune them in winter: the best times are after flowering in April and after fruiting in August. Exact pruning details depend on whether you are growing a bush tree or fan training in the open or against a wall. In essence, April pruning is to shorten abundant new stems and allow new branches to develop. August pruning aims to remove crossing branches or large branches whose fruiting value is diminishing.

Harvesting

Cherries swell rapidly in their final fortnight and in wet summers they may split – while still good to eat, they will not keep if this happens. Pick them with stalks attached if they are not for immediate eating, but their allure makes the passage to table a very tenuous one!

Problems

The scourge of cherries is **birds**. You will probably need to net or cover the tree or to use some other failsafe way of keeping birds off the fruit. Stark Gold's yellow fruit are sometimes less attractive to birds. Netting small trees on Gisela 5 rootstock is entirely feasible, because their full height and spread will be about 3m (10'), even without much pruning, although cropping will be better for it.

PEACHES AND NECTARINES

Variety	Character		Height
	Spread (m)	Years to fruit	Harvest
DIXIRED PEACH	Early fruiting, resists canker & leaf curl		2.5-5.0
	up to 5.0	2-4	Aug
REDWING PEACH	Dark red, late flowering, less leaf curl		2.5-5.0
	up to 4.0	2-4	Aug
JALOUSIA PEACH	Sweet, flat fruit		2.5-5.0
	4-5	2-4	Early Sep
FANTASIA NECTARINE	Reliable, yellow flesh		2.5-5.0
	4-5	2-4	Late Aug

Modern breeding has helped, but peaches and nectarines are still plagued by leaf curl, originating in excess moisture on their buds in winter and manifesting as curling, even shrivelling leaves through spring and early summer, sometimes to the point of trees dying. See below for remedies.

Varieties

The chart reveals some of the many possibilities – a variety with leaf curl resistance is definitely worthwhile. On the other hand, flat peaches such as Jalousia and Oriane have flavour that compensates for extra work in combating their susceptibility to disease.

Rootstocks

Two main choices are St. Julien A for more vigour, and Montclaire for less vigour.

Planting

If you have a wall or fence with a southerly orientation, this will be good for peach and nectarine. Fan training allows heavy yields, while less vigorous rootstocks such as Montclaire and Myrobolem can reduce vigour enough to make growth more manageable.

Pruning

Early spring is good for pruning – after flowering and before leaf emergence: being able to see the pretty white flowers helps conserve them from secateurs. For young trees, train larger stems into a fan shape behind wires on walls, shorten them by about a third and cut off all branches coming away from the wall. Also in summer, cut off all outward growing branches and clear leaves away from developing fruit. Thinning any clusters or pairs of fruit will help growth and ripening of the remainder.

Harvesting

Fruit may colour for a fortnight before ripening, which is revealed by touching to see when they start to soften up. You may even smell their fine fragrance, and tasting them is a notable experience.

Problems

Without chemical fungicides, there are still solutions to the dreaded **leaf curl**. Probably the safest and most reliable is to make a shelter of wood or plastic that protrudes from wall or fence above the tree to at least half a metre, sufficient to keep most rain off stems in winter. Another is to spray Bordeaux mixture (copper sulphate) on bare stems in February and March.

Drier parts of Britain are definitely most favoured; the wetter west and north carry more risk of problems. Leaf curl can strike rapidly: my Newhaven peach cropped well for three years without protection or spraying, then suddenly died the following July. This could happen to any unprotected peach and nectarine trees after a wet winter. So I have planted a pear instead.

PEARS

Variety	Character	Height (m)	Spread
	Approx. years to fruit	*Harvest*	
BEURRE HARDY	Round pear, resists scab	3.0-3.5	3.5
	3/4	Late Aug/Sep	
CONCORDE	Longish pear	3.0-3.5	3.5
	3/4	Late Sep/Oct	
CONFERENCE	Long, adapts to wet & cold	3.0-3.5	3.5
	3/4	Oct	
GOURMANDE	Round, succulent flesh	3.0-3.5	3.5
	3/4	Late Sep	

Varieties

With apples, a crop is almost certain, but not with pears. They are more prone to disease and to late frosts on their early blossom. Even when a crop is achieved and picked, they can go soft and become inedible for want of being checked regularly for ripeness.

Plant the variety of your choice in as frost-free a part of the garden as you can spare. I have tried many varieties and find Conference, the most readily available, to be one of the most reliable. Consistent yields of fruit ripen reasonably slowly, in mid autumn, without going soft too quickly. Another interesting variety, ripening slightly later with some resistance to scab is Beurre Hardy. Resistance to scab is especially important in wetter regions, while those in the drier south-east stand more chance of healthier crops.

Pollination and fruit set are generally improved by the presence of more than one variety. Concorde, although self-fertile itself (like Conference), is an especially good pollinator.

Rootstocks and Planting

There is much less variation in rootstock vigour for pears than for apples. Most pear trees are sold on the same rootstock, Quince A, which requires a spacing of about 3.5x4.5m. Staking is recommended for at least three years, more likely five. If on Quince C, trees can be planted a little closer together, will be about a metre shorter and may fruit a little earlier. Planting against a wall with some southerly aspect is good both for extra warmth and for the pruning disciplines imposed by training growth in two dimensions.

Pruning

Pears are keen growers and readily make long vertical stems that rise out of reach, especially after hard winter pruning, which should usually be less severe than for apples. Summer pruning is invaluable to cut back long new stems, to remove unwanted ones and, for example, to shape branches into a fan pattern against walls.

Harvesting

This can be tricky to judge as pears are best picked unripe – but not too unripe if you want good flavour. Move the bottom of a pear gently outwards in a circular motion: if its stem comes away from the tree, then picking time has arrived, but if it holds firm then wait another week or so before trying again. Pears are usually firm when picked– except for early varieties such as Williams – and need laying out to watch for yellowing and softening, sometimes over many weeks. Keeping them cool will slow ripening but may also stop them becoming tender, although they should still sweeten up.

Problems

Fungal scab on leaf and fruit is quite likely to infect your tree after a season or two. In wet regions it may be worth trying a variety such as Improved Fertility, as well as trusty old Conference.

Dorset window pudding

This is a very useful pudding topping that lends itself to many fruit – rhubarb, apples, plums. Fits in a 26cm flan dish.

250g pears, peeled, cored and sliced
50g butter, 50g soft muscovado sugar, 1 egg
75g wholemeal flour (25g ground almonds can be substituted for 25g flour)
1 teaspoon baking powder, 2 tablespoons milk

Butter the flan dish and lay the pear slices in a nice pattern. Cream together the butter & sugar, add the egg, flour and milk. If very stiff, add a little more milk. Spoon onto the pears. Bake at 180⁰C for about 20- 30 minutes.

PLUMS AND GAGES

Variety	Character	Harvest
CZAR	Early culinary / dessert purple plum	Late Jul
VICTORIA	Benefit from thinning	Late Aug
VALOR	Large late plum, magenta-yellow colour	Early Sep
REINE CLAUDE DOREE	Top flavour gage, some frost resistance	Late Aug
DAMSON MERRYWEATHER	Large juicy fruits	Early Sep

My observations on plums concern rootstock, above all. Nursery trees are grafted on to different roots, and I have compared various grafted plum trees over the years with some that I have grown from suckers, therefore growing on their own roots. I find that the latter have cropped better and grow more healthily, above all with no infection from silverleaf (see below).

However, they make more suckers themselves – annoying if they are close to some cultivated ground, which they also feed from. Also they grow large, up to 6m (20') high quite easily. Their shape is quite different to apple trees – more vertical and graceful.

For bought trees there are often two choices of rootstock: Pixy is the one for small gardens; otherwise the more traditional St Julien A makes a medium-sized tree. Greengages are more difficult than plums as they need extra sun and warmth, and crop a little less readily.

Varieties

The table above contains only a few of the most common varieties, so there is plenty of choice. Notice that you can have plums and gages for more than a month by combining early and late varieties. Thinning is really worthwhile if you want decent-sized fruit and can prevent boughs breaking with too many plums in good years. Smaller trees on Pixy rootstock are much easier to manage in this respect.

Planting

Note the different planting distances according to rootstock: 3x3.6m for Pixy and 3.5x4.5m for St Julien A. Staking is advised for at least three years, and five is better.

Harvesting

The first fruit to drop may have maggots inside, rather like early ripening apples with codling worm. Then from mature trees there can be an avalanche of fruit in seasons when late frosts have not damaged the blossom. Pick soft fruit off the tree or shake the trunk to make ripe ones fall, giving you some interesting opportunities for jam making and bottling.

Pruning

Most pruning consists of removing branches that are crossing or duplicating others, and the main consideration is to avoid doing it in winter—see below.

Problems

Silverleaf is a fungal disease which kills plum and gage trees, usually through access to a tree's wounds in winter and early spring, after pruning is done when the tree is dormant. Hence it is always recommended to prune plums and gages between May and July – preferably in June, when rapid growth will heal cuts quickly.

Plum moths and **sawfly** are the source of maggots in some fruit. Moths can be caught by hanging pheromone traps in trees at the end of May for about ten weeks. One trap can look after three trees, but you may well have enough good fruit to do without them.

Clafoutis

The classic recipe is for cherries, but it lends itself well to other fruit such as gooseberries, and raspberries

750g plums, 80g flour, 80g sugar, 2 eggs
1 sherry glass of brandy or other alcohol (optional)
1 pinch of salt, ½ litre milk

Stone the plums. Put in a buttered gratin dish or a circular dish of 26-8cm diameter. Sprinkle over the alcohol. Make a batter, whisking flour, sugar, salt and eggs. Heat the milk to boiling point, then whisk into the batter. Pour over the fruit and cook in a hot oven c.180ºC for 35-40 minutes. Serve warm.

OTHER FRUIT

Figs and grapes are two other worthwhile fruits to grow, especially in warmer regions or sheltered gardens. They are covered in less detail here because more rarely grown, but are not especially difficult if you respect the basic points I mention.

FIGS

Fig trees are difficult to bring into fruit unless their root run is restricted, to dampen their vigour – see container growing below. They are also susceptible to late frost if leaves emerge too early. Baby figs form in late summer but are killed by frost, while eating figs start to develop in May and need plenty of warmth to ripen by August. Brown Turkey is the standard and a very reliable variety, while Violetta is unusual for its ability to fruit without a restricted root run. Some pruning each winter will encourage fruit of better size and quality, and make it easier to find amongst abundant foliage.

GRAPES

Grapes of suitable varieties will yield well in sheltered, sunny spots and in drier regions. Look for varieties with mildew resistance, because crops are easily lost if mildew-prone varieties suffer damage to their leaves in wet summers. Four outdoor varieties for eating grapes are Alphonse Lavalée, from 1850s France, with small dark red fruit, Dornfelder for slightly larger red fruit, Phoenix for small almost seedless white grapes with a hint of Muscat flavour, and Perlette for almost seedless larger white grapes. Picking is usually through October and hard pruning is needed in late winter or early spring – pay attention to instructions with plants, and do not skimp on pruning.

TREE FRUIT IN CONTAINERS

Small fruit trees will grow and crop in containers, but remember that watering is a regular necessity for about six months, and some feeding will also help growth. An organic tomato feed is suitable.

APPLES

If apples are grafted onto M27 or M9 they can be grown in large pots, with some extra summer pruning to restrict their growth. A dwarf variety, Croquella, with red fruit in September, is well suited to pot growing.

CHERRY

The variety Cerasus Maynard Mini Stem grows no higher than two metres, requires no pruning and offers fruit in early August.

FIGS

Since fig trees fruit better in restricted root runs, containers suit them well. Any variety should be possible in a pot of about 60cm; note that some are heat-loving and fruit most reliably in a greenhouse or conservatory. Check the details when buying a young tree. Yields will not be huge off small trees, but they are ornamental too, with their dark green, indented leaves.

NECTARINE

A variety called Nectarella is sufficiently slow growing to be viable in a large pot. Keeping it in a dry place between November and March will reduce the risk of leaf curl, as long as you are strong enough to move the pot and tree.

PEACH

As with nectarines, pot growing offers the chance of minimising leaf curl by hibernating trees indoors. A variety called Bonanza is extremely slow growing and should require no pruning.

PEAR

Yields of pears can never be large in containers but some fruit are definitely achievable. Look out for Garden Pearl, which needs no pruning and has a maximum height of two metres.

NUTS

ALMONDS

Almonds can be grown in Britain, having similar climatic tolerance to plums and flowering at about the same time – therefore vulnerable to any late frosts. They are vigorous, up to 6m high, and two trees are needed for good pollination. Their leaves resemble those of peach trees and so do the nuts, encased in green flesh that can be mistaken for an unripe peach. Most available varieties have resistance to leaf curl.

HAZELNUTS

These grow so, so easily, and squirrels are so, so good at finding them before we do. I know of no easy answer, but cobnuts (large hazels) such as Kent Cob are still worth a try, edible as green nuts from late August, on bushes which grow as clumps of upright stems, 3-4m in height. Older bushes will yield heavily.

WALNUTS

Walnuts suffer similarly from squirrels and take much longer to grow, as well as needing much more space – say 8-10m between trees – and it is recommended to plant two different varieties for cross pollination and good yields. Modern varieties claim to bear within five years, about half the time previously needed, and usually come into leaf late enough to minimise risk of damage by late spring frosts.

Chapter 19

Soft Fruit (Berries)

To refresh you in summer

Soft fruit covers a wide range of summer and autumn berries. They are easy to grow, respond with tempting, juicy fruits to an annual dressing of good compost, and are much appreciated by birds, depending on who's nesting locally!

Harvests of berries are time-consuming to pick, but a great blessing in the kitchen, offering sorbets, ice creams, jams, summer puddings, liqueurs and plentiful bowls of mouth-watering fruit whose flavour, freshly picked at peak ripeness, repays, and more, the time and effort required.

SOIL PREPARATION

Soil preparation is the same as for perennial vegetables: clean the soil thoroughly. Any perennial weeds like couch grass and ground elder that are present at planting time will plague you for years to come.

Soft fruit likes plenty of humus so annual dressings of compost are most worthwhile. On top of this in spring and summer you can mulch around bushes and canes with grass mowings, straw, leaf mould and cardboard to help conserve moisture and prevent growth of annual weeds. Most bushes and berry plants have lots of surface roots and cool mulches help these.

Birds are often quicker to pick fruit than we are so netting of some kind may be necessary. However, fruit cages are quite an investment in time and money and only need one small hole to much reduce their effect, so I recommend waiting a year or two after planting to see how hungry your birds are.

BLUEBERRIES
(container-grown unless you have acid soil*)

Variety	Character Years to fruit	Height (m) Start harvesting	Spread (cm)
BLUECROP	Compact upright habit 2/3	1.2 Late Jul	0.8
SUNSHINE BLUE	Unusual pink flowers, self-fertile 2/3	1.2 Late Jul	0.8
HERBERT	Slightly larger plants and fruit 2/3	1.2 Late Jul	0.8

*acid soil in your area will be revealed by any rhododendrons, azaleas, camellias and blue-flowering hydrangeas.

Blueberries grow to over two metres high in open ground, and live for two decades or more. Their cousins are bilberries – also known as huckleberries, hurts, whimberries and whortleberries – which hug the soil in acid woodland and bear slightly smaller, darker fruit.

The recent popularity of blueberries is justified by their delicious, nutritious fruit and the ease of growing it, provided you have either acid soil or large pots of ericaceous compost. As well as fine fruit they offer pretty, small flowers and gorgeous bronze to dark red leaves over a month or more of autumn.

Varieties

More varieties are becoming available all the time; the three above all have different merits. Better yields come from growing two or more together, for pollination, but Sunshine Blue does well on its own. Most varieties crop from late July to early September, although Earliblue starts a little before.

Growing

Birds may mean that netting is necessary – a small piece draped over the plant should work. Watering is a constant ritual for pot-grown bushes. Large 45 or 60cm pots are ultimately necessary for good yields of fruit, and to maintain this some feeding of organic liquid feed is necessary, or of home-made comfrey or nettle water.

After three or four years, when your bush has spent a couple of years in your largest pot, it will benefit from being lifted out and up to one third of its compost teased or tapped out of its roots. Then re-pot it with some new ericaceous compost.

Harvesting

Blueberries are restrained and steady in ripening: a few daily over a long period for most bushes. You need several bushes to have large bowlfuls, and if I had acid soil I would plant lots of them in the garden! But in pots they are rather more work.

Pruning

Remove any dead wood, cut out branches that duplicate, and in late summer pinch out the tops of long, new canes to keep plants bushy.

Problems

Apart from **birds**, there is nothing to report here – another reason for the popularity of blueberries.

CURRANTS

Variety	Character		Height (m)
	Years to fruit	Start harvesting	Spread
BEN LOMOND	Popular for consistent fruiting, large berries		1.2
Black	2	Late Jul	1.5
BEN SAREK	Smaller bush, plentiful fruit		0.9
Black	2	Mid Jul	1.0
BEN CONNAN	Reliable cropping, large currants		1.2
Black	2	Mid Jul	1.5
ROVADA	Heavy yields for four weeks		1.2
Red	2	Mid Jul	1.5
BLANKA	Lower yields, sweet ivory fruit		1.2
White	2	Late Jul	1.5

Currants come in three colours, of which blackcurrants are the most popular. Their season is mainly July, so some bird prevention may be required. If allowed to fully ripen on the bush, which I warmly recommend, black and white currants in particular can become sweet enough to eat as raw berries. On the other hand, cooking currants tends to emphasise their acidity so added sugar is usually necessary.

Bushes can grow large, needing as much as 150cm (5') between them – although one good bush should be enough for most households.

Planting

Some compost in the planting hole will help bushes if soil is poor. Prune according to the supplier's recommendations.

Harvesting

Flavour and sweetness will improve for up to a fortnight after fruit changes colour in July, but watch for birds at this point. Picking individual berries takes a long time – pulling thumb and fingers through really ripe whole bunches of fruit is quicker.

Pruning

After one summer's growth, cut out all weaker branches to leave five or six, which should fruit next summer. The next winter, do the same to new branches of the summer just gone and cut two year old branches (which should have fruited) back to two buds, whence new branches will emerge.

Simply trimming off new growth is risky, because currants form on second-year's wood, which must therefore be allowed to develop. If no pruning is done you will still have currants, but bushes may grow large enough to make picking difficult and fruit tends to be smaller.

GOOSEBERRIES

Variety	Character		Height (m)
	Years to fruit	Harvest	Spread
INVICTA	Heavy crops, pale green berries		1.2
	2	Late May-Jul	1.5
PAX	Red dessert berries, few thorns		1.3
	2	Jun-Jul	1.0
HINNONMAKI	Yellow dessert gooseberry		1.2
YELLOW	2	Jun-Jul	1.3

Varieties

Vicious thorns and high acidity have given a bad name to gooseberries, to the point that 'Old Gooseberry' is a nickname for the Devil. However, choosing the right variety can help, for instance Pax has almost spine-free canes. Then if you manage to bring dessert gooseberries to ripeness, by waiting and by netting against birds, you will enjoy remarkable flavours that few people know about, partly because ripe gooseberries are too soft to travel well.

The best variety for jams and cooking is currently Invicta, with high yields of less sweet berries.

Planting

Best planting distance varies according to variety, check the chart and add 20-30cm to the spread for distance between bushes. Invicta makes a large and sprawling bush with many thorns, while Pax is more upright and less vigorous.

Pruning at planting time is only necessary if the supplier has not already done it. Ideally you want a short main stem of 15-20cm and four or five stems off this of about 15cm each.

Harvesting

Wait for berries to soften and to change colour so that sweetness can develop. Gloves will make it easier to pick berries off thorny bushes. Yields in the second summer are 2-3kg per bush, and rather more thereafter.

Pruning

Prune out older branches and any younger ones that are crossing or duplicating. This makes picking easier and helps ensure fruit of a good size.

Problems

Mildew used to be a major problem, but all the varieties in the table are resistant.

Birds are usually the main difficulty, so netting may be necessary. Blackbirds even eat immature green berries in May – they must be good for baby blackbirds.

Gooseberry and elderflower fool

500g gooseberries
2 tablespoons light muscovado sugar
1 tablespoon elderflower cordial
250 ml Jersey or double cream

Top and tail the gooseberries, and cook gently with the sugar and cordial in a puddle of water with the lid on the pan for about 20 minutes. Allow to cool and check the sweetness. Depending on whether you like your fools smooth or lumpy, either mash or liquidise the fruit. Whip the cream and fold the two together. If you need to sweeten the mixture, add more elderflower cordial.

RASPBERRIES

Variety	Character		Height (m)
	Years to fruit	Start harvest	Spread (m)
1. Summer			
MALLING MINERVA	Early fruit, smooth canes		2.0
	2	Late Jun	0.5
GLEN AMPLE	Midsummer fruit		2.0
	2	Mid Jul	0.5

Variety	Character		Height (m)
	Years to fruit	Start harvest	Spread (m)
2. Autumn			
AUTUMN BLISS	Long season, large fruit		1.7
	1	Aug	0.6
JOAN J	Even larger berries		1.6
	1	Aug	0.6
ALL GOLD	Sweet yellow berries		1.6
	1	Aug	0.6

High in vitamin A and potassium, fruiting deliciously over a long season, leaves that make a nice tea – what more can one ask?

Raspberries are of the bramble family, adapted to woods and hedgerows and needing plenty of dampness to do well. This means that long-cropping autumn raspberries are well worthwhile, compared to summer raspberries which, in drier parts of England at least, often suffer from heat and drought.

Two words of caution: be careful of the innocent-looking but prickly hairs or spines on most stems (Minerva excepted), and pull out the suckers sent up by raspberry canes' far reaching roots, which are somewhat invasive.

Varieties

A few canes of each of the first three varieties in the table would, in good soil with sufficient moisture, give raspberries all the time from late June to October. I find that the autumn varieties have larger berries and a fuller flavour – Autumn Bliss is extremely reliable, while Joan J has even larger fruit and superb flavour. Yellow-fruited varieties such as All Gold are worth growing for the sweetest, almost ambrosial fruit, and birds may notice them less.

Autumn Raspberries

These should really be called 'late summer': they crop steadily from August to end September, and through October in milder parts, but become more acid and prone to rotting in the darker days and wetter weather of autumn.

Planting

Planting in winter is best, preferably by the end of March. This will allow enough growth for autumn raspberries to crop in the first year, even after cutting stems back to 15cm at planting time. Summer raspberries should not be cut back after planting, and will not fruit until the following summer, unless you plant more expensive long canes and keep them well watered.

Autumn raspberries are shorter and can be grown without supports, but summer raspberries need tying in to wires or canes. Picking and weeding is much easier if rows are kept tidy by some combination of posts and wire.

Growing

Netting will be necessary in some situations. I do not net our autumn raspberries because their cropping time coincides with elderberries and blackberries, so birds are busy elsewhere.

Harvesting

Once berries start to ripen, picking will be possible every two or three days. Spells of wet weather are tricky because fruit may go mouldy as soon as ripe; pick these off on to the ground so they do not infect any berries they are touching.

Pruning

Summer raspberries need pruning in summer, as soon as they have finished cropping. Cut off all their old woody stems at ground level, leaving just the soft new growth for next summer's crop. Long stems may benefit from tying in to canes or sticks, depending how you are supporting them.

Autumn raspberries need pruning in winter and before the following March: cut off all stems to about 15cm (6") above the ground. Fruit develops on new growth of that season, quite different to summer raspberries.

Problems

The aforementioned **birds** are chief problem, and fruit turning mouldy in wet weather, when more frequent and thorough picking is needed.

Rhudidrew

An old-fashioned recipe handed on by a neighbour. It requires a nice old jelly mould.

500g fruit – mulberries or rhubarb or raspberries
30g sago
Sugar to sweeten and draw the juice out.

Soften the fruit with sugar over a gentle heat. Soak the sago in a cup of cold water for 5-10 minutes. Strain. Pour the sago into the fruit and cook over a gentle heat (the bottom oven of an Aga is ideal) for 15 minutes. Wet the mould and fill with the fruit mixture. It should set after 2 hours. Turn out onto a plate.

STRAWBERRIES

Variety	Special character	Start harvest	Height (m)
MARSHMELLO	Sweet, mellow, conical fruit, vigorous	Late Jun	0.2
PERFECTION	Tender fruit, fine flavour, good yields	Late Jun	0.2
MAE	Best for early crops, even in late Mae!	Early Jun	0.2
ROYAL SOVEREIGN	Old variety, top flavour, smaller yields	Mid Jun	0.2
CAMBRIDGE FAVOURITE	Reliable for jam, smaller, pale fruit	Late Jun	0.2
AROMEL (EVERBEARING)	Medium-size fruits all summer, tasty	Late Jun	0.2

Strawberries were adored by Henry VIII, perhaps as a remedy for his gout. In his day and for two centuries after, the only available fruits were small alpine ones, until French breeders at Versailles in the 18th century started crossing larger fruited species from the Americas. Breeding has continued, and we now enjoy the results.

The normal cropping season for strawberries is mid June to mid July, a time to really look forward to. Recent propagation of 'everbearing' varieties such as Aromel and Malling Opal makes it possible to have strawberries until early autumn as well. I find these intriguing but somehow less exciting, and slightly more difficult to grow.

Maincrop varieties

Beware the offerings of certain garden centres and nurseries where there are lots of Elsanta. They grow well and are the most common commercial variety, but not the tastiest. Almost every other variety I have grown tastes better. Three good ones, among many others, are Marshmello, Perfection and Royal Sovereign. And if a friend or allotment neighbour recommends the flavour of their strawberry, ask if they might let you plant a few of its runners.

Strawberries are one of the few crops about which one can say: 'They do well in clay'. They also love compost and manure, preferably every year, applied after cropping or in winter.

Being a woodland plant, they will tolerate some shade, but not too dry a soil.

Late frosts

Strawberry flowers are killed by frost, so early flowers will benefit from protection with fleece, if you want an early crop. Alternatively leave alone and more flowers will appear later.

Planting

New plants are actually runners – rooting nodes on stems running out of established plants, during and more especially after cropping. Once rooted, the stem can be cut and they can be lifted and planted elsewhere. Usual spacing is 45x45cm (18") each way on beds or 30cm (12") in rows, planted shallowly with the knobbly bulge (called a 'crown') above soil level.

August plantings will ensure a fair harvest the following summer. Planting as late as October is possible, but first year's crops will be small, unless plants are large and well rooted. Such plants can even be set out in March or early April to crop in July. Everbearing strawberries, like autumn raspberries, will fruit through their first summer from a spring planting, and often fruit from their new runners.

Growing

Runners are more of a curse than a blessing in bare soil, because they insert and root themselves into all the gaps between plants, leading after a few months to a densely planted mass. If left unthinned, any fruits growing under such a canopy of leaves can only grow small and may rot rather than ripen.

Three ways to help prevent this are:

- Plant through a mulch, which also helps to keep the fruit clean – traditionally a straw mulch was applied in spring. Modern plastic mulches allow air and moisture through, but are expensive and make it difficult to apply more compost for the three years or so of their presence.
- Use a good dressing of well rotted and weed-free compost or leaf mould, and repeatedly cut off any unwanted runners through August and September. Allow a few if you need more plants of that variety.
- Strawberries are adaptable to many systems of growing, and some growers have long bags of compost at waist level for easier picking. They grow well in containers, often hanging invitingly over the sides, and can be kept going for a second year of fruiting in the same pot or bag, with plenty of watering.

After fruiting has finished, cut off all foliage to just above the crown. This helps to reduce numbers of slugs and snails, and to control growth of new runners.

Picking

First fruits are the largest and juiciest, while 'jam' strawberries are the final picking of small fruit. Three weeks is an average season for most plants; the starting date will depend on variety (see chart) and whether cloches or fleece have been used to bring fruiting forward. High season of maximum fruit is mid June to mid July.

In damp weather, mouldy fruit is best removed so it does not infect neighbouring berries.

Clearing plants

The average productive life of plants is three years, sometimes more. I recommend clearing a bed or row after three or four years, having first established another. You can use your own runners unless virus has infected the plants, see below.

Problems

Be prepared for **birds** to show a keen interest, even in semi-ripe fruit. Draping a net over the bed or row should keep them off, but may not stop any **badgers**.

Avoid watering when fruit are ripening, because excess dampness encourages **fungal rots**. That is another reason for keeping space between plants.

Slugs and snails like strawberries: I often find some while picking fruit and remove them. A dry season is best; some years are simply too wet for strawberries, hence the proliferation of polytunnels to grow them in.

Virus can infect plants, making their leaves stunted and weak, with small yields of fruit. In the rare event of this happening, they should be dug up and burnt and a new bed planted elsewhere.

Strawberry ice-cream

2.5kg strawberries squashed with a potato masher
600g light muscovado sugar
5 x 284ml pots of Jersey cream
8 free range eggs separated into yolks and whites

This makes industrial quantities for the freezer. It sets like a brick and requires an hour or two to defrost, but tastes delicious. Beat the egg yolks and sugar till light and fluffy, add the sugar and strawberries. Whisk the egg whites and fold in to the purée. Freeze in suitable tubs.

OTHER BERRIES

BLACKBERRIES

Garden varieties are larger fruited and mostly less sweet than hedgerow blackberries. They are vigorous and thorny, but Oregon Thornless, Loch Ness and Loch Tay deserve a special mention for being thorn-free and somewhat slower growing, making them suitable for smaller gardens. They will still benefit from a trellis or a two-metre stake at least, and should start cropping in mid to late August for about a month. Allow about two metres from other fruiting plants.

BOYSENBERRIES

These are a combination of raspberry, blackberry and loganberry, offering a large, dark red to black fruit whose flavour is more sweet than acid, akin to hedgerow blackberry. Grow as for blackberries.

JAPANESE WINEBERRIES

These have significant ornamental value as well as fine fruit. Of the bramble family, their leaves are purple-veined and dusty white underneath, while the orange to dark red fruit are borne in pretty clusters and have flavours closest to raspberry, but perhaps more acid. Plants are vigorous, up to 3m high or long and suited to growing over a fence or trellis, with stems that are bristly more than thorny. Like summer raspberries they are 'biennial', fruiting on last year's stems which then need removing.

LOGANBERRIES

Loganberries were one of the first crosses between raspberries and blackberries. They crop between the two in late July and August, with quite long berries that need to be dark red for their acidity to diminish. I recommend Thornless LY654 to facilitate training their stems and picking the fruit.

TAYBERRIES

Tayberries are another cross between raspberry and blackberry, and usually grow vigorously with many nasty thorns, with a spread of up to five metres. However a recent variety called Buckingham has been bred without thorns, and makes tayberries more interesting. They crop late July and through August, with large, juicy fruits needing to be dark red, even purple, to be ripe enough to eat. Late flowering makes tayberries suitable for frosty sites, and their vigour makes wall or fence training a good idea.

BERRIES FOR PATIOS

Make sure you have suitable varieties and the right pots – large 45cm ones ultimately for older bushes. Use organic multi-purpose or ericaceous compost, according to species, and organic liquid feed if available, making sure it is an ericaceous feed for plants in acid soil.

This section is more to point you in the right direction than a complete growing manual. Bushes bred for patio growing will come with precise instructions for correct pruning which will be different to bushes growing in open soil. All varieties mentioned here are self-fertile, therefore needing no companions for pollination.

BLUEBERRIES – see above

CRANBERRIES

The cranberry is a creeping, low-growing plant, which requires moist, acid compost. Its dark red berries ripen through the autumn.

CURRANTS

Some currants are being bred to grow in small spaces and are usually supplied as cordons with a single stem. For example, Rovada is a suitable redcurrant variety, with long strings of large fruit and somewhat restricted growth. Grow in multi-purpose compost.

JOSTABERRIES

A cross between blackcurrant and gooseberry, with no thorns! They look like a blackcurrant bush and can be trained to a wall or trellis. Spring frosts may damage the foliage, while the fruits are shiny black and rather acid, for cooking more than eating fresh. Grow in multi-purpose compost.

LINGONBERRIES

Also known as cowberries, and related to blueberries and cranberries. More acid than the former and less acid than the latter, they are well suited to sauces and preserves. They should yield better than cranberry and offer ripe fruit in both late July and in September. They need ericaceous compost.

The Answer <u>is</u> in the Soil!

Gardening has so much to offer – being outside with the weather, birds, insects and plants, and developing the ability to help plants grow. Watching beautiful leaves, flowers and fruits develop from tiny seeds is an excitement and a privilege.

Growing food deepens the relationship considerably, as we eat and share the fruits of our efforts, and realise that we can influence the flavour, freshness and quality of our fruit and vegetables.

Continuing to grow food crops over many years offers the chance to glimpse some of nature's relationships, especially if we do it without using chemical short-cuts. I feel grateful for the opportunity to glimpse a few of the laws and principles which underpin the growth of plants, to be able to share the sheer wonder of it.

So often, in seeking to understand more I am drawn back to the soil, the key to all life. We understand it so little, and probably do not respect it enough. Since the invention of chemical fertilisers, soil has come to be seen by some as nothing more than a reservoir of nutrients, akin to a bank account.

Yet every hectare of living soil has about twenty tonnes of living organisms, from bacteria and fungi to earthworms and spiders. It is truly and literally alive, as much as a person or animal. Quality and quantity of plant growth stem from quality of soil life. Enhancing its aliveness is the basis of good gardening, leading to better health of plants and humans.

I hope that using this book helps you to achieve a wonderful garden, many great meals and vibrant health.

Resources

ORGANISATIONS

Biodynamic Agriculture Association, Painswick Inn Project, Gloucester Street, Stroud GL5 1QG. www.biodynamic.org.uk. Biodynamic advice, books, preparations, courses.

Garden Organic (HDRA), Ryton Gardens, Coventry CV8 3LG. www.gardenorganic.co.uk. Information, advice and events. See www.organiccatalog.com for their extensive range of seeds and accessories.

The Good Gardeners Association, 4 Lisle Place, Wotton-under-Edge, Glos GL12 7AZ. www.goodgardeners.org.uk. 'Moving Beyond Organic' project aims to grow food for nutrition. Information on no-dig, soil ecology, nutrition in food, human nutrition, research and education projects.

Royal Horticultural Society, 80 Vincent Square, London SW1P 2PE. www.rhs.org.uk. Help with all aspects of gardening.

Soil Association, South Plaza, Marlborough Street, Bristol BS1 3NX. www.soilassociation.org.uk. Advice, information, books and inspiration on all matters organic.

SUPPLIERS

Agroforestry Research Trust, 46 Hunters Moon, Dartington, Totnes TQ9 6JT. www.agroforestry.co.uk. Fruit and nut trees and bushes, many unusual ones.

Blackmoor Nurseries, Blackmoor Liss, Hampshire GU33 6BS. www.blackmoor.co.uk. A wide range of fruit trees, bushes and soft fruit.

Edwin Tucker & Sons Ltd, Brewery Meadow, Stonepark, Ashburton, Devon TQ13 7DG. www.edwintucker.com. Seeds of all kinds and a helpful catalogue.

Implementations, PO Box 2568, Nuneaton CV10 9YR. www.implementations.co.uk. Copper tools of high quality and information on Victor Schauberger, who understood water better than anybody.

The Real Seed Catalogue, Brithdir Mawr Farm, Newport, near Fishguard SA42 0QJ. www.realseeds.co.uk. An eclectic range of good, home-grown seeds and advice on seed saving.

SEER Centre, Ceanghline, Straloch Farm, Enochdu, Perthshire PH10 7PJ. www.seercentre.org.uk. Information on minerals and rock dust, and sales of rock dust.

Tamar Organics, Cartha Martha Farm, Rezare, Launceston PL15 9NX. www.tamarorganics.co.uk. A wide range of organic seeds and sundries.

Walcot Organic Nursery, Walcot Lane, Drakes Broughton, Pershore WR10 2AL. www.walcotnursery.co.uk. Top quality organic fruit trees and bushes.

PUBLICATIONS

Gardening and Planting by the Moon, Nick Kollerstrom. Published annually by Quantum.

The Biodynamic Sowing and Planting Calendar, Maria Thun. Published annually by BDAA (see above), selling 100,000 copies worldwide each year.

ORGANIC EXTRAS

Mill on the Brue, Trendle Farm, Somerset BA10 0BA. www.millonthebrue.co.uk. For children's active holidays and home-grown organic food.

Bibliography

An Agricultural Testament, Sir Albert Howard, OUP 1940, reprinted by the Soil Association 2006. A brilliant scientist's fascinating story of discovering modern compost-making.

Humus and the Farmer, Friend Sykes, Faber & Faber 1946. Inspiring account of converting a poor upland farm to organic methods.

The Living Soil, Eve Balfour, Faber & Faber 1943, reprinted by the Soil Association 2006. An original look at health of soil and humans, which triggered the founding of the Soil Association – still a great read.

Mother Earth 1946-64 (quarterly journals of the Soil Association). Not currently in print, but worth reading when they are for entertaining distillations of timeless wisdom.

Nutrition and Health, Sir Robert McCarrison and H. M. Sinclair, Faber & Faber 1953. Everybody should read this demonstration of the effects of good and bad nutrition.

Nutrition and Physical Degeneration, Weston A. Price, Price Pottenger Foundation 1945. Another must-read— you won't want to eat cake after this graphic, far-reaching account.

The Organic Salad Garden, Joy Larkcom, Frances Lincoln 2001. A rare combination of beauty and information from a pioneering gardener.

The Roots of Health, John Reeves, self-published 2003 (Tel: 01594 861196). A ground-breaking look at the mineral contents of food crops grown in different ways.

Secrets of the Soil, Peter Tompkins and Christopher Bird, Harper & Row 1989. Just in case we think we know it all – a lot of this information still needs to be used.

The Weed Problem, F. C. King, Faber & Faber 1951. An original exposition of the value of compost.

Main Index

Index of Recipes

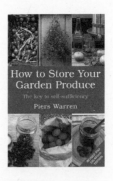